Thorns

and

Roses

Thorns

and

Roses

A Life in the Context of History

by

Almut Metzroth

Fiction Publishing, Inc.

Ft. Pierce, Florida

Fiction Publishing, Inc.
This Book Is Non-Fiction
5626 Travelers Way
Ft. Pierce, Florida 34982
772-489-5811
fictionpub@bellsouth.net

To Bert,
Veit, Riko and Eitel,
and grandsons
Erik, Alexander, Richard, Ryan and John.

In memory
of my parents
and our son Nicord.

Contents

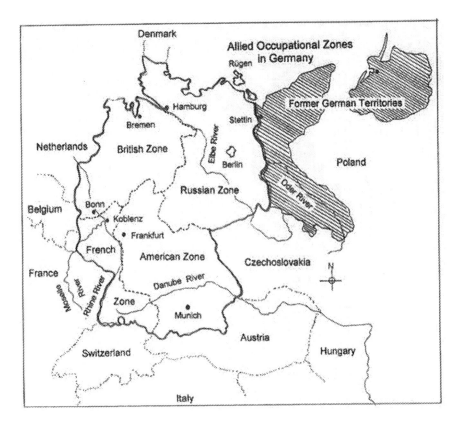

Denmark

Allied Occupational Zones
in Germany

Rügen

Former German Territories

Hamburg

Bremen

Stettin

Netherlands

Elbe River

British Zone

Berlin

Poland

Russian Zone

Belgium

Bonn

Koblenz

Oder River

Frankfurt

France

French

American Zone

Czechoslovakia

N

Moselle River

Rhine River

Danube River

Zone

Munich

Austria

Hungary

Switzerland

Italy

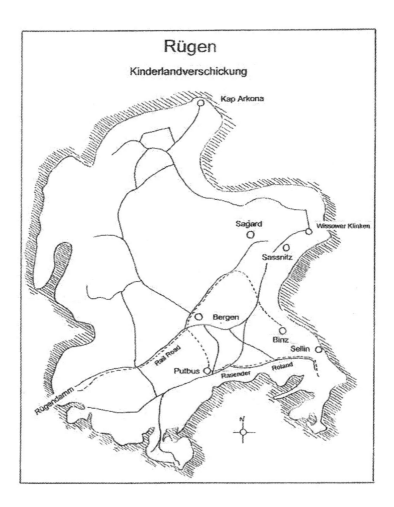

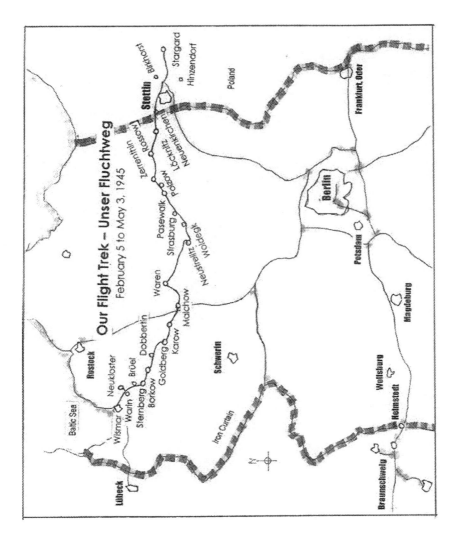

Our Flight Trek – Unser Fluchtweg
February 5 to May 3, 1945

Preface

In this book I called up many memories of people and places significant to molding me into the person I am, and of events and experiences shaping my attitudes.

Some of the characters I described, especially the hundreds of students, are composites of those who crossed my thorny or rose-strewn paths. Friends granted permission to use their names. For the protection of certain individuals, I assigned ficticious identities. In rare instances, I changed the names of places or adjusted their environment.

Almut Metzroth

Stuart, Florida
Spring, 2007

Almut 1942

CHAPTER 1

An Emotional Roller Coaster

I WAS FIFTEEN YEARS OLD in 1945, hiding from Soviet soldiers in a loft under mountains of unbaled hay on a German farm. During the days, Soviet troops searched my hiding place for suspected troves: German soldiers, women, weapons, and jewelry. With swords they had taken as loot or pitchforks found in the barn below, the Mongol soldiers went step-by-step, piercing the hay under their feet. They raped the women and it was

1

death or Siberia for German soldiers. Torture was always a possibility at the hands of drunken Soviets.

In the hours between those harrowing probes and during the nights I had time to think, mostly about how to escape my situation. Since the purpose of my hiding was to avoid discovery by the Soviets, an early escape during the first days of May 1945 was not an option. Thus, my thoughts revolved around one question: What brought me to this predicament?

My childhood had not prepared me for this deviation of the life I had envisioned and my parents had encouraged. *Some day I'll write about these unimagined turns.* In my innocence, I thought I should share my experience with the world, which I assumed did not know the horrors human beings were capable of inflicting on one another. At the time of these nightmarish events I relied on my life's motto: *Besser machen.* You do better.

*   *   *

M Y E A R L I E S T R E C O L L E C T I O N S were of living on my maternal grandparents' farm and orchard in *Neu-Podejuch,* outside of Stettin, Pommern. Before the end of World War II, Pomerania was the German province that faced the Baltic Sea, east and west of the Oder River. In February 1945 the eastern region of Pomerania became part of Poland, in accordance with the Allies' Conference at Yalta.

In Neu-Podejuch my friends were my cat, *Mieze,* and the farm animals.

I was happiest when I could be outdoors, especially riding with my father on his horse, *Schwarze,* Black One, as we surveyed the workers' progress in the fields. I also enjoyed the walks we took through the woods and meadows. We always had a ball with us, and *Vati,* Daddy, thought of many games. From him I learned my first lessons about the weather and fauna and flora.

"What grain is growing here?" he might ask me.

"How can I tell?"

"Look at the spikes, on rye hair is longer than that on the wheat across the road."

My father had been the farm's administrator at Neu-Podejuch. When inflation and unemployment lingered, he lost his job, despite the fact that he was married to the owner's daughter. In the hope that he could find work more easily in the city, my parents rented an apartment in Stettin. For years my father did odd jobs, working as a packer for a moving company or as a stevedore.

Eventually, Vati found employment with the Pomeranian State Department of Agriculture, where he could apply his skills and education. As Germany lifted itself slowly out of the inflationary times, so did my parents. They were able to buy fresh meat and vegetables again.

Although I missed the farm life and the animals, I liked the excitement of city life and the friends I made in the neighborhood. Our five-room apartment was on the second of four floors at Pionerstrasse 2. There were two apartments on each floor in the *Vorderhaus.* Our living and dining rooms faced the street. The kitchen, bedrooms and bath were arranged in a curve so that the last room of every apartment adjoined one of the living quarters of the *Hinterhaus,* so called because they were behind the *Vorderhaus.* Two garages and a high stucco wall closed the quadrangle that enclosed the *Hof,* the courtyard. Here we children played marbles, skipped rope and liked ball games in which we had to perform intricate moves between throwing the ball against the wall and catching it on its return. We played hide and seek in the staircases, much to the annoyance of the renters. To find out who would be "it" first, we stood in a circle. One girl or boy pointed a finger from one player to the next, saying this rhyme:

"Eins, zwei, drei, vier, fünf, sechs, sieben,	One, two, three, four, five, six, seven,
Meine Mutter kocht die Klieben,	My mother is cooking breakfast soup,
Meine Mutter kocht den Speck,	My mother is cooking bacon,

Und du musst weg!"   And you are gone!

The last one standing was "it" and had to find us. As for the rhymes, traditional native songs and sayings definitely lose their charm in translation and seem, at times, pointless. *Klieben* are wheat dumplings cooked in sweetened milk, a breakfast soup.

*   *   *

S C A R E D O U T O F M Y R E V E R I E, I heard someone setting up a ladder from the barn floor to the loft. Fear of discovery and bodily harm filled my senses. Then I heard my father's voice.

"Almut, I have your breakfast. The Russians who are bivouacked in the yard are milling in the kitchen, frying potatoes. When they leave I'll tell you whether it's safe to go to the bathroom and wash up."

I nodded and could only hope that the troops would not carry out one last search in my hayloft before the next detail came to stay at this farm for the night and start the terror all over.

With fear for my life a constant companion my stomach nerves fluctuated between hunger and revulsion to food. I took some bites of the buttered bread and returned to my memories.

*   *   *

W H A T A H A P P Y M E M O R Y my first school day was! For this important event in my life, my parents gave me a *Schultüte,* a decorated conical container half as big as I was tall, closed on top with pastel-colored crepe paper. On my back I carried my new leather backpack. It held the tools for a first-grade student: a wood-framed slate tablet with lines for my writing exercises on one side and, on the other, squares for number work. A slate "pencil," a tin to keep the sponge wet and ready for cleaning the tablet, and a dry rag to use after the sponge. These two were hanging outside the backpack and became an impediment when boys were chasing us on the way to school or back. Our pursuers could easily grab the strings of sponge and rag and twirl us around before running away.

I loved going to my school, *Pestalozzi-Schule für Mädchen, 28. Gemeindeschule,* 28th Precinct School for Girls, in Stettin. Fräulein *Krause* was my first grade teacher, an old lady who was willing to let thirty antsy children advance at their own speed.

"Today, we will have our spelling drill," she said once a week, "I hope that you are well prepared and ready to defend your seats." As she was facing our four columns of two-seat benches, eight rows deep, Fräulein Krause explained the order of competition.

"I will call out a word. The first student with a hand up will give us the definition and spelling. If correct, that student moves to the back seat in the window column. She will keep that seat until another student can replace her by giving more correct answers than she did." With this system we were in constant motion, up and down in the ranks. We had great fun.

The seating arrangement applied to all our graded efforts in reading, dictations, and compositions — yes, in first grade — arithmetic and social events. Did I ever defend my number one seat! Only after absences because of illness did I have to move a seat or two down in rank for short periods until I caught up with the class again.

*   *   *

VATI'S FAMILIAR WHISTLING in the barn let me know that I could come to the farmhouse to freshen up. With unsure steps I crossed the yard, anxiously looking around for any of the monsters in their earth-tone uniforms. As my parents and the farmer's family stood watch at the front of the house, back doors and windows, I hurriedly washed up. We did not take baths in the early months of Soviet occupation because we never wanted to be found naked in case the foreign soldiers were roaming through the houses of the residents.

I assumed that I was returning to the hayloft when my father said, "I was offered a foreman's job at a neighboring farm. The owner is a prisoner of war in France. His wife has two small children. Her few elderly farm hands need direction."

"Can I hide there?" I felt panicky.

"Not really. We will move into a provisional 'apartment' in a former henhouse."

"In a henhouse?" I interrupted, visualizing the usual arrangement of roosts.

"Hear me out," Vati said calmly. The place has a kitchen with running water and a large stove on which people used to cook mash for chickens and pigs. A crude table and two benches stand under the windows next to the latched entrance door."

"Latched? Can we lock it?" My panic grew. "I know we need to earn a living but will we be safe from future round-ups by Societ troops?"

"No, there is no lock. When we are inside we must push the table and the benches against the door."

"As if that could keep any invaders out," I blurted out in desperation.

"What about windows?" *Mutti,* Mom, asked.

"The windows near the entrance are small and high above the floor. That means no one can easily look inside. We will have to stand on the benches to look out."

At noon, my parents and I walked unmolested to the Lehmann farm. Vati introduced us to Frau Lehmann who lent us cooking and eating utensils, as well as blankets and sheets to cover our straw mattresses.

I entered our new living quarters with trepidation. What a dingy place *this* was. Mutti covered her nose. "I smell Lysol. Somebody must have tried to rid our new 'lodging' of any hint of the original dwellers."

The darkbrown floorboards had dried out over time and showed spaces between them, which were filled with dirt and provided a haven for fleas and other pests.

"Oh no! Look at this: Fleas hopping on my legs already. We'll be devoured by these varmints," I moaned, slapping at the lively black spots. "How can people live here?"

"This place is better than the woods or hayloft, isn't it?" Vati asked, discouraging any more arguments.

Mutti supported Vati's efforts. "We have to try out this shelter. Let's see what's beyond the kitchen door."

"Two bedrooms," Vati said. Crossing the threshold, he looked at me, "This one will be yours."

In my room, a chair lay on the straw mattress of the bedstead; a recessed area functioned as a closet. Besides my work clothes, plundering Soviets had left me with only a dress, a blouse, and a skirt. "I wouldn't hang them up here in plain sight for the next marauders to swipe them," I remarked. "Better to ball them up in the wash bowl and hope the fleas won't get into them."

Vati opened the door adjoining my closet. "Our bedroom," he said to Mutti. Two actual iron beds stood alongside walls, framing a window. Crates turned upside down served as tables.

I pointed at the bare windows, "Unlike the kitchen windows, these are no more than one meter above ground. The troops can break them with their rifle butts and enter. Good luck to us."

Mutti was as apprehensive as I was about this layout. Denying her fears, she contemplated, "This side is at the rear of the building. Perhaps there won't be as much traffic as in the yard. We'll cover the windows with rags."

"I guess the Lehmans converted our 'apartment' in a row along with four others to furnish shelters for the steady stream of refugees who came from the eastern provinces through Mecklenburg on their treks to the west, fleeing from the advancing Soviet troops," Vati observed.

After our inspection, we borrowed pails and scrub brushes, lit a fire in the stove and boiled water for our initial cleaning chores. When we poured the water on the floors, the fleas jumped out of the crevices. Soon they covered our legs, hungrily biting us. From then on until the day we left in September 1945 to flee to West Germany, my parents and I were never without flea bites. I learned the meaning of mind over matter: no scratching.

In the upheaval that Germany experienced immediately after World War II, we could not obtain insecticides. We were tempted to relieve the itching by scratching but were afraid to cause infections on the skin. My mother had ugly sores that saved her from the fate of many German women. Soviet soldiers did no longer go near her.

I did not sleep much during the first night in our apartment. Between listening to cajoling and prowling drunken Soviets and trying to ignore the creepy crawlers on my body, I sought refuge in my thoughts again.

*   *   *

I N S E C O N D G R A D E, *Hefte,* thin notebooks, replaced our *Schiefertafel,* or slate boards. Inkpots and pens took the place of the *Griffel,* slate pencils. We practiced our homework assignments *ins Unreine,* in first drafts, or second or third, depending on our parents' judgment of the quality of our work, before they allowed us to copy it *ins Reine,* the final draft in the notebook. German children did not use pencil for work they handed in to the teacher. Thus, the early practices in neatness and in the rules of grammar and expression were good training for later studies.

School started at eight in the morning. After two hours, we had *Grosse Pause,* a fifteen-minute recess spent in the schoolyard.

We ate our sandwiches and fruit and visited with friends, walking about. By one o'clock, school was out. We went home to the big meal of the day. In the afternoon we did homework and were free to play, read, or take lessons in music or sports. To this day, many German stores and offices close for up to two hours so that workers can have the mid-day repast with their families.

During the winter months, Stettin transformed itself into a snow-covered wonderland. My parents pulled Gunhilt, my mother's youngest sister, and me on our sleds to a park, the *Quistorp-Aue*, named after a nineteenth-century benefactor of our city. Gunhilt and I did not want to wait for the weekends; so we asked *Mutti*, "May we go sledding today?"

"To the *Quistorp-Aue*? Alone? Will you find the way?"

"Oh, sure! We will follow the streetcar tracks," Gunhilt said. I trusted my aunt. After all, she was three years older than I.

"All right; but be home before dark."

When the weather was warm enough to go swimming in the lakes, Mutti took us for swimming lessons at the city lake, *Glambecksee*. I was a *Wasserratte*, taking to water like a rat. At age seven, I signed up for the *Freischwimmer* test. To prove my proficiency in water safety, I had to swim in deep water for fifteen consecutive minutes and had to execute one jump and one dive from the one-meter board. When I was nine years old, I passed the *Totenkopf* test. As proof that I had swum for one hour without interruption and had performed jump and dive from the three-meter board I received the coveted patch of skull and bones for my bathing suit.

My youthful goal was to become an Olympic swimmer. From the time my parents and I attended the aquatic competitions at the *Olympiade* in Berlin in 1936 I "knew" what I wanted to strive for. Thanks to the war, these plans never materialized.

*　　*　　*

A S I A W O K E on that first morning in our henhouse apartment I heard Vati in the kitchen, preparing to leave for work. I hurried to speak with him.

"Vati, can I go with you and work in the fields? I feel so trapped in this place. Besides, what would I do here all day?"

"If you want to be in the open I will accept two extra hands for turning hay in fields, which are not visible from the main roads and military convoys."

Although I was constantly looking across the landscape, reassuring myself that no foe was near, the familiar smell of soil and hay relaxed me enough to fall into the work routine. *How can the sky be so peacefully blue? Why does the sun's benevolent rays shine down on us, unchanged by the chaos of a lost war?*

Lessons in religion and philosophy had not prepared me with answers to the questions I raised following my recent experiences.

As I turned hay in repetitious motion for hours, I again returned to thoughts of my childhood.

*   *   *

I N H I N D S I G H T, I first recognized signs of political import in 1938: ration cards for butter (In Pomerania, part of the breadbasket for Germany?). I distinctly remember going to the grocery store with my blue sheet of paper on which I saw the space reserved for the user's name and address, and numbered squares. The grocer cut off the valid square for the current week and the quantity bought.

Ration cards were indicators of impending political changes. Germany mobilized. One morning in August 1938 the dreaded letter arrived in the mail.

"What is a *Stellungsbefehl*, Vati?"

"When a man receives a draft notice he has to report for training as a soldier," my father explained.

"But there is no war. You are a *Landwirt*. Why does a farm administrator have to be a soldier?"

"When a country needs to defend her citizens or wants to support or liberate her neighbors, she needs competent soldiers. I will probably come home after basic training."

"What kind of soldier will you be?"

"I have to report to the *Luftwaffe*."

AFTER FOUR WEEKS in the German air force, Vati had to continue training with searchlights. On October 10, 1938, German troops marched into the *Sudetenland*, the northern part of Czechoslovakia. Hitler had promised the ethnic *Sudetendeutschen* to bring them *Heim ins Reich,* home to the mother country. He annexed the *Sudetenland.* Vati participated in this campaign. I missed him terribly.

"She is her father's daughter," was Mutti's standard explanation to herself and to others when she remarked about my habit of following Vati around in fields and barns, tending to horses, learning to ride them; using farm machinery; feeding cows, pigs, geese, ducks, and chickens.

VATI WAS A TALL, handsome man with a sturdy but lean frame. His light blue eyes dominated his face despite the scar across his left cheekbone. This mark was a reminder to him of the time he did not protect his face from a strike by his opponent's épée during a fencing tournament. In the 1920s, the fencers of his fraternity, *Corps Teutonia,* did not wear facemasks.

My father, Curt Finger, was born in 1906 as the oldest son of a family, which for generations had been Pomeranian landholders. As was the custom, the oldest son inherited the estate. The second-born son often made his career in the military; the third traditionally worked in agriculture for about twenty years with the aim to buy his own farm or estate.

These keepers of the soil were interested in only one stock in which they wanted to invest and reinvest their labor and financial gains—their farms. As they entered the twentieth century, the landowners became more educated and welcomed time-and-labor-saving machinery, chemical fertilizers and insecticides.

Some farmers established small manufacturing plants for agricultural products, such as peatmoss-packaging facilities, egg-sorting houses, or nurseries for reforesting. The families did stay on their homesteads, though. Of the sons who left to serve in the military or to study at universities, most returned to the land as veterinarians, farmers or administrators.

To prepare for his chosen occupation, Vati was a student at the *Landwirtschaftliche Hochschule*, the College of Agriculture of the University of Berlin, until the effects of the inflation in 1923 ended his studies abruptly. My grandfather had lost his estate. I wondered why a progressive farmer with a three-year business plan, like my *Opa*, Grampa, lost his holdings.

"Opa had taken up loans in order to update machinery and buildings. Because the interest on the borrowed money had risen to twenty-five percent, he was faced with higher payments to the bank than his income allowed. When in 1925 and 1926 severe rains destroyed crops and added to the financial distress, many farmers went bankrupt. For years, Opa fought to hold on to his property but, in the end, it was the weather that defeated him and many of his neighbors," Vati said.

"But the farmers' success is always contingent on the weather. Was it not really the monetary problem that led to Opa's ruin?" I asked.

"Yes. Besides the weather, we are subject to social and political rules that we cannot always control."

*   *   *

MY FIRST DAY AT WORK as a farmhand passed uneventfully and allowed me to contemplate the implications of being a member of the ruled. On the way back to the farm and our henhouse home, I realized that I had not felt the fear-induced headache and throat tightness while in the field. That changed, however, as we neared the village.

We walked back to the Lehmann farm on country roads. The main road, leading northwest to Wismar, ran through the middle of Reinstorf. From afar we heard the rumbling noises we associated with moving military convoys.

"The British must be on their way here," I said. With this expectation I felt my facial muscles work into a smile. There had not been any cause for expressing gladness in months. "I told you the Western powers would not leave us in the hands of these barbarians."

As we came closer to Reinstorf, I saw that the military vehicles were identifiable by their red stars. They were moving west in great numbers. "I thought the war was over. Are they fighting the British now, Vati?" I asked with alarm. The smile vanished from my face.

We pawns did not know of the post-war plans the Allied leaders had made for the occupation of Germany. What our tired group of farm workers observed on this day in June 1945 was the withdrawal of British and American forces and the advance of the Soviets to establish the borders the west later called the Iron Curtain.

"That explains the massive presence of Soviet troops so close to the British forces in our area," Vati said. "They had waited for their orders to occupy more German territory west of here. I wonder what other developments we don't know about."

*   *   *

WE HAD LIVED WITH PROPAGANDA, rumors, and wishful thinking for as long as I, a fifteen-year-old, could remember. While German troops were successful in their drives to conquer and occupy foreign countries, the press bubbled with good news. Positive slogans encouraged the German population to work for victory. Locomotives displayed banners describing their mission, *"Räder rollen für den Sieg,"* wheels are rolling for victory. This slogan, and many others like it, did not fade away when the great retreat took place. It seemed to convince the Germans to remain positive and to believe in the *Endsieg*.

When Germany's final victory became wishful thinking, rumors spread about the surprises Hitler's regime had in its arsenal. The V-rockets were to turn the tide. But the Allied armies marched on until they met in the middle of Germany in early May 1945, according to plan.

The first weeks under Soviet rule shocked us into disbelief. Nobody cared about our suffering. Only our hope for delivery from the brutality and the desperate state of our situation kept us from giving up on life.

MY FATHER'S COMMENT about our ignorance of current affairs is an example of how suspended we felt from the life we had known. No longer were we able to make decisions for ourselves because of the tyrannical supervision. At first, we had no concerns about anything but our daily necessities.

Eventually, men who had been prisoners of war in England or the United States returned to their homes in the Soviet Zone of Occupation. They told us of the normalization of living conditions in West Germany.

"People are starting to clean up rubble and to rebuild."

"Are women safe from the occupation troops? Are schools open?" I asked.

"What about food?" was my mother's question.

"Could I find work?" Vati worried.

When the returning POWs answered our queries in the affirmative, we wondered why they chose to be discharged to East Germany. "We are at home here. Our families need us. It is legal to cross the border with our discharge papers. To try to get to West Germany *illegally* is dangerous."

These conversations planted a seed in my mind: we had to escape to the Golden West. I plotted night and day. I had to convince my parents.

"Crossing the border would have been easier when it was only seven kilometers from this farm. Why do you want to walk seven times that distance now? You can't ask anyone for overnight shelter because your plans are secret," Vati said.

14

But Mutti was ready to venture an escape. We had become more informed about our surroundings and our provisionary government through, finally, published newspapers. Although these primitive organs carried only Soviet-approved news items I felt encouraged to read that trains left regularly from Berlin to the western border.

"We will take our bags to go shopping in Neukloster. There, we can leave our bikes at the railroad station and buy tickets to Berlin. Once we are in the city, we will study our options," I said.

Because of the risks involved, Mutti and I needed weeks to convince my father to flee to West Germany. He opposed our visions of a life other than that of farm workers with diverse objections: "We can't leave Frau Lehmann before the harvest," or "We don't have enough money for tickets and a new start in the west," and "How do you know that we will make it across the border?"

The valid questions of a family man were no obstacles for the fifteen-year-old girl who saw no future for her parents and herself in a chicken coop. I made allowances for the need to bring the harvest in. Besides, two more months of employment assured us of the necessary income to underwrite our plans.

I was anxious to go back to school. In anticipation, I reviewed past lessons while working in the fields and before falling asleep on my straw mattress. The memorization of poems and theorems that my friends and I had so detested became my mental salvation.

*   *   *

FROM THE BEGINNING of my school years, Mutti had stimulated my interest in learning, *"Was du gelernt hast, kann dir keiner nehmen."* What you have learned no one can take from you. How grateful I was now that recent physical brutality had not affected my brain nor robbed me of what I had learned.

15

In 1940, my fourth year of elementary school, my parents registered me at one of the three high schools for girls in Stettin. I had to take the written entrance examination along with many other ten-year-old applicants. Passing a dictation and an essay assignment for the one-hour test in German was another requirement. The second hour was reserved for the math exam. Students who successfully completed these tests were accepted; others were given a chance to improve their scores in a follow-up oral session.

Some of my new classmates had been at the *Pestalozzi-Schule* with me. I made friends with girls from the suburbs, too. Soon, we became known as ABCDE, Almut, Brigitte, Christa, Doris, and Evelyne. We liked our English class. I still remember the first expressions taught to us: pen, ink and inkpot.

THAT SAME YEAR, 1940, I received my notification to report for induction into the *Jungmädel-Bund,* the branch of the Hitler Youth for girls ten to fourteen years old.

Attendance at public schools was mandatory for children aged six to fourteen. So was membership in the age-appropriate levels of the Hitler Youth. Non-compliance or frequent unexcused absences from Wednesday and Saturday afternoon meetings resulted in reprimands to the marked family.

Our *Jungmädel* uniform consisted of a standard short-sleeved, white blouse with two buttoned front pockets, and a dark-blue skirt; a waist-long brown jacket of heavy imitation suede material completed our uniform.

The skirt featured recessed pockets, one each to the left and right of a front pleat. Buttons secured the flaps, and a belt kept the blouse neatly inside.

After rolling up a black, triangular kerchief into a *Schlips,* or tie, we fed its two ends through a brown, woven-leather ring, or *Knoten,* and pulled it up to the collar.

At the Wednesday meetings, we listened to our young leaders, thirteen to sixteen years old, give a short review of the political structure of the Nazi party before they taught marching songs.

As the war progressed, stores offered less merchandise. Raw materials, as well as labor, had to support the war effort. Obviously, toys became a rarity. Now our Wednesday meetings became workshops. I liked to use my jigsaw to cut out plywood patterns of animals, pictures and building blocks. The hardest job was to file wheels round enough to roll evenly across the floor when toddlers pulled the wooden dogs, wiggling ducks, or trains. Replenishing our supplies of saw blades and paints became a challenge. We donated our finished toys to needy children.

On Saturday afternoons we practiced or competed in sports: track, swimming, and ball games.

The German school system also stressed physical education, *Turnen*. Following the Greek tradition of healthy bodies and healthy minds, Friedrich Ludwig Jahn, *"Turnvater Jahn"* (1778-1852), founded exercise clubs, *Turnvereine*. In the United States, German clubs still exist under that name, revealing their original purpose.

The academic instruction during the twelve years of Hitler's dictatorship was richly influenced by his regime's political aims. Teachers were feeling the pressure on the population to be members of the Nazi party and to wear the party button on their lapels.

While most of my instructors kept their personal ideologies quiet, a teacher of German infuriated me enough to never forget her.

"This Dr.Hauser," I complained to my parents, "can't give a single example in her grammar lessons without glorifying the party or the *Führer*."

"Hmm," my father said carefully. "You know from experience that not all Germans want to join the party. Dr.Hauser's husband is a prominent architect and refuses to join. I suspect that Dr.Hauser is trying to protect her husband and her family through her actions."

"I think she is overdoing it. The other day, she referred to Hitler's visit in Stettin. Remember that hot day, when all the uniformed party organizations, the SA, the SS, and the Hitler Youth had to assemble near the *Hakenterrasse*? The Red Cross medics could barely keep up in their efforts to rescue fainting people. Three hours is a long time to stand in the blazing sun, about two hundred meters away from the podium, trying to catch a word of Hitler's speech. And Dr.Hauser insists we are lucky to be able to tell our grandchildren someday that we saw the *Führer*."

Vati's mentioning of our experience with the Nazi party's attempts to force Germans into joining it, referred to his summons in the late 1930s to report to the district headquarters of the Nationalsozialistische Deutsche Arbeiterpartei (NSDAP). For years, rumors circulated that some individuals did not return home after they followed these orders. For security, Vati took me with him to the party office where representatives of the SA, *Sturmabteilung*, or Brown Shirts, sat behind their desks.

Members of the SA were the storm troopers used in street battles in the early days of Hitler's struggle for power.

At the party office, Vati never let go of my hand. When ordered to leave me in the waiting room, he refused. Thus, I witnessed the seemingly endless interrogation as well as threats and attempted persuasion. Vati retained his restrained demeanor for a long time. But eventually he answered the party bosses' shouts with his own. His body shook and his blood surged up his neck to his head. I was scared and cried.

My father looked at me and said, "Come, we are going home." Nobody stopped us. He had not signed any papers of agreement to join the party.

Several weeks later, a letter arrived in the mail with a membership card in my father's name, a party button, and a list of upcoming meetings. Thus Vati learned he had become a registered member.

Reminded of that incident, I was willing to tolerate Dr.Hauser's enthusiasm. This time, I said, "Hmm.You mean, you don't always know why people act the way they do?"

Vati nodded. "Another lesson learned."

L I F E' S   L E S S O N S under a dictatorship taught the German population to be vigilant in word and deed. Adults were careful when they spoke in the presence of their children. Sometimes, though, I caught snippets of the humor that veiled desperation: Farmers were restricted as to what they could feed their animals. Anything fit for human consumption was off-limits.

On a farmer's visit with his neighbor, he asked, "What do you feed your chickens? They are plump and their feathers are shiny."

"*Ach*, I give the rooster five marks and tell him, 'You feed your family, and I feed mine.'"

At other times, parents were in danger of being reported for unlawful possession of food items because authorities had not made them available for sale during a given time span. On the way to school, children shared their happiness, "We had eggs for breakfast." Later, the friends brought the news to their mothers. "Fred's family ate eggs this morning. Can we have some, too?"

"They must have exchanged them on the black market. I don't have any eggs."

M O T H E R S   C A R R Y the heaviest burdens in times of war. While taking care of children and homes, they worry about their men at the front: husbands, sons, brothers, cousins and in-laws.

During World War II, German mothers were anxious also about the availability of the daily fare for their families. Creativity became essential.

When children outgrew clothes, mothers converted some of their own apparel into garments for their offspring, for whom they could rarely buy sewing material. Either stores ran out of stock, or ration card points were not called up when needed.

B Y   N E C E S S I T Y, Mutti met her challenges competently. As the third-born child but oldest girl in her family of ten children,

Cläri-Margret was accustomed to being a caretaker alongside her mother and two nannies.

Mutti and her siblings lost their mother when Gunhilt, the youngest, was only three years old. Their father died five years later in 1935.

The two oldest brothers, Paul-Hartwig and Eberhard, took the reins of the family business. Now in the third generation, *Paul Schlegel, Glas, Kristallwaren und Porzellan,* was the largest Pomeranian wholesaler and retailer in its industry. The family accountant and a pastor became guardians for Felicitas, Enno, Edzard and Gunhilt. Mutti and Vati provided a vacation home for the three who attended boarding schools. Gunhilt came to live with us. We got along well. She told her friends and teachers, "Almut is my niece and my sister."

Gunhilt played that double role well. If she wanted to exert authority she said, "I am your aunt. Give me that doll." At Christmas and at Easter, when we had received equal quantities of candy, she ate her sweets quickly. Gunhilt knew that I liked to save some for later days. Habitually, she wheedled, "You will share some with your sister, won't you?"

W E   A N T I C I P A T E D the mail carrier's daily visit with great anxiety during the nearly six years of war. In Germany, death notices of fallen soldiers arrived by mail, usually accompanied by a personal letter from the commanding officer. My parents were the contact for family members and the business the ten brothers and sisters owned jointly.

My uncles saw action in France, Russia, including Stalingrad, in Narvik, Norway, and on a *U-Boot* in the North Sea. Counting my father's brother and four brothers-in-law, my ten uncles survived the hostilities but all became POWs. Three died in captivity. Others came back wounded or with diseases.

I N 1939, Mutti was twenty-nine years old when the family responsibilities cascaded onto her shoulders. Since Vati was drafted again into one of the Luftwaffe's searchlight units, Mutti had only Gunhilt and me, a twelve- and a nine-year old, for company. We had to help and lost some of our playtime learning new skills.

The hardest and increasingly important lesson my mother taught us was *Strümpfe stopfen,* how to repair socks. Mutti gave each of us a *Stopfpilz,* a wooden tool in the shape of a mushroom. We pulled the sock or hose over the *Pilz* and placed the offending hole in the center of the mushroom head. We held the stem inside the sock with one hand, while with the other we wove needle and yarn into a pattern that closed the hole. Initially, many tears accompanied our efforts because Mutti was a perfectionist. With practice, our mending became acceptable.

Drying dishes after my mother had washed them, was another chore I tried to avoid.

"Pick a song. Perhaps we can harmonize. That will make the time seem to pass faster," Mutti said.

"Oh, ja: das Pommernlied."

Wenn in stiller Stunde	When in quiet moments
Träume mich umwehn,	Dreams envelop me
Bringen frohe Kunde	With happy memories,
Geister ungesehn,	Then hidden spirits
Reden von dem Lande	Whisper of the country
Meiner Heimat mir,	That is home to me
Hellem Meeresstrande,	With its sun-baked strands
Düsterm Waldrevier.	And dusky wooded lands.

Singing in harmony cheered both of us. Mutti's rare smile emphasized her beauty. She always brushed her long, blonde hair back and arranged it in a wide, flat bun over her nape. Blue eyes complemented her fine facial features. Mutti might have been one of Elizabeth Arden's earliest customers. She pampered her skin. I remember the array of cosmetic jars and bottles, cotton balls, and lipsticks on her vanity. And just when she could afford these luxuries after the years of Vati's irregular employment in the early 1930s, the war prevented the import of foreign products.

My mother's tall, slender figure and erect posture caught attention in public, which she acknowledged with charm. Hidden was her short temper. Impatience with others and the desire to get her will caused her to sever relationships. She decided how long the estrangements should last. Mutti expected her *antagonists*, including her siblings, to take the first step for reconciliation, at times sending my father or me to iron out the differences.

How I hated those missions. I was eight years old when I first thought, *besser machen!* I will never be like that!

The particular instant of that resolution is etched in my mind: Mutti had a habit of degrading my friends in order to get my attention while reprimanding me. If I felt that she had wronged me I tried to explain my point of view. That day Mutti cut me down sharply. "Don't you argue with your mother. I am not Doris you are talking to."

*   *   *

IN THE SUMMER OF 1945, after many brushes with death, my parents and I lived a glum life, subdued and hoping to stay alive. Baths, showers and cosmetics were distant memories. Our one mirror shard let Mutti see the effects infected fleabites and the lack of hygiene had on her face. She complained but never lost her temper over it. Instead, she looked ahead and scrounged for flour, sugar beet syrup, butter and salt to make batches of *Printen*—hard cookies—provisions for our planned escape to the west.

We estimated that by the end of September we would have harvested early potatoes, wheat and rye, and saved most of the vegetables from early frost. While I worked with Vati in the field, Mutti helped Frau Lehmann to preserve fruits and berries, which they steamed in jars as compote, boiled to make jelly and jam, or filtered for fruit syrup.

With this routine, we had plenty of time to reflect on our past. I wondered what went through my parents' minds. They did not whine or mention their material losses. Besides our plans for the future, our greatest concern was for our relatives. Had they survived? None of them had our address, nor had we theirs. The end of the war had come so quickly and violently that we did not reach our intended goal: the home of my mother's sister Renate in Kiel, Schleswig-Holstein. Her address had been the family's agreed-upon place for contact. Even though the postal authorities in East Germany made attempts to establish basic services in the Soviet Zone of Occupation, they did not connect with West Germany for months. Consequently, we could not inform my *Tante Reni* of our whereabouts.

Raids by Soviet troops during the days had become rare but nighttime visits still occurred. The troops sought out houses now and did not bother with chicken coops. What an advantage we had…

Fear, my stubborn burden for longer than two years, now tightened its ring around my neck less often. Yet, its presence served also as a reminder of our terror-laden encounter during air raids.

Almut, February 1931, Neu-Podejuch

23

Neu-Podejuch

Great-grandparents' house, Stettin

Vati and friend, July 1942

Almut, 1935

*Mutti visits Vati in Oldenburg
September 1939*

25

CHAPTER 2

The Rain of Terror

AS I TRACED MY MEMORIES back to my first three years in high school I realized that the turbulence in my life started when I was thirteen.

I attended the *Kaiserin-Auguste-Victoria Oberschule für Mädchen.* Our curriculum in the first three years differed immensely from the basic courses during my four grades in elementary school. We now took classes in German, history, geography, mathematics, biology, English, needlework and physical education, or *Turnen.* The classes met on different days of the week as scheduled, so we didn't have the pressure of doing homework for each subject every afternoon. The emphasis was on German, math and Turnen, each taught four hours a week. The remaining subjects filled in our schedules of five hours daily.

When air raids on Stettin and Berlin became more frequent in the early 1940s, and we had to spend two or more hours in the shelters, we reported to school at ten o'clock instead of eight. We skipped the first two classes.

The tenants of city buildings had allotted cellar spaces. Air raids necessitated the provision of a common shelter. Neighbors shared their individual cellars to make room for a communal sanctuary, which they fortified with beams and support pillars.

Families staked out their own niches, supplying as many chairs as they needed. As long as electrical generators were operating we had enough lights by which to read, do homework, mend or knit. If we lost electricity, we lit kerosene lamps and candles sparingly because of fire danger and the resulting loss of oxygen.

Whenever the sirens alerted a city's population to possible attacks, every person hurried to the nearest shelter. In the case of night raids, most people were not at work but at home, usually asleep.

Awakened by the alarms, my mother came to my bed to uncover me, sit me up and move my legs over the side. *"Wach auf, Almut! Schnell! Wir müssen in den Keller."* Wake up, Almut! Hurry! We have to go in the cellar.

I did not always hear the alarm despite its piercing wail. At times, the warning came when I was in my first sleep. In later months, I was dreaming of air raids already so that an alarm sounded in my subconscious while it was also reality; or I had barely fallen asleep again after our recent emergence from the cellar after the previous attack.

Once awake, I quickly dove into my laid-out clothes, reached for my assigned load to carry into the shelter and joined my mother and neighbors on our flight down the dimly lit stairway, observing the mandatory blackout. Every person lugged suitcases, blankets, pillows, some food, and candles to the shelter. People helped each other, lending support to the elderly or carrying a neighbor's child.

Not all alarms were sounded in time for us to reach the shelter, even if it was located on our own building. Then, fearful cries of rushing, stumbling people mixed with the tremendous noise that was always part of direct attacks: the droning of hundreds of planes' engines, the screeching of falling bombs, booming salvos of anti-aircraft guns; rattling machine gun bursts of bombers and fighters; the shattering of windows; the muffled collapse of buildings; and even the barking of pulled-along dogs. Often, casualties occurred before we reached our cellar.

People who arrived safely in their shelters settled in for an unknown duration, which depended on the target of the raiders. If they crossed the air space over Stettin to open their bellies over other cities and returned to their bases on a different route, we could leave the shelter within a short while. When raids on Stettin were carried out by waves of attackers, we trembled inside the shaking earth for hours.

Single able-bodied persons, usually belonging to Red Cross or *Luftschutz,* Civil Air Defense units, circulated in the shelters or made occasional checks for damage on the street level.

For a time, so-called *Dachbeobachter,* or rooftop observers, were supposed to watch for and announce the start of fires after hits by incendiary bombs. Pomerania's *Gauleiter,* or governor, had issued an ordinance to that effect, but authorities in Stettin, the capital city of Pomerania, soon realized that such an assignment on rooftops amid falling bombs was absurd. Instead of being able to report burning roofs, those observers were killed or maimed without anyone realizing the loss before the end of that particular raid. At other times, when the observers did report that the building's own or adjacent roof was on fire, panic broke out among the tenants in the shelters.

The governor had to be shown the tragic results of his ordinance. Therefore, Stettin's *Polizeipräsident,* or Police Commissioner, organized a demonstration of the effect of incendiaries and other bombs on the environment to which he invited the governor, as well as political and military administrators. The bombs used in the demonstration were duds dropped during the aerial attack on Stettin on April 21, 1943. Later, the police commissioner reported with satisfaction that the governor had been visibly impressed by the destruction. Consequently, this remote decision maker withdrew his order.

The governor's behavior raised doubt that he experienced an air raid in a shelter, rather than in one of Stettin's thirty-eight bombproof bunkers, which survived all attacks and could not be harmed by incendiaries. Most of the city dwellers were not that fortunate. We hovered under five floors of apartments. There we listened to the rhythm of carpet or pattern bombing. We had learned that the explosives screaming on the way down would not fall directly above us. It was ironic to identify the degree of danger by the sound of the bomb, the name of which was derived from the

28

Greek word *bombos,* meaning a deep, hollow sound. When the bombs detonated, buildings shook. If carpet bombing was applied to entire boroughs the shaking in its regular intervals never stopped until the end of the bomb run. It had the effect of an earthquake. No wonder that we felt caged rather then sheltered at the time. The world seemed to come to an end.

Whose idea was this madness? In their post-World War II research, historians and biographers noticed one recurring statement, which dominated the placing of blame for actions taken in the pursuit of eliminating opposition to political policies or fulfilling military objectives: "I only followed orders." Following orders was the routine that deadened anxiety and independent thoughts.

As for the aerial attacks on cities, the same sentiment was expressed by Allied as well as German participants in the war, from the lowest rank to commanding officers.

The aim of these political strategies by the Allied governments was to demoralize the German civilian population socially, economically, and psychologically. We could not shake off the terror of the air offensive after the first experience of an actual direct attack. After having survived one air raid, the anticipation of the next one manifested itself in various ways, sometimes as physical pain, such as the tightening of muscles in my neck. I called it my "iron ring." Others developed psychological fears and superstitions, or they adopted an "I don't care" attitude. The desired total breakdown of the population's will to live and to work did not materialize, if only because the best remedy was to go on with living.

This attitude reflected the feelings of the Allied and German bomber and fighter crews who carried out the raids or fought to abort them. The Allied flyers were counting the number of operations, which would fulfill their individual missions. After twenty-five missions they would leave the European front while the Germans kept defending their territory of dominance that had been shrinking daily since the loss at Stalingrad in 1943. But all these pawns in the hellish game of politicians and desk-bound militarists lived with fear. "We were doing our job at a particular time in a particular place," was their refrain.

The loss of comrades, the anti-aircraft hits, and the air battles caused burnout among the air crews, which was called cowardice by the Royal Air Force and labeled L.M.F., lack of moral fibre. This phenomenon was kept secret from the general public as it would reveal the ferocity and the human cost of air raids on German cities, according to a comment made by a U.S. veteran on NBC on June 2, 1984, in commemoration of D-Day.

How did German city dwellers deal with the ferocious assault on their everyday life? While no one could develop a routine to which a person was able to adhere confidently at a time when homes became frontlines, people embraced patterns of response to the air raids in World War II.

A F T E R   W E   H E A R D   T H E   S I R E N' S monotone signal at the end of the attack, the *Entwarnung,* the *Luftschutz* warden gave us a report on the condition of our building.

"We were spared this time. I guess you can go back to bed."

Increasingly, second then third air raids followed the first. When attacking cities, which were to receive their first massive aerial attack, bomber squadrons employed the full *Hamburg* treatment, so called for the method applied.

Dropped explosives broke windows and tore apart roofs over a wide area. The following incendiaries set fire to the buildings. Resulting sparks penetrated roofs and apartments; curtains and furniture went up in flames.

Stettin lost its virgin city status during the night from April 20 to 21, 1943. April 20 was Hitler's birthday. For that reason, German authorities correctly aniticipated a major air attack on Berlin, the capital. Additional *Fliegerabwehrkanonen,* Flak, or anti-aircraft, were to defend the city. Several of the relocated units had been stationed on the perimeter of Stettin. Because Allied bombers met with ferocious anti-aircraft fire around Berlin, they returned to their original flight route over the Baltic Sea, unloading their cargo on the way over the more weakly defended Stettin.

Mutti and I rushed out of the cellar after the last *Entwarnung,* all-clear, during that night. As soon as we set foot on street level we skated on glass shards, covering every one of the five floors of our tenement building.

Where did the heat come from? And this eerie orange glow? Why does it hurt to breathe?

In our apartment Mutti wet linen napkins and towels under the dripping faucet of the kitchen sink before the water ceased to flow completely. We knotted the napkins behind our heads, covering our noses and mouths. We took the towels to the windows that were facing the street and slapped at the incoming sparks. The raging firestorm sweeping through the street blew the sparks through the window openings and on us.

"Watch out," Mutti said, "I have to wet the top of your head. Check my hair, quickly."

"You're all right. I'll fetch two kerchiefs." As I tied one around Mutti's head, tears ran down my cheeks. "I can barely see what I'm doing. The smoke burns in my eyes and nose; acrid taste fills my mouth."

"Mine, too. Smoldering rubble will keep this smell in the air and on our clothes for days."

I wore the bulky brown cardigan Mutti had knit for me that year. The big stitches allowed incoming sparks to settle in their recesses. Consequently, Mutti and I swung our wet towels not only at windowsills and frames but on each other's backs, too.

FIRESTORMS ORIGINATE when separate fires become linked. As they heat the air above, an updraft occurs and attracts fresh air, pulling it to the center of the fires. The force of the movement is greater than those of normal combined winds. Temperatures in firestorms can exceed 1500 degrees Fahrenheit.

These infernos and the developing black smoke slowed or made escape of fleeing neighbors on the ground impossible. Many burned to death, while others suffocated.

31

Where fire fighting was possible, neighbors helped neighbors, watching each other's backs, manning bucket brigades; retrieving few possessions, stacking them in the street, loading them on handmade wagons, or tying them to bicycles. Children watched babies; grandparents guarded the last belongings until the mother was able to say either it was safe to return into the house or that they would have to find alternative housing.

The most frantic rescue missions took place where buildings had been hit by detonator bombs and lay in rubble. There were never enough cranes available after aerial attacks. People began to dig with spades, hoes, and their hands in attempts to free neighbors buried alive. One of those incidents is edged in my mind.

Mutti's youngest brother, Edzard, was on Christmas furlough from the Russian front. When the alarm had sounded for the air raid on January 6, 1944, he joined us in the shelter. He acted strangely out of place, pacing up and down among people who had sat down in *their* corner. It was Edzard's first experience as captive of an aerial attack after four years of frontline service in the infantry. "This is worse than sitting in a foxhole," he said, then went to the street level where he felt more in control of his life. Periodically, he returned to the shelter to reassure us of his well-being and to see how we were holding up.

On one such visit Edzard asked Mutti, "Was there always a street across from your building?"

"No," she answered with apprehension.

"One of the bombs we didn't hear coming while I was down here with you took out that structure. That was the cause of the earth-shattering burst we felt," Edzard explained.

Everyone in our shelter knew someone who had lived in that house. One of my classmates with whom I used to walk to school every morning was not found. I cried.

Margit's death pierced my invisible armor that had protected me from thinking that the "rain of terror" was more than a new routine to practice and, of course, survive. *It could have been our house... a split second sooner, or later, releasing the bomb...*

The personal loss of relatives and friends soon affected all German families. In addition to the heavy toll of lives on the battlefronts and in air raids
, there were also those casualties that occurred unexpectedly at rescue missions or wherever unexploded bombs detonated accidentally or due to their delayed fuses. Other untimely deaths befell hospital patients and others who depended on medication and could not find a supply in a burning city.

The casualties happened as much during daytime air raids as those in night attacks. Identifying the dead, however, was more difficult or even impossible after daytime raids because of the many people in transit. Most were going to work or school, or returning home. They were perhaps shopping or visiting doctors or relatives. Thousands of commuters swelled the cities' populations during the day. Moreover, in 1945, millions of refugees from the eastern provinces were passing through the cities west of their original homes.

All these segments of the population found themselves included in the helpless masses under the rain of terror.

Fear became my steady companion with which I learned to live. Different kinds of fear emerged under attack. While my uncle felt caged in our air-raid shelter, I would long for one, shaking during aerial attacks on trains I was riding.

If an alarm was sounded for the city and trains were about to enter the city limits, they stopped, literally in their tracks. All passengers could do was pray. They had no place to hide.

At other times I had been on trains during daytime several miles away from Stettin or later Stargard, East Pomerania, when the bomber squadrons and their fighter escorts appeared. Then all passengers had to vacate the trains and run into the fields or, if possible, into nearby woods. To watch from there an aerial attack on one's hometown where most of us had family and friends was another fearful experience. While fragments of anti-aircraft shells were falling all around us, we watched the bomb runs of the Flying

Fortresses and Liberators and the dog fights between escorting planes and German fighter planes. We also observed the crashing of incapacitated aircraft.

Gradually, the sky over the attacked city turned red, reflecting the inferno. Black smoke rose thickly and the wind carried the smell of massive burning across the Oder River. The memory of the daytime raids I witnessed made subsequent stays in air-raid shelters unbearable. I had come to understand my uncle's aversion to that confinement.

Contrary emotions, such as wishing for a shelter when none was within reach and wanting to be in the open when huddling below street level, expressed the great desire for an end to all that harassment and killing we call warfare. By the spring of 1945, warnings of approaching aircraft or full-alarm signals became useless because Allied aircraft were taking off from airfields on the European continent. They were present most of the time. Fewer bombers were needed for on-the-spot attacks.

WITH INCREASED EFFICIENCY of the bomb runs, the self-help measures of the city dwellers under attack diminished. The fire brigades often could not reach the burning areas because of the firestorms and the heat that developed instantly due to dropped bundles of incendiaries, which broke upon impact and scattered burning phosphorus.

Rescue missions after aerial attacks became increasingly difficult. To avoid trapping people in their cellars, wall breaches from one shelter to the adjacent building were to provide escape routes. This preventive measure was a blessing in instances where other exits became closed off by rubble or a wall of fire.
Some other time, the blast effects of the blockbuster bombs blew out the heavy doors and caused additional casualties.

The resulting losses of human lives along with the number of homeless, as well as the types of expended bombs over German cities were included in the official reports which the *Polizeipräsident* of the attacked community issued after each air raid. These reports also contained the precautionary measures, which city government agencies took in anticipation of possible aerial attacks.

Another great concern was the supply of water for fire-fighting. Manning the hoses of available fire engines was a challenge despite planning and organization. Since all able-bodied men from sixteen to fifty-five were serving in the military, only handicapped veterans or older men were available as firemen. Their diminished physical strength limited their endurance of the heavy demands made on them.

After bombing raids, we suffered interrupted telephone service, severed electric cables, gas lines, and water pipes. The damage to the utilities represented a tremendous hazard to all people involved in rescue or cleanup operations. Even people walking past ruins in search for relatives, or leaving their former, now destroyed, neighborhoods were exposed to the dangers of escaping gas, exposed powerlines, and gushing fountains of precious water.

Along with the utilities, the transportation network was out of commission after major air raids. Repairs to the streetcar system involved restoring the overhead leads, tracks, and cars. Service was usually reestablished in an amazingly short time.

As the war progressed, the attacking aircraft numbered more than two hundred. Stettin's harbor took substantial hits with losses of ships, docks, warehouses and bridges. Several of the fires burned for days and thick, oil-fed smoke spread inland, darkening the day.

Polizeipräsident Grundey wrote a comprehensive report after the war. In it he mentioned all Allied air raids on Stettin but treated the details of only the six major attacks on the city and its harbor. He included also the seven bombing raids on the *Hydrierwerke,* or oil refineries, in the northeastern borough of Pölitz.

Most of my memories of the rain of terror are very sad as the one of my missing classmate. One event, nevertheless, was so unique that I think people had to see the following scene because not even with good will would they believe that, as stated in our newspaper, *Pommerscher Anzeiger,* a hundred meter by one-and-a-half meter high mass of sugar, burnt into caramel, was the end of thousands of tons of sugar. According to his report, Polizeipräsident Grundey had tried to have the sugar stored in different warehouses, away from the refinery, but he had met with opposition. When the people of Stettin learned of this loss in January1944, they wondered how many rations of sugar that syrup mess represented. *Would there be any candy rations left for Easter?*

As I recount this incident, I am grateful Mr.Grundey's report verified that phenomenon. I saw this brown sea of syrup with my own eyes. Mutti wanted to find out about a friend's circumstances in Stettin-Zülchow.

"See whether the tram can reach her neighborhood," Mutti said. "Who knows when we'll have telephone service again? Ask if we can help her."

The streetcar tracks ran along the main street but several feet higher so that the trains could slowly proceed on the clean surfaces. We passed Marie's house. It had only broken windows and a pockmarked façade. I did not leave the streetcar to walk in the syrup. Mutti understood.

S O C I A L   A G E N C I E S tried to meet the needs of the individual *Ausgebombten,* people now homeless. In central locations, social workers distributed emergency rations of food, clothing, and blankets. Since the agencies had catalogued all types of dwellings, they knew where they could assign people to share habitable apartments.

The social impact of the air raids manifested itself most severely in these assignments and in the evacuations. While under duress and fire, people generally pulled together and acted in a brotherly spirit. The horrible experiences and ever-present fears, however, wore everyone's nerves down so that the slightest friction would often cause emotional eruptions between the original tenants of the apartments and the assigned Ausgebombten, or the rural population and the *Evakuierten,* evacuees. Difficulties arose especially in shared kitchens and bathrooms. The assigned people often had lost everything but their lives. They entered the homes of others with the need to share all household articles without joining the families.

To ease the increasing shortage of habitable apartments and the intention of saving lives led to evacuations. Residents considered non-essential to the functioning of the city experienced a change from their urban to an unfamiliar rural lifestyle.

Evacuees who could relocate to the country and stay with relatives or friends did so without government help. For others, special agencies found accommodations previously requisitioned for victims of air raids or, later, for refugees from the advancing Soviet troops.

After the disastrous aerial attack on April 21, 1943, Stettin's authorities issued a proclamation that schools were no longer open for students aged sixteen and under. Youths above sixteen had to remain in the city and perform social work with assigned agencies when needed.

Most high schoolers were evacuated with their teachers to Rügen, an island in the Baltic Sea. There we joined students from the Ruhr Valley who had arrived months earlier.

I was then thirteen years old. Because of the absence of water, gas and electricity as well as the condition of our devastated apartment, Mutti suggested she and I seek lodging in the countryside.

Gunhilt's legal guardians placed her in a boarding school in Saxony.

*   *   *

V A T I H A D R E T U R N E D to civilian life in late 1939. The government realized that the majority of farms were without heads of household to carry out successful planning and directing the work at their farms. Better to recall one agricultural administrator from the military than twenty-six farmers.

In his new assignment, Vati made his rounds at the farms. He advised the families about planting and harvesting, animal husbandry, and bookkeeping. He could spend only weekends with us in the city. Vati watched the air raids on Stettin from afar with great fear for the lives of his family. He received many offers from his clients to relocate us.

My parents wanted to choose an emergency residence from which I could commute to another high school. By invitation, we stayed three days on a trial basis on a farm in Birkhorst on the eastern shore of the *Dammscher See,* the lake that separated this rural area from Stettin.

When the news of the evacuation proclamation and its details reached us in Birkhorst, the first phase of the *Kinderlandverschickung,* KLV for short, or evacuation of children to the country, had already taken place.

"Du hast den Zug verpasst, im wahrsten Sinne des Wortes," Mutti said to me. You missed the train, literally.

"How did other families get their children ready so quickly? Many had no clothes to pack. Were they able to buy some? Are stores open again?"

"We'll have to go back into the city and try to find answers to your questions, Almut. Lots to do before your assigned train leaves."

A week later, we met the other schoolmates and latecomers of my school at Stettin's severely damaged *Hauptbahnhof,* the main railroad station.

There, the farewells were heartbreaking. Many months, even years ago mothers had to let their husbands go to war; now their children left.

After hugs and promises to write, we children took our seats on the train.

"Let's open the windows," I suggested.

We stretched out our arms to touch hands one more time. Most mothers were in tears, but only the youngest children among us cried. We were glad to escape the city and its dangers and looked forward to summer in vacation paradise.

When the train followed the curve of the tracks and we could no longer see our waving mothers, we sat down to anticipate our future in Sellin on the Pomeranian island of Rügen.

View from the cliffs of Rügen

CHAPTER 3

Kinderland

"TO WHICH HOTEL are you assigned?" Jutta asked me.

"*Haus Preussen*. That's where our class is staying. You must go there, too. Check your notice."

Jutta was as tall and thin as I was. Not many youngsters were plump after three-and-a-half years of war, except Gisela, the greengrocer's daughter. We were always hungry though not starving. Amid good-natured banter, we soon broke out the sandwiches that our mothers had lovingly prepared for us.

The first leg of our journey took us through a landscape of neatly partitioned fields in a northwesterly direction from Stettin to Stralsund, a harbor city on the Baltic Sea. The serenity of the sun-bathed countryside affected our war-scarred minds.

"I forgot what long stretches of our world look like without bomb craters," Brigitte Stengel mused as she motioned her head toward the springtime scenery. Winding her blonde braids around her right hand, she continued, "Perhaps we can pick some wildflowers on the island."

"*Ja,* press them and enclose some in the letters to our mothers," Lisbeth Braun added.

An early tinge of homesickness?

AFTER ABOUT TWO HOURS, our train crossed the Strait of Strelasund over the *Rügendamm,* the 1.5 mile-long causeway

40

connecting the mainland with Rügen, the largest German island. In Putbus we had to change trains. The so-called *Rasende Roland,* Racing Roland, a narrow-gauge train, huffed and puffed its cargo to the seaside spas.

Although tired after our five-hour excursion, we wondered about our accommodations at Haus Preussen.

"It will be great to see many of our classmates again," Kiki Waller said.

"The train is slowing down. We must be there," I exclaimed and stuck my head out the window.

"Sellin!" the conductor called out after the train had stopped at our destination. A teacher from another of Stettin's high schools greeted us with shocking news.

"Haus Preussen has been put under scarlet fever quarantine for six weeks. During this time you will be housed in the *Strand-Hotel* with our students. We have several rooms available and will try to place you with your chosen roommates," she said.

Meanwhile, hotel employees had loaded our luggage on a horse-drawn wagon. We followed this rig on foot to our new location.

On the way, we tried to decide who would be our roommates.

"Jutta, do you want to share a room with me?" I asked.

"Gladly, but how do we know whether they'll assign us to doubles, triples, or more?"

"We won't know that before we get there. Who else do you think, could share a room with us?"

"Let's wait."

Finally, we reached the last turn on our hike as we entered the *Wilhelm-Strasse.* On this uphill street, hotels and full-service private guesthouses had catered to tourists and summer residents for decades. In the early 1940s the German government requisitioned them for the Kinderlandverschickung.

Halfway up the street, familiar faces and voices from our school, the KAV, greeted us enthusiastically from the balconies of the three-story Haus Preussen.

"Hello! Where have you been? Do you realize you could be shut-ins like us if you hadn't missed our train? Where are you going?"

"The Strand-Hotel," we shouted.

"What? To *Gesenius-Wegner?* You poor lambs!"

That was all we needed: to feel like lambs going to the slaughterhouse because of the traditional competitive spirits between the high schools in Stettin.

Our reception at the Strand-Hotel, situated on the promenade, was cordial. Jutta and I shared a double on the fifth floor.

"Living under the attic has one advantage," I remarked looking out the window. "Above the trees, we have an unimpeded view of the sea."

"I suppose we should give our room a name and paint a sign for the door, like others did," Jutta said.

"How about *Kap Arkona?*" I suggested, thinking of our lofty room at the northern edge of the hotel and naming it after Rügen's cape at its north shore.

We reported to the dining room shortly after our arrival. The head teacher welcomed us and promised cooperation, calling us guest students. While this expression meant that our school, KAV, paid the monthly tuition received from our parents, our hosts intended to treat us as guests, not as poor lambs.

We didn't know any of the teachers and few of the students of the Gesenius-Wegner school but had expected our teachers to fulfill their daily responsibilities *in loco parentis.*

Following the welcoming speeches and introductions, our new fellow students taught us our first lesson. They were hungry and did not want to wait any longer for their food. Thus they sang out in unison,

"Wir haben Hunger, Hunger, Hunger,
haben Hunger, Hunger, Hunger,
haben Hunger, Hunger, Hunger,
haben Durst."
"Wir müssen warten, warten, warten

müssen warten, warten, warten
müssen warten, warten, warten, bis's was gibt."

We fell in quickly to express our sentiments. We, too, were hungry and thirsty, obligated to wait until the student waiters of the week could serve us supper.

In Germany, the big meal, *Mittagessen,* is usually served during the middle of the day; *Abendbrot* or *Abendessen,* the evening meal, is often a cold supper. So, no dinner for us that day; sandwiches on the train and again at night. The food in the KLV was always tasty and nutritious—there was just never enough of it for active teenagers.

On our first full day in Sellin, we received textbooks to share and work materials, such as pencils, erasers, pens, and paper in moderate quantities. These rations taught us thrift, which became a habit for life.

We attended classes daily in former conference rooms. Our attention was never undivided because of our worry about family members in the city.

Rügen was declared a Red Cross sanctuary on account of the thousands of evacuees from German cities and the required absence of military installations.

Whenever the sun shone from a blue cloudless sky we said, "This is a perfect day for air raids." Often, the alarm sounded in Sellin when Allied planes approached the mainland from the north. Then we had to leave the buildings and seek shelter in the nearby forest. We stared at the messengers of death and their pregnant bellies, hoping they would spare our loved ones. From radio broadcasts we learned which cities had been the targets on a given bomb run; but it took days before we received personal reports by phone or mail from home.

After mail call we asked one another, "What did your mother write?"

"She let me know that no bombs fell in our immediate neighborhood this time. But did you hear that Anke's brother was killed in Russia?"

We shared the good and the bad news.

Mutti wrote that Vati was drafted again and sent to the *Ostfront,* or eastern front.

We couldn't even say good-bye, I thought. For the first time since leaving Stettin, my eyes welled tears.

Despite our anxieties we were learning in our classes, perhaps because we wanted to cover our angst with new impressions and experiences.

We liked our hands-on science classes in nature and the sports we practiced on the lawns and the beach the best.

During blueberry time we went with our class to pick the abundant fruit for the hotel kitchen. We returned from those outings with stained hands and faces, looking forward to delicious desserts. Before supper, however, we had to remove ticks from our arms and legs.

Another organized activity supporting our upkeep was that of *Kienäppel sammeln,* or gathering pine cones. On Saturdays maids lit fires under the huge copper vats in the hotel laundry room. The pine cones supplemented firewood for our once-a-week hot water bath. We also did our personal laundry on these occasions.

*   *   *

RARE VISITS FROM OUR FAMLIES and field trips were the highlights of our stay on Rügen.

"Did you know we are going to see the *Kreidefelsen* on Friday?" Jutta said jubilantly as she entered our room.

"Prima! Das wird eine Tagesreise," I said, looking forward to a day trip to the white cliffs.

Our class left early Friday morning. We hiked for about five miles through the forest from Sellin to Binz where we boarded an excursion steamer for Sassnitz. This harbor is called the "gate to the north" because of its active maritime commerce with Scandinavia.

On our short enjoyable voyage we looked up at the white cliffs, known as *Wissower Klinken,* from the level of the sea. What an impressive sight!

"We'll have another hike before we are up there," Fräulein Schneider, our homeroom teacher, said. She guided us along the *Uferwaldweg,* the coastal trail. It led through a forest of beech trees in *Jasmund National Park.*

Of course, Fräulein Schneider was well prepared for our lessons *in natura.*

"Rügen has its origins in the cretaceous period and is a cretaceous island, saturated with moraines at different levels. The action of glaciers probably caused this deposit of debris."

"There you have history and geography rolled into one," Kiki Waller whispered, ever the ungrateful teenager. "What's next?"

She did not have to wait long for a lesson in botany. We learned to identify trees, grasses, rare orchids, and the different varieties of horsetails, one of which we collected and dried to make tea.

"In zoology we'll probably study ticks again. Wonder how many we'll catch today," Kiki joked.

Instead, Fräulein Schneider directed our attention to the osprey and falcons circling over the cliffs and sea. Even teenagers could marvel at the birds' powerful flight and dives.

When we reached the majestic *Wissower Klinken,* we were struck dumb with amazement. Our view of them from the boat had dazzled us with their starkly white cliffs rising out of the blue sea, framed by the green forest. Now we could rub our fingers against them and recognize their composition.

Fräulein Schneider touched on economics when she told us of the value of the chalk deposits on the island.

"For the people of Rügen this plentiful sediment supports an industry. In the process of whiting, pulverized fine chalk is prepared for use in toothpaste, metal polish, and artist's paint."

Over the years these products have reminded me of the Kreidefelsen.

*　　*　　*

R E U N I O N S   W I T H   O U R   P A R E N T S were cherished and memorable occasions, especially if fathers or brothers spent part of their furloughs from the front near us. Then they had to rent rooms from local fishermen's families, farmers or *Pensionen*, bed-and-breakfast lodgings, because all hotels housed children of the Kinderlandverschickung.

Before we met my, or Jutta's, mother at the Racing Roland, we picked wild flowers or blueberries for them in the woods adjacent to the Strand-Hotel. At the railroad station, we joined about fifteen other girls from among the hundreds of evacuated students living in Sellin.

Once our visitors disembarked and we exchanged our reunion hugs, our happiness spilled over.

"Mutti, if you sign Jutta and me out every day of your stay, we can be with you. We can go to the beach, or we can visit some of the *Hünengräber,* these impressive prehistoric burial sites. Or shall we go to Binz to see Jutta's brother? That's where all the boys' schools have their accommodations. Or…"

"Hold it!" Mutti interrupted. "First, take me to my lodging. There we'll catch up with the news. Then we'll go to the Strand-Hotel, where I'll meet your teachers and you can show me your room. Tomorrow, I'll pick you up after your classes and we'll go exploring." She stretched and breathed deeply. "How wonderful the fresh air feels … how peaceful and removed from the war this island seems to be …"

We anticipated family visits with eagerness, knowing that *Vorfreude ist die beste Freude,* anticipated joy is the greatest joy. As happy as the days spent together were, the renewed farewell felt as raw as the one at our leaving Stettin. The unspoken question troubling us still was, "Will we see you again?" Handkerchiefs in hand, we wiped away our tears and waved *Auf Wiedersehen* as long as we could see the train.

S C H O O L   A C T I V I T I E S helped us back into our routine. The regularity of instruction eased the move to Haus Preussen after the end of the quarantine.

Our daily exercise on the beach included walking, timed sprints—difficult in the sand—swimming and *Burgenbau,* building sand castles. The higher the walls, the more protection we had from the sea breeze and the air-borne sand. In competitions, every castle had a name, which we spelled out with shells on the outside of the wall.

Collecting amber was an informal competition.

"Look at the size of this piece. Is it amber or just a brown pebble?" one of my classmates asked.

"Here: Rub it against my wool sweater. If it picks up a tiny piece of paper, it's amber," I said.

"Rügen, the Queen of the Baltic, has her own buried treasure," Jutta remarked.

For centuries, local artisans have taken advantage of this natural find to create amber jewelry, which they sell in small stores and boutiques.

*   *   *

I N   T H E   F A L L   O F 1943, the evacuees of Rügen prepared for winter. Students went back to their families for a week to exchange their summer clothes for winter garments. The challenge for mothers was to provide their teenagers with warm apparel at a time when many families themselves were evacuees or homeless. They had neither hand-me-downs nor sufficient points on their *Kleiderkarten,* or ration cards for clothing and shoes to properly outfit their children. Nor did those families own valuables that could help them trade on the black market.

Children improvised by borrowing and lending a jacket here, a skirt or slacks there. It seems that nearly every female over the age of eight learned to knit or crochet. My mother used to unravel old sweaters so she could knit new ones, or mittens, hats or socks.

Per doctor's orders, I could not spend the cold months at the Baltic Sea coast because of my bout with rheumatic fever when I was nine. Instead, my parents placed me with my father's brother, Ulrich, and his family in the country. In Friedeberg, fifty-five miles southeast of Stettin, I continued the odysseys of my education as a guest student.

Vati on furlough,
Sellin, Summer 1943

Jutta, Kiki and Almut with classmates in
Sellin, Summer 1943

Mutti's visit in Sellin, with Almut
and Jutta on the beach. Summer 1943

CHAPTER 4

Friedeberg

BY REPEATEDLY TRANSPLANTING seedlings into increasingly larger containers, they develop into stronger plants, capable of growing further with less care if provided the necessary environment.

Just like a plant's guided growth, my frequent changes of environment and schools contributed to molding me into the person I became.

When Vati's brother Ulrich and his wife Gerti invited me to spend the winter months with them before I could return to my school on Rügen for the summer, my parents were grateful and I was elated.

Onkel Ulrich was a fun-loving and entertaining man. He played card games with me and challenged me to discover his cheating.

"You have to watch your opponent at all times," he said. "Which card is missing?"

"*Der schwarze Peter,*" Black Peter, the cat and character in a game comparable to Old Maid.

"Why can't I ever win against you? Which cards have you hidden now?" I asked.

With a smile he retrieved cards from his sleeve and from under his feet.

Like my father, Onkel Ulrich was again a civilian in 1943. Drafted at the beginning of the war, he returned home to help secure food for the German population. My uncle oversaw an installation to which farmers delivered their quotas of eggs. Through careful inspection of the eggs as they passed through light chambers, employees graded this harvest. Incubators received the prime specimen while the others went to market.

In contrast to Onkel Ulrich's imposing figure, Tante Gerti was of diminutive stature. Her friendly disposition allowed her to channel my uncle's ebullience into calm. She guided their two-year-old twin boys and one-year-old son with love and purpose.

Joining this household was quite a change for me. An only child, arriving from a camp-like atmosphere shared with hundreds of preteen girls, I now assumed the role of big sister to Wolf, Peter and Uwe. I was happy and never tired of playing with my little cousins or pushing their carriages on our excursions through their neighborhood of Friedeberg.

This scenic town, situated east of the Oder and north of the Netze Rivers in the area called *Neumark,* has a rich history. Friedeberg received its name when in 1260, Count Konrad had a castle, the *Friedeberg,* built for the protection of the old trade route that passed through. While there have been many changes of the spelling of Friedeberg from the thirteenth century to the present, the symbolic meaning of the name is *Berg des Friedens,* mountain of peace.

And peaceful was the impression I had as I came to live among the town's estimated six thousand residents. Despite the presence of noise from industries, such as sawmills and machine-producing factories, agriculture was the most important resource. Friedebergers expressed their love of the land in colorful and well-cared-for gardens and parks.

I attended the only local high school, the *Gymnasium.* Originally, a Gymnasium accepted only male students. The war, however, changed this arrangement in many communities. As evacuees from city high schools sought refuge in the country, schools became co-ed by necessity.

To be the new kid in school is stressful enough; to be gawked and snickered at by ten-to-eighteen-year-old boys—and boys they were—required stoicism in the hallways. In class, I enjoyed the directness and precision of the teachers' presentations and the students' discipline. The few months I spent at that school provided me with an appreciation of the value and satisfaction of academic achievement.

Eventually, the female enrollment grew to a handful of guest students from Berlin and Stettin and the cities of the center of heavy industry—the Ruhr Valley.

Dating back to times when every able hand helped with bringing in the harvests, German schools recessed for autumn vacation. In 1943, we students thirteen and older, received our orders to gather potatoes in farmers' fields.

"You have read in the papers that you will report on Monday morning at half past six in front of the main gate of the Gymnasium," our class advisor told us at the end of the last class before vacation.

"That early?" the class clown piped up.

"You can sleep all day on Sunday, Rudi, to be rested for your participation," Herr Schmidt recommended.

"Do we bring our bicycles?" Gerhard Kurtz asked.

"No, trucks will take you. You will need your strength for work. Most likely you will not even know how you arrived back here after a full day in the fields because you will fall asleep on the truck," Mr. Schmidt said.

For the following two weeks, we gathered potatoes that machinery had unearthed. At seven o'clock in the morning, fog hovered over the land. Our clothes were damp, our hands numb.

The fields met the horizon. At the starting point, the workers faced the assigned field: in a row life-long farmhands alternating with students. The purpose of this arrangement soon became painfully clear to us. The speed with which the women picked up the potatoes and dropped them into wire baskets left us breathless. We were expected to maintain the set tempo.

"Do you think they'll slow down after a while?" Annemarie, from Berlin, asked me as we were looking at the women's backs.

"I doubt it. Better learn to keep up."

"Oh, my aching back!"

Men displaced from eastern European countries moved among us, leaving empty baskets as they carried full ones to waiting trucks and trailers. From seven to ten o'clock we did not have a break unless the trucks had not returned from the farm after transferring their loads, and all baskets in the fields were filled. But at ten they brought us farmers' sandwiches.

"I can't remember when last I had such a rich sandwich, buttered and liverwurst," Renate, another guest student said.

"I can," one of the Friedeberger boys volunteered. "Last year. Here."

Our drinks were piping hot. We poured *Ersatzkaffee* from big enamel coffee pots into enamel cups. Roasted barley was the usual ersatz for coffee beans.

"Back to work!" the supervisor called out.

"We'll have lunch to look forward to," Hans said.

The lunch break was about thirty minutes longer than the ten-o'clock recess.

We were able to enjoy delicious thick potato soup or stew, and socialize. In this setting we met students who were not in our classes. They were frisky boys. Wandering hands tried to make contact. We girls effectively discouraged them.

In mid-afternoon, coffee and *Marmeladenstullen,* rye sandwiches with butter and homemade preserves, broke up the strenuous routine.

"Eleven more days like this one? I guess the food and the money will bring us back," Burkhard Bauch said.

"As if we had a choice," I mumbled.

The strain on the body eased and became more tolerable with each following day. Sleep during those nights was fitful, though. If leg cramps did not wake me up, recurring dreams of endless potato fields and my fear of falling behind disturbed my rest.

Potatoes were a major crop in Pomerania. Children helped with more than just the harvest. In the spring, before our evacuation, classes collected the foraging Colorado potato beetles. Armed with glass jars, we gathered these bugs, turning leaves plant-by-plant, row-by-row. When the jars were filled, we emptied them into pails. Farm workers doused the beetles with kerosene and burned them.

It was important to remove the yellow or orange, black-striped, three-eights-of-an-inch-long aggressors before they laid their eggs and larvae hatched. Their ferocious appetite could defoliate entire fields of potato plants and destroy a crop.

Besides our missions in agriculture, young students went into action when Allied airplanes had scattered massive amounts of aluminum strips over cities and the countryside to create static interference with German radar defenses.

"Who will turn in the largest ball of aluminum strips? I have a prize for the winner at the end of the month," said Herr Henze, our class advisor and math teacher.

On the way to school, returning home, going to the grocer's and of course on the class trips scheduled for this activity, we rolled this resource for the war effort into balls. I did not win the prize, but even after the war I rolled aluminum foil from chocolate and chewing gum wrappers into balls before discarding them.

*　　*　　*

DURING THE TWO WEEKS of bringing in the potato crops the guest students became an accepted part of the Gymnasium's student body in Friedeberg. Initial disbelief by the natives about the city kids' backgrounds and experiences turned to respect and empathy.

"Are you sure you went to see plays or operas in your *Stadttheater,* city opera, every month?" Paul Spies asked.

"Yes, my parents gave me an *Abonnement* for my birthday," I said.

"What did you see?"

"Schiller's *Don Carlos.* One evening an air raid interrupted Goethe's *Faust.* So, I never saw the last act."

"You visited Belgium and Holland?" Manfred Meier questioned Lisa Werth.

"That wasn't difficult," said Lisa. "My hometown *Aachen* borders both countries. But I love your beautiful countryside with its lakes, meadows and the fragrant fruit trees and soil."

"Yes, and the people are hospitable," added Klaus Schneider from Köln. "I was dubious about coming here because of your reputation: *die sturen Pommern.*"

"We aren't stoic people—just like to think before we speak," said Gerhard Steindorf, called Stein.

"Best of all, no air raids here, no sleepless nights, no constant angst," said Lisa.

The guest students felt welcomed and our Friedeberger schoolmates learned a little about life beyond their then-peaceful county.

We became more sociable with the relaxation of tension between our two camps. For the first time, a boy, Paul, accompanied me home after school and carried my books. He was Gerhard Steindorf's best friend. Gerhard was a leader in any group he joined, admired and respected by his fellow students. A class above me, I could fancy him only from afar. Besides, he had a girl friend. Years later, we accidentally met in West Germany.

MY BLISSFUL STAY IN FRIEDEBERG ended abruptly when Mutti visited me at Onkel Ulrich's house. She was strong-willed and did not appreciate opposing views. Thus, after an argument with Tante Gerti, she pulled me out of school and took me back to Stettin.

I had no time for goodbyes and was sad to leave my cousins and friends. Where would I go next?

The ride from Friedeberg to our home led east along the Warthe River toward the Oder via Vietz. In this area, we saw settlements dating back to the 1770s and 1780s. Under Frederick II, or Frederick the Great, settlers drained the swamps and cultivated the land. Influenced and inspired by the news of the

54

American Revolution, villages called their new communities Yorktown, Hampshire, Saratoga and Pennsylvanien. For some settlers, America represented a goal they dreamed about.

Like the eighteenth-century settlers I dreamed of far-away places without war and frequent uprootings, no matter how beneficial oft-repeated transplanting is for plants.

Almut and cousins Uwe, Wolf and Peter Finger

CHAPTER 5

Hinzendorf and Stargart

ON THE WAY BACK TO STETTIN, I asked my mother, "Now what? Where am I supposed to go to school?"

"I will call *Tante Dorle,* and ask whether you can stay with her," Mutti said.

"She lives in Hinzendorf. What high school is near that village?"

"You will probably have to go to school in Stargard."

What planning. My aunt, Mutti's sister, did not even know about, let alone consent to my intended stay at her house.

As the oldest sister in her orphaned family of ten, Mutti was accustomed to making arrangements for her younger siblings, along with their court-appointed guardians. Consequently, my aunts and uncles respected my mother's wishes and directions. It was no surprise to me that Tante Dorle agreed to welcome me to her household.

My aunt was a pediatric nurse when she met Justus Grassmann, called Beppo. At twenty-four, Tante Dorle married Onkel Beppo, a much older man. He had been a pilot in *the Richthofen-Geschwader,* the "Red Baron's" squadron, during World War I.

In World War II, he was too old for active duty. As the *Forstmeister,* or forest superintendent, over an area that included more than one county, he was responsible for not only the flora but also the fauna. The game wardens kept precise records of every

56

stag and doe. Game became part of our meat rations during the early years of the war.

When I joined their family in the winter of 1943, Tante Dorle and Onkel Beppo's only child, Dietrich, was five years old. Once again I had "a little brother" to entertain. On one occasion, I read one of his books to *Dieter,* as we called him. Looking at the pictures, he asked, "What is that?"

"A banana."

"And that?" He pointed at an orange. "What do they do?"

"They are fruit. You can eat them. They taste good."

"Why don't we have any?"

It was up to me, the thirteen-year old to explain to my cousin the habitat of tropical fruits, and one consequence of war: Embargoes and sea battles prevented many imports. Dieter was always inquisitive and grew up to achieve a doctorate in chemistry.

In Hinzendorf, we lived in the *Forsthaus,* the official residence of the Forstmeister. A barn and stables framed the farmyard; a small park bordered on the herb and vegetable garden. I participated in farm and garden chores in my free time.

On school days I had no free time. Awakened at six o'clock, I rushed to catch the Post bus to Stargard forty-five minutes later. In areas that could not be reached by rail, the postal system, as well as the railroad, provided bus service as they delivered mail and freight.

The bus took about an hour to arrive in Stargard, a city I had only known as a waypoint on trips to more eastern areas of my home state. In school I had learned that Stargard, situated on the Ihna River, is about thirty-two kilometers from Stettin. I recalled textbook descriptions and facts of the city's history and development on my commute to school.

Later events in my life crowded out the exact route through Stargard's streets to the bus depot and the walk to the *Königin-Luise* school. I do remember, though, the idyllic inner city reflecting the architecture of Stargard's beginnings, tribulations, and growth.

First mentioned in documents in 1124, the early settlers of the town included merchants, craftsmen and monks. During the Thirty-Years War, 1618 –1648, Stargard burned repeatedly and was nearly destroyed. However, because Stettin became part of Swedish territory at the end of that war, Stargard rose to be the capital of non-Swedish eastern Pomerania.

We guest students could not forge friendships with our Stargarder classmates because of our bus and railroad schedules. At times, we were late coming to school because of air raids on the way, or we had to leave early to catch the last bus or train leaving Stargard in our respective directions. We became aware nonetheless of our classmates' backgrounds. Many of their families worked for local industrial plants, distilleries, and cigar manufacturers, which processed products grown in the area, such as rye, sugar beets, and tobacco.

But I went there to further my education. In this field, too, Stargard had an old and glowing reputation that dated back to the early seventeenth century.

When I entered the assigned classroom on my first day at the *Königin-Luise Oberschule für Mädchen,* a girls' high school, I was surprised but glad to see several of my Stettiner classmates. These girls lived in Stettin's suburbs east of the Oder River. Instead of taking trains from Finkenwalde and Altdamm to Stettin, they now traveled in the opposite direction to Stargard. Some of our teachers who did not join the move to Rügen found jobs at schools with increased enrollments away from metropolitan areas.

Attending school in Stargard was not as peaceful as it had been in Friedeberg. With Stargard's proximity to Stettin we often had to evacuate our classrooms and dash to shelters when Allied bombers crossed over the area on their flight path to Berlin or Stettin.

The guest students felt greater urgency than the local students to seek cover before the aircraft dropped their deadly loads. We were the experienced children, survivors of earlier raids.

"Hurry up," we yelled at the stragglers. "You don't want to die in the staircase, do you?"

"Your city makes another good target with its railroad junction, an important link to the Russian front," my friend Doris added.

"Not again," Helga Wittmann sighed. Her family relocated from Essen in the devastated industrial Ruhr Valley to re-establish its business in the quiet but productive countryside of Pomerania.

I liked the qualities of, *meine Heimat,* my home state, which I quietly observed on my daily bus rides to and from Stargard and Hinzendorf.

At the *Forsthaus,* I had my own comfortable, spacious room and bath in the attic. For a girl who had left a city apartment with blown-out windows and splintered furniture, I felt like a queen as the only tenant on the third floor. From here I could see the sun rise over the village and the surrounding beech and pine forests in a panoramic view.

Here, too, I paced routinely back and forth, memorizing assignments given in our German class, such as the famous epic writings by Germany's great poets and writers, Goethe and Schiller. Their poems, *Erlkönig* and *Die Glocke,* respectively, are standard lessons in German schools and take days to memorize. They were practical assignments for our teachers. No matter how much class time and instruction were shortened due to air raids, students could start memorizations at home or on the way.

"I absorb less education in school than in shelters and on the road," I told my parents. "I spend more time there, too."

Transportation became ever more irregular. Bus and train schedules were unreliable, so we caught the next available conveyance. In the winter, I left home in the dark and returned in the dark; my serving of the noontime meal had dried and shrunk in the warming compartment of the stove. Doing homework gave way to needed sleep.

Because of these conditions, we commuting students were no competition for those living in Stargard. Poor grades hurt my pride.

CHAPTER 6

My Last School Days In Pomerania

IN THE SPRING OF 1944, I had to return to my class in Sellin, Rügen. By that time, I was used to frequent changes in my life and the necessary goodbyes.

Dieter did not want me to leave, "Will you come back tomorrow?" he asked me.

Will I ever return to Hinzendorf? The war taught us not to think too far ahead.

I found it difficult to leave my pleasant room at the *Forsthaus* behind and to give up the walks in the forest. On occasion, Onkel Beppo had allowed me to accompany him on his rounds.

"Today I want to look for an old stag. I saw him limp the other day but let him go. Now I have to determine whether his injury is life-threatening."

"How will you find him?"

"We have to walk to an elevated blind where we will sit and wait for him to pass. I know his routine."

On the way to the blind, my uncle motioned me repeatedly to avoid stepping on twigs or dried leaves. "Don't make any noise!" As I tried hard not to upset my uncle and ruin our mission, I perceived his silent gait. I admired his sure foot as he peered through the underbrush.

From our lookout we observed deer, rabbits, squirrels and birds. I would have liked to ask many questions but, obviously, I could not talk while we waited for the stag. I saved my queries for the dinner table.

Onkel Beppo pointed at a clearing shortly before sunset. I saw a majestic animal surveying the glade. When his family of does and fawns caught up with him, he trotted off to scout the meadow ahead to protect the herd.

My uncle smiled, indicating that the stag was no longer limping and still in control, able to defend his position.

I, on the other hand, felt like a ball being bounced back and forth by players: my parents who wanted to keep me safe from the war's intrusions, and the government's decreed solutions to the same problem. They were in control, though limping. Unlike the stag, they had to send their "fawns" away.

AFTER A WEEK'S SPRING BREAK that brought all evacuated children from Sellin back to their mothers for outfitting with summer clothing, I rejoined my original class. What stories we had to tell each other about our experiences during the past six months. My classmates reacted to my accounts of attending a Gymnasium, "A boys' school, oo-oh! How was it? Were they fresh?" They also listened when I told them how I was reunited with some of our friends in Stargard.

"But how was the winter on the island?" I wanted to know.

"Cold, bitter cold. These summer palaces were not designed to having guests in the winter. Only common rooms like dining halls and rooms converted to classrooms were warm enough for us to be able to hold a pencil," the veterans of the *Kinderlandverschickung* told me.

"*Ja,* we'll still have cool temperatures until the end of June: don't you remember from last year?" I said.

Like the weather, much of life in the KLV on Rügen was what I recalled from my previous stay. One incident, however, was momentous enough to stay memorable.

For me, that particular mishap began with a Sunday evening meal of individual cold platters. Our open-faced sandwiches featured toppings of sliced gherkins and tomatoes. When I took a bite of the liverwurst sandwich and its gherkin decoration, I felt sharp pains at the roof of my mouth as well as my tongue.

"Ach, du liebe Güte, was ist das?" I said as blood was oozing out of the corners of my mouth, goodness, what's that?

Those were the last words I could pronounce coherently as my tongue swelled up quickly and the sharp pain returned every time I moved my mouth. The wire of my braces had snapped behind the upper front teeth; one end boring into my tongue, the other into my palate.

"You are lucky that the government dentist will be in town tomorrow. She will help you," my math teacher reassured me. I could neither eat, nor drink, nor speak and had to wait until the next day before I could expect help.

"I am not allowed to administer treatments other than fill cavities," the dentist said.

"Can't you cut the loose ends of the wire off?" I wrote on the pad she gave me.

"No, you have to see your dentist back home," she said.

"What? Go to Stettin? Alone? My mother does not have a telephone," I wrote.

"I can call your doctor for you," she offered.

"But she will not know when I can be at her office. I have no idea what train connections I can find."

"I will contact your teachers to check the railroad schedules to send you on your way as soon as possible."

The Racing Roland left the coastal towns for Putbus in the morning and returned in the early evening. Consequently I could not begin my trip to Stettin for another day.

On the morning of my departure I was hungry and felt weak. People stared at me and my bloody swollen lips. When they asked whether they could help, I shook my head. Every time I wanted to speak, the broken wire dug in and scratched along my tongue. The resulting grooves became permanent.

In Stalsund, I sat in the *Bahnhofsrestaurant,* the railroad station's restaurant, painfully sipping an orange-flavored drink through a straw. The loudspeaker competed with the din of the talking, walking and dining travelers. From time to time an announcer informed them of the arrival or departure of scheduled trains.

"Achtung! Achtung! Sondermeldung!" Attention: special report.

"Alliierte Truppen sind heute morgen an der Küste der Normandie gelandet. Schwere Kämpfe sind im Gange." Allied troops landed this morning on the coast of Normandy. Heavy battles are being fought.

Heavens, how quickly will they come here? Will they carry out more air raids while I am on the train, and later in Stettin? Mutti does not know I left Sellin today. Vati is on the Ostfront. Where will I go? I have little money and only one change of clothes with me. Will Tante Doktor expect me?

These and other thoughts swirled through my head on this Tuesday, June 6, 1944. People in the restaurant fell silent for a little while before engaging their neighbors in discussions.

"Nein, oh nein! My husband is stationed in Caen."

"My brother is in Cherbourg."

"Well, don't panic. Our troops expected an invasion. They will prevail."

While the people in the restaurant expressed their fears and their hopes to one another, I decided to follow through with my plan to seek treatment at *Tante Doktor's* office. *Will she be there?*

Dr. Elfriede Scheddin was a long-time friend of Vati. They both had taken pre-med courses at the Berliner Universität. Vati used this background in the field of animal husbandry. Dr. Scheddin became a dental surgeon. I visited her office for the first time when I was three years old. From then on, I called her Tante Doktor.

Soon the train to Stettin was announced. I went to the assigned platform, looking all around me. *Everything looks as it did two hours ago. The people go about their business. Are the Allies not landing here, too?*

During the entire ride to Stettin I looked out the windows, scanning the sky, searching for Allied airplanes.

I was relieved when I arrived in Stettin. A feeling of being home washed over me. I knew my way. No matter how bad the destruction disfigured my city, and what detours I had to take with streetcars, I was able to arrive in Braunsfelde, the suburb where Tante Doktor practiced.

When she saw me in the waiting room, she gasped, "Almut, what did you do? Where are you coming from?"

"Didn't the KLV dentist call you?" I wrote on my pad.

"No. Does your mother know you are here?"

"Barnheims, the farmers at whose house she now lives, do not have a telephone."

"Well, let's have a look at you. Tonight you'll stay with me. If the swelling is reduced tomorrow you go out to Birkhorst and let Mutti know that you are not in Sellin. Tell me what happened."

After recounting my story of the broken braces, Tante Doktor said, "We will replace them. I have to remove these first so your wounds can heal. In a week we can take impressions."

"What about the Allied troops, will they be here by then?"

"No, they are fully engaged in France," Tante Doktor answered.

My concern on that fateful June day in 1944 was to see my mother as soon as possible.

After a quiet night with nothing but cold liquids for nourishment, I traversed Stettin on the streetcar system from the western suburbs to the east to catch a ferry on the Oder River. On the ride in the trams, I hungrily drank in all the familiar yet now disfigured landmarks, especially along that part of the way, which had been my daily route to the Kaiserin-Auguste-Viktoria

Schule. More than a year had passed since my last school day in Stettin…many disturbing events ago.

The ferry left her dock on the Oder and entered the *Dammscher See,* the lake that conjoins the *Oderhaff.* This bay has a connection to the Baltic Sea through the Swine River, pronounced *Sveene.* Having taken a northeasterly course, the ship tied up in Bergland within an hour.

To reach Barnheim's farm in Birkhorst, I had to walk into the village before I turned north for two kilometers on a sandy road. As I entered the yard between horse stables, I scanned the farmhouse. To my surprise, my mother was at the open window of her room. I will never forget Mutti's face at seeing her daughter below. "Almut!" she cried out and turned away from the window. Moments later we hugged on the front steps.

"Why are you here? How did you get here?"

"Don't worry, I didn't run away from Sellin and I'm fine," I said to calm my mother's fears. "Everything is all right on Rügen; no troops landed on the island."

Mutti noticed my swollen lips and the missing braces right away. I retold the events of the previous three days, as well as the timetable set by Tante Doktor.

"Well, come in and say hello to the Barnheim family," Mutti said. "Did you bring ration cards for your stay?"

"No. Nobody thought of that. Besides, we didn't know how long I would be away from Sellin."

"Oh, weh!" Oy vay! "We will have problems obtaining some for you. Perhaps the mayor's secretary can contact your teachers for verification of your emergency visit here."

The Barnheims were willing to have me share their meals until my ration cards arrived.

Meta Barnheim, a statuesque woman in her forties, had two extraordinary skills: preparing health foods and weaving. Both were rooted in the past but only the first one has been making a comeback in the general population during the last few decades. In the Germany of World War II, practitioners of these two skills had to live on farms to have access to the necessary components and ingredients, such as wool and organically grown fruit and vegetables.

Meta believed in *Rohkost,* servings of raw produce in a variety of salads and as an addition to *Müesli,* the Swiss prototype of cold cereals containing oat, wheat and millet flakes, raisins, nuts and similar components.

The two grandmothers in the house oversaw the meticulously tended kitchen gardens, which included more herbs than I had known or tasted before. These gardens, the fields of grain, including buckwheat, and the livestock provided Meta with the products she needed to perform her culinary magic.

Just as her meals echoed the diets of earlier civilizations, so did her artistic weaving on two big wooden looms. Both were always set up and ready to use. One of them might have colorful yarns strung through which to send the shuttles back and forth to weave material for dresses, shirts or jackets.

On the other loom, Meta wove fabric for kitchen and table linens. I was fascinated with the preparation as well as the work at the looms. In this endeavor, too, both grandmothers helped, starting with spinning the wool shorn off Barnheims' sheep.

"Do you think I could learn to weave some day?" I asked Mrs. Barnheim.

"That requires a lot of time. But I will be happy to teach you when you are ready."

Obviously, one week's stay was not the time to learn an intricate craft. But I kept watching.

*   *   *

A S   P R E D I C T E D, after ten days my gums were ready for Tante Doktor to plant my new braces and send me back to Sellin. By this time I was no longer scanning the skies for airborne Allied invaders.

In Sellin, however, my schoolmates and I observed rockets streaking brightly over the Baltic Sea. We wondered why anyone would launch them from the mainland without having visible targets to shoot at. After the war we learned that Wernher von Braun and his circle of scientists and technicians designed, developed and perfected the *Vergeltungsraketen,* V- or revenge rockets, in Peenemünde, at the mouth of the Peene River. In their straight northern flight path we could easily observe them from Sellin.

U N T I L   T H E   E N D   O F   S U M M E R season at the seashore, my classmates and I enjoyed the advantages we had over city dwellers as well as the population of the Baltic countries and *Ostpreussen,* the German province of East Prussia. The majority of them fled their homes and land from the advancing Soviet troops.

On Rügen, we continued our routine of class instructions, field trips, berrypicking, and our favorite activities on the beach and in the sea. We lived in the *Kinderland,* the closest thing to a children's paradise. Every so often, bad news about war-related deaths or missing-in-action notifications in our families punctuated our idyllic life. At the same time during which we supported each other emotionally, we were careful not to knit our bonds too tightly. We experienced too many goodbyes because of the many changes the war caused German families.

When winter approached, I had to bid my friends and my beloved Baltic Sea adieu again. In the fall of 1944, my mother decided I was to live with her in Birkhorst, on Barnheim's farm. Soviet troops were pushing the *Ostfront* evermore west.

"It is better not to be separated anymore," Mutti said.

"What about school? The nearest *Oberschule* is in Stargard. How am I going to get to that high school?" I asked.

"You ride your bike to the Bahnhof in *Arnimswalde.* A train will take you to *Altdamm.* There you catch the connection to Stargard. It will arrive at 7:30 a.m., in time to make it to school before 8:00."

"How far is Arnimswalde? When will I have to get up?" I asked.

"Seven kilometers to Arnimswalde. If you get up at 4:45 a.m., leave at 5:30, you can be at the Bahnhof for the 6:30 train.

After two stops, you are in Altdamm where you board the train to Stargard."

Mutti had planned my route throroughly.

"I'll be tired by the time school starts," I grumbled. "I suppose this regimen will be fine in September. After that it will be dark in the morning and at night when I return. And what about winter weather?"

"You'll be all right. You'll get used to it," Mutti said. "You can start your homework on the train and in the Bahnhofsrestaurant in Altdamm in the afternoon."

"Did you ever work so hard just to get to school?" I asked.

"No, I didn't have to commute to school during a war."

"It depends on when and where you are born, doesn't it?" I complained. "I wish I were in Sellin where we ate, slept and learned in the same building."

Besides obeying the law of compulsory education, I liked school, and not only because I met my friends there. As in the previous winter, when I took the postal bus from Hinzendorf to Stargard, I shared my classes with Christa and Doris of the former ABCDE quintet. We laughed at our reunion, *"Junge, Junge! Bist du aber gewachsen!"* Boy, oh boy! Did you ever grow."

"Du auch." So did you.

During the winter of 1944, I needed all my enthusiasm for school to endure the hardship of reaching the classroom.

After a healthy breakfast of fruit-enriched cereal and hot milk, I started my daily journey to school. The two kilometers to Bergland were difficult to navigate, no matter what weather prevailed on a given day. The soil of the narrow pedestrian path on which I rode my bike was more solid than the sandy road. If a person walked in front of me, I had to push my bike around them before I could continue my ride. In the early morning, not many people were walking, but at night I had to mount and dismount my bike frequently.

In September, I liked to watch the sunrise over the fields to my left and listen to the awakening of nature: the birds and the roosters, and the dogs barking when I passed their domains.

Ferries, tankers, and ships signaled their departure as they blew their horns on the Dammscher See. Across the lake, I saw the silhouette of Stettin.

I was glad to trade the sandy road for one paved with gray brick-shaped stones in Bergland. On my way to the Bahnhof, I observed farmers on horse-drawn wagons delivering milk to the nearest dairy, or to the railroad for transport to the cities.

After I pedaled for four kilometers on that paved road, I left it for a wide asphalt bicycle path along a high wire fence backed by a hedge of tall bushes. During the dark hours, this path was never illuminated by streetlights. Only my bicycle generator had my lamp throw a dim light ahead of me. The population learned from workers in the plant that behind the fence was a weapons factory. Adjoining the installation ran the railroad. *I hope I will never be near this potential target in the case of air attacks.*

The local in Arnimswalde was always on time as it served the hinterland of the cities. We could not rely on the connecting trains in Altdamm, however, because of war-induced delays, such as enemy actions, damaged tracks, or troop transports.

In cold weather, we stood on the platform, shivering.

"We better not go into the building. We might miss our train," Doris said.

"*Ja,* why can't the announcer give us a forewarning before our *Bummelbahn,* steams in here?" I said, referring to the dawdling train.

"Because the station administration has to react to all the delays from different directions. That's a confusing situation to handle," contributed Christa, our deep thinker.

Consequently, despite my rising early in the morning, I often arrived in school late an hour or more, along with Christa and Doris. We were tired and cold by then. Trains were no longer heated. Usually, their windows were broken or boarded up.

When we finally took our seats in the classroom, teachers were annoyed at the interruption, though they understood our predicament.

"Get the class notes from those who were here from the beginning of class. Now, where were we?" was the teachers' refrain. They were as frustrated with teaching in the course of the last months of 1944 as we students were with our efforts at furthering our education.

Those struggles were over early in the new year.

On the Ostfront, the Soviets advanced and German troops withdrew. By January 1945, *die grosse Flucht,* the Great Trek, was rolling westward through Pomerania.

Vati was missing in action on the Ostfront. When I urged my mother to leave Birkhorst before the Soviet troops occupied *Ostpommern,* she hesitated.

"This address is the only one Vati has to contact us. Let's wait a little longer. We might hear from him," Mutti said.

"Vati has our Stettin address. We could always pick up mail from the post office in the city. Do you want to wait until we can't cross the Oder anymore because all the bridges are blown up?" I asked.

"Hm, perhaps our military will defend and hold Stettin," Mutti hoped.

When the Barnheims readied their wagons for the flight west, loading bedding, linens, food, one disassembled loom and yarns, chicken in crates, grains and hay for the livestock, and, finally the family and some trusted farmhands, Mutti knew that we could wait no longer.

CHAPTER 7

The Great Trek

ON FEBRUARY 3, 1945, my fifteenth birthday, Mutti and I loaded as many belongings as we could on our bicycles and pedaled thirty-five kilometers to the nearest bridge across the Oder River.

Mutti had awoken me at 4:30 that fateful morning. "Almut, get dressed quickly. I did not go to bed last night. The artillery shells came closer. Look out the window. Lübzin is burning. That's only six kilometers away, down the sandy road.

"Here, put on everything I laid out for you: underwear, your ski pants, the blue dress, this sweater I finished knitting just an hour ago, and the winter coat. Don't forget shawl and knit hat, gloves and mittens."

"Where are our bags?" I asked.

"By the door. Stack them in the baskets on our bikes and tie them down. *Schnell, schnell!*" Mutti urged. Hurry, hurry!

With shaking hands we secured our bags and did not take time to eat. We left Birkhorst under a red sky.

"Go, go!" the Barnheim family called out. "We'll see you west of Stettin!"

So this is the last time I'll ride my bike on this path. And I thought it was hard to steer when I had only my school bag on the Gepäckträger behind the seat.

Footprints and ruts from bicycles and hand-drawn wagons were frozen in snow and ice and slowed our passage; they made it

71

difficult and dangerous. We could neither afford to fall down and get hurt, nor to have our bags shift so that we would have to arrange them all over again.

God, don't let the Russians catch up to us.

From the time we reached the paved road, farmers' wagons dominated the Great Trek west. Whenever minor roads intersected highways, the junctions became clogged. Often, the families on wagons already on the highways, had left their homes weeks before. I don't recall any tempers flaring, though, as the latest refugees maneuvered their horse teams into the endless wagon trains. The mood of the people was stoic rather than excited as they tried to outrun advancing Soviet troops.

Mutti and I wove our way in and out of the refugee columns like braiding hair as we passed the horse-drawn open or covered vehicles.

At times, people called out to us, *"Sind Sie nicht Herrn Fingers Familie?* Are you not Mr. Finger's family?"

These refugees were from the farms Vati had supervised in the absence of the farmers called to military service. Occasionally my mother and I had accompanied Vati on his rounds. Then Mutti and I took walks in the country while Vati checked the bookkeeping, livestock, and crops in the fields.

"Have you heard from your husband, Frau Finger?"

"Nein, not since October."

"Well, good luck to all of us!"

When evening came, the glow of not-too-distant fires never allowed total darkness. Mutti and I reached the Oder and a bridge to cross the river. After an hour of threading our way around craters and piles of rubble in Stettin's streets, we arrived at our apartment.

"Thank God, the building is still standing. Now we can stay for a few days," Mutti said.

"It's freezing here. No windows, no electricity, and I'm starving," I said. "I'll look for some candles."

"Surprise!" Mutti called out, "Can you believe that we have gas? I'll light all burners and the oven of our stove. We can warm up the kitchen and food from the pantry."

When I looked at the soup in my *Suppenteller,* or soup plate, I did not know whether I could eat. Besides being exhausted and cold, I had stomach cramps because we had not eaten for more than twenty-four hours.

"You have to eat, Almut. How can we leave from here to ride hundreds of kilometers under conditions we experienced today or worse, if you don't eat?" Mutti said.

Little by little, I finished my soup…and fell asleep at the table.

"Let's go to bed and stretch out our tired bodies," she urged, tapping me on the shoulder.

I really did not want to leave the warm kitchen and lingered.

"Mutti, I know you stayed up all night yesterday to finish my present but today you didn't mention my birthday."

"*Auch das noch!*" In addition to everything else. "How could I forget that? Come here."

We hugged and Mutti caressed my hair. "Of course, all my best wishes are for you always. But it was not a happy birthday, was it? At least, we put the Oder between Ivan and us."

We rushed into the chilly bedroom, crept into our beds and heaped featherbedding on us, not bothering with sheets.

T H E   N E X T   D A Y, we scraped the necessary ingredients together, or those we could find, to bake *Printen,* a kind of spice cookies.

Mutti had a recipe for these traditional Christmas cookies.

500 g (grams) Weizenmehl	4 cups wheat flour
1 Päckchen Schokoladenpudding	1 pkg. Chocolate Pudding
½ Päckchen Dr. Oetker *Backin*	1 tablespoon baking powder
375 g Zucker	15 oz. sugar
½ Teel. Zimt	½ teaspoon cinnamon
½ Teel. gemahlene Nelken	½ teaspoon ground cloves

Backaroma Zitrone	lemon flavoring
200 g Honig oder Sirup	1 ¾ cups honey or sugar-beet syrup
2 Eier	2 eggs
5 Essl. Milch	5 tablespoons milk
125 g Butter (Margarine)	1 stick butter (margarine)
125 g Haselnusskerne	1 cup ground filberts
Backzeit: 15-20 Minuten	Baking time: 15-20 min.
bei starker Hitze	at high temperature
Mandelkerne oder Zuckerguss	Sliced almonds or frosting
zur Verzierung	for decoration

To obtain thin, hard Printen we omitted the baking powder and all ingredients we did not have in our semi-deserted apartment, such as eggs, milk and butter; we omitted filberts and used water and margarine. In Pomerania, most households kept syrup in their larder, especially in Stettin, thanks to its refinery. We did not decorate our Printen.

We mixed the dough, kneaded it, and rolled it out; then we cut it in strips, creating small rectangles. The baked and cooled Printen we stored in cookie tins as our "iron ration". From now on we could not expect to have regular meals. Moreover, our bicycles were overloaded with clothing. If we added food packages, we could not swing one leg over the bike to reach the pedal. Both Mutti and I had bicycle frames with a connecting rod from the handle bar to the seat. We strapped briefcases with important documents to the rods.

"One more night in our beds," Mutti said.

"I hope it doesn't snow," I worried.

"We have a few more hours of daylight. I'd like to check for mail at the post office and then tell Onkel Postel we will leave Stettin tomorrow. The streetcars are still running. Let's try to see him at the warehouse."

Mutti's oldest brother, my godfather, ran the family business since his return from Stalingrad. When we said goodbye to him, I asked, "Where will you go when you leave?"

"Able-bodied men have to stay to defend the city. I received my orders to report to the barracks in Braunsfelde where I am to lead a company of streetcar operators."

"But you must not waste another day. We have not received mail for days; if Curt is alive he will find you," Onkel Postel assured Mutti. "Almut, choose a present I can give you."

"I would like that figurine," I said and pointed at a porcelain reproduction of the statue *Sonnenkind*, child of the sun. The figurine represented the joie de vivre that was so absent from our lives in the winter of 1945. From that moment on, my Sonnenkind has accompanied me without a scratch through dark as well as happy times.

*   *   *

I WAS TIRED ENOUGH TO SLEEP through our last night in Stettin, which was recently declared a fortress. The noise created by the battle south and east of the city was so constant that only an interruption of the devastating action would have drawn our attention.

On February 5, 1945, we locked the door to our apartment in the *Pioneerstrasse* for the final time and continued our flight on overloaded bicycles ahead of the legendary brutality of the Soviet troops. Stettin's streets were eerily devoid of traffic as we departed my hometown, heading in a westerly direction.

"Where are the wagon trains?" I asked Mutti.

"I suppose the bridges are either heavily defended by our troops; or they were blown up, stranding many refugees east of the Oder River. I tried to listen to a newscast this morning but Stettin's station was not on the air and Berlin gave useless advice to its residents," Mutti said.

"Useless?"

"Yes, reporting that their *Führer* is among them, ready to defend their city," Mutti remarked with disdain.

We were well within reach of the artillery of both the defending and the attacking forces when suddenly I heard an unfamiliar sound whizzing by.

"What was that?" I yelled.

"A close call from a *Stalinorgel,* a Soviet rocket," Mutti shouted back. "They come in multiple bursts. Just keep pedaling. There is nothing we can do to protect ourselves if we want to make it out of here."

Stoically, we continued on our way, ignoring our fears. On occasion, we overtook other people fleeing from the Soviet threat. Aged couples pulled their last belongings in wooden handwagons; others fled in their cars. They had permits to operate them in government-sanctioned jobs that no longer existed.

German soldiers followed orders and walked in small groups toward the front. *They did not march. Are these the troops that will stem the advances of the red machine?* Not every soldier had a rifle; a few carried a *Panzerfaust,* an anti-tank weapon.

My back and legs began to ache from the strain of having to balance the load on my bike as I pushed the pedals. *So far, we have reached only Stettin's city limits, six kilometers down, hundreds to go.*

"How are you feeling, Mutti?" I asked her over the din of arms.

"All right. No time to think about it," Mutti said, adding, "Why is the sky so blue? How can the sun shine so golden on this hellish scene?"

I had not paid attention to the weather, worried earlier about snow. "At least we're not getting wet from above," I answered.

Because of the physical exertion we sweated under our triple layer of clothing despite the below-freezing temperatures and the blowing wind at our back...*the only good thing coming from the east: lucky, we don't have to fight that, too.*

IN EARLY AFTERNOON, we caught up to the last wagon trains that had been able to cross the Oder River. Every few miles, we noticed abandoned wagons with broken wheels. Other vehicles seemed intact; they were probably left behind when horses died of exhaustion or broken bones incurred in falls on icy roads. When mares foaled, their owners left them with local farmers.

The well-being of his human dependents was the trek leader's foremost concern, but only maintaining the horses' fitness enabled people on the wagons to continue their journey. After weeks on the road, the number of draft animals succumbing to the long pull's strains grew daily.

The loss of forty-five horses meant giving up about twenty wagons. The families on the remaining vehicles took in people of the abandoned wagons. Everyone had to part with some personal belongings, which was distressing to them. This disposal of cargo littered ditches on the side of the road and adjoining fields for hundreds of kilometers.

A T D U S K, Mutti and I learned the nightly routine we were to follow during the weeks of our life on the road. We stood in line at the *Bürgermeisteramt,* or mayor's office, to obtain an assignment to quarters for the night and ration cards for twenty-four hours. The latter we gave to our hosts, who fed us supper and prepared sandwiches for the next day.

I cannot praise enough the selflessness and empathy of the farmers and settlers of Vorpommern and Mecklenburg. Night after night, from late 1944 through April 1945, they opened their homes and barns to give shelter to the fleeing masses.

"I can barely walk," Mutti moaned. "My legs want to rotate."

"Mine, too. I have become used to driving this load. To balance the bike alongside of me is tricky."

The farmer's wife greeted us at the door, "Come in. You must be tired. Where are you from?"

"Thank you. We left Stettin this morning," I answered. "Where can we park our bikes?"

"Bring them into the house, the corridor. You don't want to lose your last possessions."

After our hostess showed us our room, she said, "Come to the kitchen when you have freshened up. You'll eat with my family and the help."

Left alone, Mutti fell on her bed, "White linens and downs! I don't want to go eat."

"Now remember what you told me two nights ago. We can't do this trek if we don't eat. Besides, I need to drink something, *anything*. I am parched."

A S   W E   W E R E   S E A T E D at the kitchen table, feasting our eyes on the evening meal, inhaling the promising aromas of meat, potatoes and vegetables, our fears and the strain of the day seemed to have been a bad dream. Or was this gathering a mirage?

Even with the Soviet troops less than twenty kilometers away from the farm, its owner set an inviting table with serving dishes for the diverse offerings, rather than ladle the food out to the hungry group at this sitting.

"Please have some of these potatoes," the farmer's daughter urged me. "Do you like Brussels sprouts?" she asked my mother.

"Yes, do eat," our hostess said. "What we consume now, Ivan can't take from us."

Ivan. That brought us back to reality and robbed us of the joy of the moment.

"Will you leave, too?" Mutti asked the farmer's wife.

"Where would we go? You are aware of the multitudes streaming west. They are clogging up the roads, slowing everyone down. Will they reach safety? And you? What is your goal?"

"We are trying to reach Kiel. My sister, Renate, is the only one in our large family who left Pomerania when she married," Mutti answered.

"Kiel?" the woman gasped, "how long will that take you? Do you have the strength? Will you find lodging every night?" she asked.

"Those thoughts have been on our minds, along with worries about the conditions of our bikes, their tires and innertubes," Mutti sighed. It's about five hundred kilometers from here to Kiel. As long as the Soviets are kept east of the Oder River

78

and we progress steadily on our trek, we should be able to achieve our journey's objective."

"Our best wishes are with you. I'll pack you a lunch tomorrow. Get a good rest tonight."

THE NEXT MORNING, February 6, we awakened early to the *hü* and *hott*, gee and haw, of the wagon trains' team leaders as they prepared their vehicles and passengers for the next leg on their trek. Mutti and I, too, hastened to get underway after gratefully taking leave from our hosts.

It became more difficult with every passing day to overtake the wagons on the left because they could not always maintain a straight line. On their right, forlorn pedestrians walked doggedly at the road's edge. *How long could they keep up their flight on foot?* Mothers pushed baby carriages; grandmothers pulled handwagons. From time to time they had to veer out into the road to walk around broken-down wagons or abandoned cars, which had run out of gas. From these, people had joined the wagon trains; they took turns walking with those who were riding.

On the opposite side of the road, military vehicles had been abandoned for the same reasons the farmer's wagons and the private cars were left behind. Others had taken direct hits from artillery or strafing planes.

Strafing became a daily threat now that enemy lines came closer in the west, and the Soviets could station their planes on conquered territory. Because German troops, no matter how large or small their numbers, were always present on our escape routes, we refugees were part of the targets of opportunity.

During the attacks, Mutti and I dove or fell with our bikes into the ditches along the roads. When it was all-clear again, we pulled our bikes upright and led them to the nearest tree. Then we put one hand on the handle bar and the other on the tree trunk as we mounted our heavy bikes and pushed off. Sometimes, walkers helped us on our way.

The scene after every attack was utter chaos: horses reared, straining in the bridles, neighing desperately, eyes bulging. Men needed to combine their strength to keep the horses from bolting with the wagons. Children screamed; the wounded, military as well as civilians, called for help.

Chaos has many faces. I thought back to the day when I first saw this word on a banner in the main hall of the *Stettiner Hauptbahnhof.*

"What does that word mean, and how do you pronounce it?" I had asked Vati.

"Chaos describes a situation of great confusion and distress, such as when people flee from an eruption of a volcano and its flowing lava," he had explained to me.

On the sign in the station, the slogan proclaimed "Ohne Sieg, Chaos!" Without victory, chaos. *The one time the Nazis were right,* I thought in February 1945.

*   *   *

"W H A T W A S I T H I N K I N G when I suggested we make this trek on bicycles?" Mutti wondered out loud as we continued our odysseys. "My entire body aches with the slightest effort, even getting dressed is difficult."

"Too late now to give up," I reminded her. "We haven't gained anything yet. Our family doesn't know where we are. The Soviets will be here before long, and our purpose is still to avoid contact with them. Let's not dally."

Every day, the obstacles to our flight multiplied. The roads were riddled with potholes and craters so that vehicles crawled forward as best they could, at times proceeding laboriously over fields.

Shards of glass and shrapnel inflicted wounds on the horses' hooves and walking refugees' shoe soles, which showed wear and tear after months of pounding the roads. Our bicycles, too, needed frequent repairs.

"Ich hab' einen Platten," I called out to Mutti, pointing at my flat tire.

"Again?" Mutti sighed. "We'll run out of patches and adhesive before we reach Kiel."

"From now on, let's stop at every village store and try to buy another repair kit, although I have little hope that we'll find any along the route," I said. "Can you help me unload my bike so I can turn it upside down?"

With each repair we lost precious time. To spot the hole in the innertube, we needed water in which to submerge it. We thawed the snow covering the ground in our hands and helped the sun to melt it into puddles. After drying the damaged area and roughing it with sandpaper, we cut a patch sparingly to size, applied the adhesive and kept our hands on it for about fifteen minutes to ensure contact.

"Now pump it up and submerge it again," Mutti said.

"It's holding air; no more bubbles in the puddle," I reported. "Next time, I hope this happens near a settlement, so we can ask for a bowl to hold under a faucet."

"I worry about the tires that are pressed hard into the ground by all the weight on the bikes," Mutti murmured. "We have only one spare and one innertube replacement for four wheels."

"Na, denn!" I said. All right, banish that thought! "Let's pack up again and get moving."

We had been aware of the increased action, the rhythmic machine-gun fire, the billowing smoke and red glow over the hamlets in the east. But war was all around us, and we ignored its impact if it did not explode in our midst. That attitude was our chosen resolve for daily survival.

*   *   *

WHITE BED LINENS, down-filled covers, and tables set for dinner were a cherished memory during our arduous flight. We did not enjoy them again until April, and then only briefly.

Increasingly, Mutti and I spent nights sitting up in chairs lined up in farmers' kitchens or adjoining rooms, along with many other refugees, their children and dogs. We balanced stew-filled plates in our laps, holding glasses of milk with hands that shook from the intense grip on our handle bars during the day.

"The food the farmers serve us is hearty and tasty. How can they afford to feed transients so well night after night in these chaotic months?" I asked Mutti.

"They see people in distress day after day. Besides, how much longer before Ivan overruns this area? So farmers share their products with the fleeing masses."

"I drank more milk in the last two days than in a week on Rügen, especially whole milk."

"Milk is no longer collected for sale at the distant towns. You didn't see any delivery conveyance on the roads, did you?"

"No, thank goodness. They might not reach their destination. Imagine: spilled milk coating everyone and everything during an attack."

"Only a fifteen-year old could conjure up such visions amid our hardships," Mutti said, shaking her head as she smiled at me.

I was glad that I could make my mother smile. Her psyche had been jolted repeatedly under the heavy strain since the Great War began. As the oldest sister of ten orphaned siblings, she was apprehensive about her five brothers' military deployment; her husband's fate on the eastern front was not known; property and personal belongings were reduced to what two bicycles could carry.... Could she retain the strength needed for our continued flight?

Soon, Mutti left most of the decision-making to me.

B Y   M A R C H, after a month on our sad journey, we left Pomerania and entered the state of Mecklenburg.

One evening, the local mayor's office assigned us to a farmer's barn for our overnight stay because we had traveled until late and all private homes were filled.

Wagons were crammed into the farmyard; the horses found needed rest in stalls where they could lie down, a rare treat for them because only the first ones to arrive gained this luxury.

For the wagon train it meant turning in early, thus losing time and its place on the trek the next morning. Following wagons had moved up, filling the vacant spaces.

In the barn, refugees slept in the loft as well as on hay and straw on the barn floor. Since Mutti and I wanted to stay near our bikes we chose to rest in front of the stalls. I was fond of horses and did not mind the odor.

At night, children fell asleep quickly by the dim light of wagon lanterns. Women took turns watching over their families' belongings, and men periodically checked their teams.

On their watches, people talked to each other in low voices. The woman closest to our nest in the straw asked us where our *Heimat* was.

"Stettin," Mutti answered. "And yours?"

"Schlochau."

"Oh, yes; a victim of the Treaty of Versailles," I said. "I remember learning that only one fifth of your county remained in Pomerania; the rest became part of the Polish Corridor, before being reunited with Germany in 1938, isn't that right?"

"Ja. And now we are homeless."

"When did you leave Schlochau?" Mutti asked.

"On January 23, nearly two months ago, treks from Ostpreussen and the land along the Warthe River had been coming through for weeks. They told of atrocities the Soviets committed on people who had stayed behind in their towns and homes. When German troops retook some of the recently lost territory, they found that women and girls had been violated and nailed to barn doors and men had been tortured to death.In Nemmersdorf forty French prisoners lost their lives."

"The news of the outrageous mistreatment of people by the Soviet troops in Gumbinnen, Goldap, and Nemmersdorf traveled fast and sent millions fleeing." Mutti said. "We will manage our burden in the hope that we can escape the fate of the people in Soviet-occupied territory."

At that point, the woman's husband and leader of their trek, stopped by, "Is everything all right?"

"Yes. We're exchanging travel talk," Mutti answered. "Why did you leave so late from Schlochau?"

"Not by choice," the trek leader answered. "While the German authorities in the Baltic regions and Ostpreussen told the population to evacuate in the fall of 1944, we Pomeranians had to wait for permission to leave. I suppose the government thought our troops would stem the Soviet onslaught before they reached our *Heimat.*"

"Yes, imagine an abandoned hinterland," his wife added. "There would be no more food and dairy production; our troops would not be motivated to defend a wasteland."

"Now look at us. We left Schlochau in the worst of winter weather, made it over the pontoon bridges across the Oder but are at the end of the wagon trains, worrying that we will fall into the Soviet hands anyway," the trek leader said as he shook his head.

The man had lost an arm earlier in the war and was discharged, thus he could be with his family and guide this wagon train.

"How many people are in your trek?" I asked.

"Everyone in this barn, except you, your mother and about two hundred. We have been fortunate not to have lost anyone to the cold, old age, childbirth, disease, food poisoning or warfare. We did lose horses, though; their legs broke due to the constant pulling by day and standing on asphalt by night."

I rose up and looked over the gate into the nearest stall. "They are getting a rest tonight," I said. "Do you have an area in mind where you can resettle?"

"No. I expect the government will direct us to agrarian states, Schleswig-Holstein or Oldenburg, once we reach the Elbe River.

"I better resume my rounds; you catch some sleep. Tomorrow we struggle on," the trek leader sighed, rubbing his tired eyes and adjusting his hat.

During the three to six months the wagon trains were on their flight west, each leader assumed the responsibilities of commander, father, husband, negotiator, veterinarian, treasurer, friend, inventor, and counselor. In some cases, the only able-bodied men were prisoners of war who had worked on farms, particularly French POWs who were heading home under the protection of their former keepers.

"Why are those Russian POWs accompanying treks?" I asked Mutti.

"Your uncles, Postel and Edzard, told us while on furlough from the Ostfront that the Soviets treated Russian prisoners as deserters when they "liberated" them. That's why these men want to take their chances in the west," Mutti explained.

A FEW DAYS AFTER THIS EXCHANGE, I gasped as we passed a lifeless figure hanging from a tree at the side of the *Chaussee,* thoroughfare. The body was clad in civilian clothes but his combat boots must have given him away: He had tried to end the war for himself. A sign, hung from his neck, proclaimed, *"Ich bin ein Deserteur,"* I am a deserter. Passing doomed soldiers took this image with them as they walked alone or in small groups to the front, about five weeks before the end of the war.

* * *

"WELL, HOW FAR are we from Wismar?" Mutti asked me.

"I'll check the map," I said. "We are coming to a fork in the road again. Either we go north to Bützow, then west to Neukloster before meeting the road to Wismar; or we ride to Sternberg in a southwesterly direction and, via Brüel, directly to Wismar. The distance is about the same, about forty-five kilometers. The traffic and danger will be the same, too, because our troops use all roads leading east."

"You decide," Mutti sighed.

"Na, denn: I choose Sternberg."

MUTTI AND I SUMMONED our energy daily. By April we had reached *Wismar*, a port on the Ostsee, more than three hundred kilometers from Stettin. This city was to be our *Zwischenstation.* We had been invited to this interim station by our neighbor in the Pionierstrasse. The Schmidts' apartment was two floors above ours.

"Da sind Sie ja!" You made it, Frau Schmidt called out joyfully.

"Park your bikes in the back entrance. We can unload them later. First, have some refreshments," she said. "Come and meet my parents."

We had come to the childhood home of Frau Schmidt. The three-storied house with some boarded-up windows and a pock-marked façade showed otherwise little damage after past air raids. The interior was impeccable. *How can this be? Aren't these people in the same war we're in?*

"Mutter, Vater, meet Frau Finger and her daughter, Almut. They are my neighbors and friends whom we had expected." Frau Schmidt introduced us to her parents.

"Willkommen in unserm Haus," they said, welcoming us.

"Thank you...for your gracious... invitation," Mutti stammered through her exhaustion, seeking support against a wall.

"Would you prefer to rest before eating?" Frau Schmidt asked.

"Yes, could... I have some... water, please?" Mutti begged.

"Gladly. Let me show you to your room." Frau Schmidt led the way. When she opened the door, I marveled, "Feather bedding and white sheets! Thank you."

She gave us a carafe with water and two glasses.

"After your nap come downstairs for supper. Sleep tight." Frau Schmidt closed the door behind her.

Mutti headed for bed.

"Wait, Mutti. Wash your hands and face. I'll help you take off your outer layers of clothing before you lie down," I encouraged my mother.

I, too, fell into a heavenly bed after my *"Katzenwäsche"*, cat's licks. We did not wake up until we heard a knock on our door the next morning.

"Frau Finger? Almut? Guten Morgen!" Frau Schmidt called. "Would you like some breakfast?"

"Ach, du liebe Güte!" Goodness. "Yes, thank you. What time is it?" Mutti asked.

"Nine o'clock."

"We slept for seventeen hours," I said, adding, "We'll be with you in a moment."

"Katzenwäsche again and dirty clothes in this spotless house." Mutti shook her head disapprovingly.

"We'll bring our bags upstairs after breakfast, clean ourselves up and ask whether we might do some laundry," I suggested.

At the breakfast table our hostess asked us, "Do you like goat milk and cheese? We have two goats. They help us stretch our ration cards."

"I've never had goat milk but I'll try it," I answered carefully.

The first spoonfuls of the hot breakfast soup went down slowly. *You are hungry. This soup is better than anything you had during the last two weeks. Get used to it.*

"Have some home-baked bread," Frau Schmidt's father said. "We occasionally barter goat cheese for food we don't produce, like flour."

Mutti and I appreciated this family's generous hospitality. Our eyes feasted more on the offered nourishment than our stomachs could accept after weeks of limited intake.

When I wanted to help with the dishes, Frau Schmidt said, "You can assist me in the kitchen tomorrow. Now we'll unload your bags and take them to your room. I started the hot-water heater so you can take baths."

"How long ago did we soak in a tub, Almut?" Mutti asked.

"I don't remember. Where did we? In Birkhorst?" I wondered.

"If you feel up to it, you can wash your clothes in the laundry room, where your bikes are. I'll show you," Frau Schmidt suggested.

When I hung our laundry on the clothesline in the back yard, I stepped around Schmidt's chickens and noticed cages propped up on stilts alongside the garage. Rabbits were watching me with their big eyes, twitching their noses.

Beyond the cages, Herr Schmidt had seeded lettuce, carrots and other vegetables in neat rows, four each to a bed. In late April the young vegetables had barely broken through the soil. This peaceful oasis made me homesick. *Is anything sprouting in the cratered countryside surrounding Stettin?*

Wailing sirens shocked me into reality.

"How far away is your bunker?" I asked Mr. Schmidt.

"Too far to reach it safely in a direct attack. So we stay in our house, where we have a better chance of survival than by being in the streets," the tall gentleman said, surveying his yard and pushing me gently into the laundry room.

Soon we heard the heavy droning of the Allied bombers overhead. From the back entrance of the house I observed the planes in perfect formation as they passed unhindered over Wismar. *Heading for Berlin? Where is the Flak? Run out of ammunition? Of men? Of cannons?*

Mutti must have had the same questions when she stated, "Well, we will not have shrapnel or planes raining down on us. But the poor people who are targeted by these messengers of death…"

Facing acute dangers every day forced us to concentrate on decisions we needed to make trying to survive the next twenty-four hours. Because of Mutti's exhaustion the Schmidt family offered us shelter until Mutti could continue our trek west.

"Thank you for your kindness," I said. "After the all-clear signal we'll report to the Bürgermeister's office and obtain a temporary permit for lodging and ration cards."

At city hall, we learned that Wismar allowed local residents to share their homes exclusively with refugees who were blood relatives.

"Oh, no," Mutti groaned, "I need a break."

"We can transfer you to lodging in the country," the clerk declared.

"Where would that be?" I asked.

"I have a nice room in Neukloster." She pointed at a map in front of us.

"But that is east of Wismar. We came from there two days ago!" I said dejectedly and looked at Mutti.

"Give me two days. Please," she pleaded.

I gave in. *You don't want her to collapse five kilometers from here. Then, what would happen? Hospitals are filled beyond capacity.*

The Schmidts were sad that we could not rest at their house. Other transients would be assigned to them after we left.

"Why don't you take only three days' change of clothes with you and store the other bags in our attic. When you continue your flight to Kiel, you stop in and pick up your belongings," Frau Schmidt's mother offered.

We gratefully accepted and left for Neukloster the next day.

"I AM DOING THESE TWENTY KILOMETERS to the east under protest," I muttered. "So much time and energy wasted."

Mutti ignored my complaints.

In Neukloster, we registered at the town hall, showing our transfer papers.

"Your room is at the Kellers' house. Here are the directions," a secretary said.

The town's streets were clogged with wagon trains and military vehicles.

"Hallo, Frau Finger! Wo wollen Sie denn hin?" A farmer's wife, one of Vati's former clients, called from the driver's seat of her wagon. "Aren't you going in the wrong direction?"

"We are looking for our assigned room," Mutti said in passing. "How are you faring?"

"So far everyone in our trek has weathered the difficulties. We lost three horses, though. I am waiting for our trek leader to distribute today's ration cards," the woman explained.

"Good luck in the days ahead," Mutti said.

HERR AND FRAU KELLER were retired. Years later, when I saw Grant Wood's painting *American Gothic,* I was immediately reminded of Herr and Frau Keller. Their house was one in a row of small brick buildings of the same utilitarian style, erected for factory workers and their families.

After we rang the bell, both hosts appeared in the open door to greet and welcome us. They smiled and helped us lift our bikes over the threshold. *Their children were probably never allowed to bring their bikes into the house. Another change the war caused.*

Our eyes lit up when the Kellers showed us our room: fluffy feather bedding again, this time protected by cotton covers with blue country prints. Mutti chose the bed and I was happy with the couch under the window.

Shortly after our arrival, we heard the doorbell ring. A moment later, Frau Keller knocked on our door, "Frau Finger, a woman wants to speak with you."

At the front door, Mutti met the farmer's wife she had spoken to in the street.

"Frau Finger, your youngest sister was at the town hall looking over the list of refugees who are staying in Neukloster tonight. She saw your name and will contact you tomorrow."

"Thank you. We'll be here," Mutti said.

WHEN WE HAD NOT HEARD from Gunhilt by noon, I went to have a look at the list with transients' names and assignments. Gunhilt was not registered.

What went wrong? The woman would not have made the effort to contact us if she did not have the facts.

I gave Mutti the disappointing news. We did not meet Gunhilt during our stay in Neukloster.

MUTTI RECUPERATED WELL from the physical and mental stress of our "bike tour". Two days after checking into the Kellers' house she surprised me with an idea.

"I think we should try to catch trains, where they run, and rides with trucks going east. We could pick up our car, along with canisters of gasoline that Vati stored in a barn in Colbitzow, when he was drafted last year."

I stared at my mother. *Had she lost all reason under the stress of war?*

"We are here at the end of the great migration," Mutti continued. "The roads are no longer congested back east. We could be back in four to five days."

"What if the military commandeer our *Peter* once you drive him out of the barn? Or, what do we do when we run out of gas? And what about the Soviet troops? No, no, let's leave for Kiel now," I tried to persuade Mutti.

"Our troops are holding the Soviets beyond the Oder. I am sure we can retrieve Peter if we leave today," Mutti insisted.

Toward the end of April we set out to retrieve our car from Colbitzow, more than two hundred kilometers east of Neukloster. With only one bag of clothes and Printen, our travel food, we were able to hop on any means of conveyance available.

After two days, we stood in front of our dusty *Adler Trumpf Junior*. To remove the layers of blocks on which the car rested, we pulled out the lowest block behind every wheel with the help of a rake. Four times we circled the car poking and pulling until it stood on its wheels. *Will Mutti be able to start Peter?*

"Isn't that a beautiful sound?" Mutti asked triumphantly. "The battery is not dead, that's amazing. We'll load the canisters in the trunk and be on our way."

"How different this journey is from our previous one on bikes. There's hardly any traffic and, therefore, probably little warfare going on in this area," I said.

On the entire return trip, German soldiers on guard duty at major road junctions stopped us only at two locations.

"Ihre Papiere, bitte." They smiled when they asked for our papers.

"Where are you going with that car?" one soldier wanted to know.

"As far away from Ivan as possible," Mutti answered. "Could you spare us some gas?" she asked straightforwardly.

"Sure, we are not moving much further, it seems," the corporal said.

"Anything else you need?"

"Yes," I said eagerly, "do you have patches for innertubes?"

"For the car?"

"No, for my bike."

"Ja, I'll share some of mine with you. Like you, I plan to use my bike when the gas is gone."

That evening, Mutti parked Peter in front of the Kellers' house.

L Y I N G O N T H E C O U C H under my covers again, the absurdity of our last undertaking kept me awake. *What if the Soviets had broken through the German front lines while we were en route? What if Peter had no longer been in that barn? What if Mutti could not have started the car? What if Peter had been commandeered from us?*

From the beginning of our flight from the Red Army, I was able to suppress the fear enveloping the base of my neck like an iron ring that I had felt many times since the first major air raid two years before on April 20, 1943. The events during these stressful times demanded action and discipline if I wanted to master difficult situations. Brooding and acknowledging physical pain cloud a clear mind.

Now that Mutti's project of bringing our car to Neukloster was behind us, I was exhausted. In the dark, I asked Mutti, "What do you want to do with Peter? You know we can't obtain any gas. Civil or military authorities will certainly confiscate our Adler between here and Kiel. Moreover, with a car we have to stay in a line of wagon trains."

"We'll see. Tomorrow we have to wash Peter. *Kommt Zeit, kommt Rat,* time will show us a way," Mutti answered, yawning.

"What time? Let's take our bikes and get out of here. While we have wasted days, Ivan has moved closer," I warned.

"I'll sleep on it," Mutti murmured. "Good night,"

* * *

T R A D I T I O N A L L Y, May 1 is Labor Day in Germany. In 1945, no German was celebrating this beautiful spring day. *The weather is perfect for continuing our bike journey west.* But, no, Mutti and I vacuumed and washed Peter with implements borrowed from the Kellers.

After lunch we were changing our clothes so we might wash the few articles we had brought with us from Wismar, when Frau Keller knocked on our door, "Frau Finger, there is a soldier in the front yard. He says he is your husband."

"What? Where?" Mutti screamed as she left our room with me following at her heels.

We ran towards Vati. He smiled broadly. His tired, gray face told of the trials that were behind him. With outstretched arms he cautioned us to hug him carefully.

"What happened? Where did you come from? How did you find us?" Mutti and I flung questions at Vati.

"I'll tell you all about the last eight months and want to hear of your survival," Vati answered.

"Please come in, Herr Finger. My wife is brewing a good cup of coffee from beans she saved for a special occasion; no ersatz coffee today," Herr Keller said.

Over coffee and Printen, our hosts listened to both our report and Vati's experiences.

In his last letters to us, Vati had written that he was the driver for a medical doctor in the field. "That changed when the Soviets pushed relentlessly forward. I was ordered to join a group

93

of nine infantrymen with one machine gun. Near Königsberg, Ostpreussen, my nine comrades were killed in a skirmish, and I took shrapnel in my back. Lugging the MG34 with me, I made my way to the harbor where I received the first treatment for my wounds. As the last ships were leaving Königsberg the next day, I was immediately placed on a small passenger boat which, in better days, had cruised the Baltic Sea."

Vati took a sip of the *Bohnenkaffee* and smiled, "I forgot how good real coffee tastes. Thank you again."

"Lately, we have heard more factual news than propaganda broadcasts," Herr Keller commented. "With many people in the thick of the war, the authorities know that we are more aware of our situation. We did learn of the losses of ships and lives on the Ostsee. Was your ship hit?"

"Our crossing to Lübeck was perilous," Vati continued. "Every day, Allied planes attacked the convoy. Most ships carried military personnel as well as civilians, making all of them targets. Also, mines exacted a toll on ships and souls. Miraculously, the ship on which I sailed reached Lübeck in March with little damage, to answer your question, Herr Keller," Vati said.

"Were you taken to a hospital there?" I asked.

"No, many of the wounded, including me, went by train to Perleberg's field hospital."

"Tante Gerti's hometown," I exclaimed. "Did you see her?"

"Yes, my brother's wife," Vati explained to the Kellers. "But Gerti did not know where you were. So I hoped you had left a message with the Schmidts, or Tante Reni in Kiel, or Felix in Bad Kreuznach, as we had agreed upon years ago to cover emergencies."

"We took no time to write and had no access to telephones," Mutti said.

"How long did you stay in the hospital?" Frau Keller wanted to know.

"Four weeks. After removing the shrapnel, doctors covered the individual wounds with *Hansaplast*, large band-aids. We learned quickly that I was allergic to the adhesive. Consequently, I

94

developed infections over most of my back that took longer to treat than my original wounds."

"What were your orders after discharge from the hospital?" Mutti wondered.

"To go to the Ostfront. Since the Soviets were pushing forward from the south and the east I walked north first, trying to get to Wismar. There, the Schmidts gave me your address."

"Your boots seem to give up their service. The soles are barely attached to the uppers," Herr Keller observed. "Perhaps I can give you a pair of my shoes, if they fit."

"Thank you. I'll borrow them until I leave tomorrow."

After our coffee break, I went to the Bürgermeisteramt for our daily ration cards, while Mutti brought Vati up to date on our flight. He was not pleased to hear about Mutti's irrational decision to recover Peter. "We'll have to find a garage or storage for him until we know what future we have," he said.

On my walk to the town hall, I noticed people talking excitedly and smiling at each other in the streets. At the office, a woman asked me, "Isn't this what we've been hoping for? The British are already in Wismar. They will be here tomorrow."

I shared the good news with Vati. "Then I can give myself up to the British from whom I expect a better fate than from Ivan," Vati said, full of hope.

ON THE MORNING OF MAY 2, 1945, Vati, Mutti and I went to the market square where, to our relief, we saw British troops. They had entered Neukloster without a fight in a tank, a 2½-ton truck, and a six-wheel recon vehicle. Placards instructed German soldiers to turn in their weapons to the British contingent and report again the next day for orders.

We were glad that Vati could stay with us legally. Wearing his ragged uniform and his civilian shoes, he looked for and found a garage for Peter that afternoon.

Despite uncertainty about the coming day, I slept soundly through the night, convinced that we had ridden out the worst of the war.

THE HUMMING OF MOTORS, their changing deceleration and acceleration, awakened me early the next morning. I sat up on my couch to look out the window and saw, across a field, a military convoy.

"Mutti, Vati, trucks with white stars on their doors are rolling into town. Americans coming from the east?"

"Oh, mercy. Look at the troops emerging from the vehicles: Those are Soviet soldiers. What is going on? Yesterday the British told us to come back today. Now the Soviets arrive in American vehicles," Vati said and added, "Let's get dressed. We have to get out of here."

On the Great Trek west: Mutti and Almut. February through April 1945

Washing Peter in Neukloster, April 1945

CHAPTER 8

Under the Soviet Heel

FROM THE MOMENT I REALIZED the uniformed men were Soviet troops, I was shaking, afraid that they would practice on us the atrocities Ostpreussen's refugees had talked about.

"Herr Finger," our host called out, "try on these clothes. We'll bury your uniform. The war is over. No sense in your reporting to these barbarians. Try to avoid them."

"Oh, thank you. Without civilian clothes, I'd be a marked man, to be shot or deported to Siberia," Vati said.

After he had changed, we joined the Kellers in their yard, digging several holes into which we buried the uniform, Mutti's jewelry, my Sonnenkind, and the Kellers' valuables. We observed neighbors busy with the same activity. *Will they break under pressure to reveal the stashes of others? Will we and they live to retrieve our treasures?*

"Now let's plant these lettuce seedlings and onions in rows over the tell-tale sites and rake the area neatly," Herr Keller suggested. *How can he be so calm?*

From that day, I habitually looked over my shoulder, listening for signals that might bring harm to me. *Got to stay ahead of surprises.*

"We'll leave you for a hiding place so as not to endanger you. Ivan might think you are harboring a German soldier. Would you store our few belongings? Don't worry if they are commandeered. Be safe," Vati said in parting.

Fear marked our faces. We helped our sad appearance along, wanting to seem older and unattractive. Mutti and I wore kerchiefs tied under the chin as the three of us limped on side-streets out of Neukloster toward the forest.

Most people stayed in their homes. The only sounds came from moving military vehicles and the yelling of Russian orders.

Vati, Mutti and I entered the woods unhindered. We walked on a narrow path before leaving it for thick underbrush, careful not to break branches or trample plants.

Despite my utter despair, I thought back to happier walks in the forests of Pomerania with Onkel Beppo, how he taught me to tread quietly so he could check on the health of the game.

When Vati determined that we had found a small suitable spot without large roots where we could dig into the soil, we began our task. With our hands and shoes as implements we hollowed out an area big enough for three grown people to lie down flush with the surrounding surface. We had one gray imitation-fur blanket beneath us and a brown one to cover us.

During the day, we sat in our rectangle and whispered to each other. "How long can we stay here without food?" I asked.

"Probably three days, hoping that the Soviets' initial onslaught and searches will be over. Until then, we'll forage as the inhabitants of the forests do. It's too early for berries but we can eat the leaves of their plants. Morning dew will be our water," Vati said.

"Let's eat sparingly though, to avoid diarrhea," Mutti cautioned.

Our life of hiding continues. We are still seeking refuge from the horrors of war, still burrowing into the earth; first in air raid shelters, now in this dugout.

THE SUN'S RAYS barely reached the ground through the tall coniferous trees. In early May, the snow had only recently melted, the soil was damp and so were our clothes. The three of us tried to keep warm by doing exercises and rubbing each other's limbs and backs. We spent the clear, starry nights huddled together.

Dread of discovery kept us awake.

Our ears were constantly monitoring noises. Deer and rabbits passing by had nothing to fear from us. *We were the hunted.*

"Where do we go from here?" I wanted to know.

"That depends on how free we are to make our own decisions. Perhaps we can go to the Kellers', pick up your clothes and try to make it to Wismar," Vati said.

"When?" Mutti asked.

"It's awfully dark today. I expect rain. We can't stay here in a downpour. So, our departure might be dictated by the weather," Vati answered.

"I'm hungry," I said softly.

"Food may be a problem from now on," Mutti sighed.

O N   M A Y   6, we left our hiding place. As soon as we came to paved streets, we saw the overwhelming number of Soviet military vehicles parked alongside the pedestrian walks. Troops were milling around, some doing repair work, others painting the white stars red. All of them calling out to the few Germans who passed by fearfully, keeping their eyes to the ground. Again, the three of us put on our "ugly" faces and limped down the street. The accumulated soil on our clothes made us look like spirits of the forest.

We noticed fences around private property flattened by tanks, entrance doors in splinters, windows broken by forced entry....

Neukloster was taken without a fight. Why is there so much destruction? Will the Kellers be unhurt?

When we reached their place, we noticed the front gate dangling from one hinge. The lawn and garden showed signs of digging. *I wonder whether Ivan found our 'burial grounds'?*

The doorbell hung torn out of its housing, so Vati knocked at the door. It was the worst thing he could do to the frightened

Kellers: That was the way the Russians demanded entrance after the initial onslaught.

Herr Keller opened the door, ashen-faced. "Oh, my God, how are you? Where have you been?"

Realizing her husband was not addressing Soviet troops, a fear-stricken Frau Keller emerged from the living room.

"It's so good to see you. Look what they've done to our house, including your room. With stolen swords and knives they sliced open bedding to look for hidden things. Feathers everywhere. They punctured the sofas and chairs."

"Your bikes are gone. Soldiers swerved down the front path, falling from side to side. They did not know how to ride bikes. You might be able to find yours not far from here," Herr Keller said.

"I saw the holes dug in your front yard," Mutti said. "Did they find our caches?"

"No, but they trampled the lettuce."

"When it's safe for you to unearth my uniform, do so and burn it. I don't want them to find it and shoot you because they think it's yours," Vati beseeched Herr Keller. "I wish we could have burned it initially, but that would have attracted immediate attention."

Herr Keller agreed.

"What will you do now? You are welcome to stay if you feel safe. We still have a little food we can share," Frau Keller offered.

My parents accepted the Kellers' generosity. "May we one day be able to repay your kindness," Mutti wished.

Over lunch of bread and sugar beet syrup, our hosts recounted more of the events of the previous three days. "Have you seen the trophies the Russians strap to their arms?"

"No, we avoided looking at them."

"These marauders stripped every German of his watch if he had forgotten to remove it. If rings did not slip off easily, Ivan used force, sometimes cutting off fingers. Gold teeth or silver crowns were booty also. Imagine how they were harvested." Herr Keller shook his head in disgust.

"Well, Almut, we better take out your silvery dental braces," Vati decided. "The Russians seem to want anything that's gleaming."

With toenail cutters and tweezers Vati carried out the bloody task, discarding the installation. *What next?*

W E   S P E N T   T H E   N I G H T at the Kellers' house, cleaned ourselves up and washed our laundry. Fully clothed, we stretched out on bed and couch. When soldiers came through the front door, we stood up immediately. No one wanted to be found in a horizontal position. During that night, Soviet troops looked only for material goods, checking us for jewelry, and the closets for weapons.

After one of those intrusions, I asked Vati why those troops looked so different from the Russian POWs that had worked on farms at home.

"They are Mongols, descendants of Genghis Khan, coming from the southeast of the Soviet Union."

In the morning, we bade the Kellers goodbye, telling them we would walk towards Wismar.

"If we can survive the next six months, perhaps peace will return to our country and with it, order. We'll try to stay in touch. Thank you, again."

W E   T H E N   S E T   O U T to complete our original attempt to flee to the British Zone of Occupation. I carried my backpack because we did not want Ivan to think Vati was a soldier with an army-issue fieldpack if he had it strapped to his back. Three changes of clothes and Herr Keller's donations for Vati, as well as the last of our Stettin-baked Printen, made our meager belongings a light load. Vati and Mutti each carried one of our two blankets.

After leaving Neukloster, we chose to walk on a path above a high embankment separating the road from fields. Tall bushes shielded us from view by the Soviet troops on the road.

The more communities we passed, the more refugees joined our long line of would-be escapees from Soviet barbarism. Whenever we crossed an access road to the fields, we feared being accosted by troops.

*   *   *

IN LATE AFTERNOON, screaming and cursing soldiers on horseback rounded us up and marched us into a huge barn, lining up about one hundred men, women and children against the long walls of the threshing floor, enforcing their orders with kicking and clubbing.

The guards walked up and down the length of our lines, brandishing their weapons, leering and grinning, taunting us with their screams in Russian and broken German. One soldier pulled Mutti's kerchief off and yelled, *"Du deitsche Schwein, warum du nicht sprechen ruski? Ich sprechen deitsch."* Why did she not speak Russian, he asked, while he was able to speak German.

When officers rode in, they gave orders to the troops with their arms sweeping upward and pointing to the stables. The soldiers chose women whom they must have picked out as they guarded us. When they were tearing us out of the line-up, children started to cry and whimper. One little girl did not want to let go of her mother but one loud slap across the girl's face by the officer dimmed her screams. As we were marched out, one man tried to save his wife and was clubbed unconscious. He was lucky he was not shot on the spot. With laughter and kicks, enforced by prodding with their weapons, these barbarians drove us into the cowshed where every woman and girl was violated under the big eyes of feeding cows.

Why me, God? I'm barely fifteen years old.

More thoughts crowded my mind. Is this how wars end? Does every individual of the vanquished pay his share in his country's defeat?

Confused and bewildered I returned to my parents. The three of us embraced. Vati and Mutti tried to control their tears, not daring to weep openly. Stunned and shaken, we adjusted my clothes, fearing the Soviet troops' next move.

Before evening, the officers on horseback chased us out of the barn. We continued our walk until we found shelter at a farmhouse, where several people occupied every room. Some were related, others single travelers, most of them women and children. All of us shared the same danger and the same goal: escape to the West.

The farmer's wife heated water in several kettles and pots on her big hearth. She handed out porcelain wash basins and designated rooms in which the refugees took turns disinfecting and cleaning themselves.

The front door of the farmhouse was unlocked. *Why enrage the drunken Soviets by making them break down the door and shooting their way in?*

*   *   *

E V E R Y   N I G H T   D U R I N G the first weeks of their occupation, the Red soldiers looked for women, *"Frau komm! Davai!"* Quickly! Yelling their command, and with drawn weapons, they urged their prey on. Sometimes, the Soviets led me and other women to houses they had confiscated. There they forced Vodka down our throats to make us drunk and rob us of thoughts of resistance or escape. They answered refusal with beatings.

This was the soldiers' idea of having a party. They served their army's molassses-colored, flaccid bread, and wurst and cheese seized from Mecklenburg farmers' pantries and smoke houses. After the meal, each soldier took his detainee to an unoccupied room in the house or doubled up with another "couple" to violate us. In the morning, the soldiers reported to their units; I and the others went back to our families, or continued the flight west by joining like-minded groups.

O N E   N I G H T Mutti, Vati and I stayed overnight in an abandoned house on a side-street of a village. All doors were missing or dangling off their hinges, and many windows were broken. In an upstairs room, we laid down in our clothes on the only piece of furniture, a twin-size bedstead with a mattress. As we did in the woods, we spread one blanket beneath us and covered ourselves with the other. Our fieldpack became Mutti's footrest. Although lying pressed against each other like sardines in a can, we fell asleep.

Suddenly, the beam of a flashlight scared me upright. I had not heard Ivan come up the stairs. Vati, Mutti and I put on our "ugly" faces and made incoherent sounds. The soldier turned and left.

"That was close," Mutti said relieved.

We could not fall asleep again but were lying in the dark, listening for intruders.

SEVERAL DAYS OF DISTRESS had passed since we parted from the Kellers. "We can't go on like this," Vati said. "We are dirty, tired and hungry. The border between the British and Soviet occupation forces is still kilometers away. I am going to try and find a job at one of the farms. This is the end of May, the time for sowing, planting potatoes, and weeding. Yet, I don't see any workers in the fields."

"You'll need horses and machinery besides people. Who knows how many animals the farmers have left in their stables after the Soviets opened the gates on many farms to herd livestock to Russia?" Mutti argued.

"What passing madness that was," I said, reliving my ordeal.

Soviet soldiers had seized me and several other women from our column of refugees to drive confiscated cattle eastward.

The tempo was slow because the cows were not milked and thus reluctant to move. We stopped at a deserted farmyard at night. An older woman warned me about the soldiers' evening activities.

Not again! I've to get out of here!

Petrified, I skirted the side of the herd farthest from the farmhouse. The soldiers were drinking and frying their daily dinner of potatoes, drenched in oil.

While it was still light, I stole away. Bent low, I walked behind elder bushes growing between the road and the field. *I hope dogs will not alarm my tormentors.* I did not notice any traffic on the road, but at dusk I decided to hide out in a prickly hedge of wild roses, tearing my clothes in many places.

Suddenly, I heard a truck approach. I froze, my heart pumping wildly, the "iron ring" closing around my neck. *They must have parked. Where are they?*

A young officer had come to relieve himself...and found me. As I attempted to flee, he yelled, *"Stoij!"* Stop. He gripped my shoulders and turned me around. With one hand under my chin he forced me to look at him: a white Russian, not a Mongol.

He pointed in the direction of the vehicle loaded with Soviet troops and pushed me towards them. They greeted me with the usual howling and their suggestive gestures. *They'll be the death of me... just shoot me.*

As we neared the truck, the officer shouted sternly at the troops; they quieted down. Opening a door of the truck, he motioned me to get in and then sat down beside me. With a wave of his hand, my captor ordered the driver to be on the way.

"Where do you want to go?" he asked in German.

"My parents are near Krassow."

I did not want the officer to know where I had last seen my parents, so when we came to that village I pointed at a house and said, "Here."

He nodded, gave the order to stop the truck, and helped me out of the cab.

"Auf Wiedersehen," he said.

I don't want to see any of you again!

"Danke." I nodded and left.

On the way to the outlying farm where I hoped to find Mutti and Vati, I picked up some clothes from the ditch by the side of the road to replace my tatters. After plundering houses and stranded treks, the troops threw away the artifacts, dishes, and clothes they did not want. Thus, I was able to look for garments and shoes to fit me.

A black silk blouse with three-quarter-length sleeves, German army tan fatigue pants, one right black combat boot and one left ladies' ankle-high shoe with laces, early twentieth-century-style, became my work clothes for the summer months. In my "uniform," I did not look any stranger than many of my fellow workers.

Mutti and Vati shed tears of relief at our reunion. I have cried rarely since 1945.

LATER THAT NIGHT, I asked my parents, "How far do you think those herds made it? When I was ordered to join that drive, nobody thought of feeding people or animals. We didn't have enough water. Cows, heavy with milk, were whipped forward. Horses ran away, some of them were shot. People fainted and were left behind. When I saw that, I knew I had to escape before too long."

"Who supervised the drive?" Vati wanted to know.

"No one for any great length of time or distance." I thought back. "The Soviets who put the drive together didn't seem to meet replacements. Other drivers told me they ended up slaughtering a cow each night for their barbecue. Some animals could not get up in the morning; they died where they had collapsed. You saw their dead bodies along the roads."

"Yes, the stench in the summer heat was unbearable. That disaster caused the outbreak of typhoid fever as water became contaminated and cows were infected," Vati said.

"And people drank the milk and made butter," Mutti added.

"Those cattle drives are another reason why I want us to stay off the roads. You have experienced how the troops commandeer people to work as herders. What would be your fate next time?" Vati asked.

WE WALKED TO A NEIGHBORING VILLAGE, Krassow, and entered the driveway to a large farmhouse. Through the open entrance door, Vati greeted on old man he could see inside.

"Do you have need for a laborer? I was a farmer in Pomerania."

"I surely do. Come in. My son is not yet back from the war. Our help disappeared. The daughter-in-law and grandchildren have been milking the few cows we have left."

"My wife could help in the house," Vati offered. "Our daughter we would like to hide from the hordes, though."

"I understand. You can take her to the hayloft. Identify yourself and tell those concealed there your intentions. You might neither see anyone nor get an answer," the old farmer warned.

ONE MORNING Mutti came to the hayloft. "Where is Vati?" I asked.

"Soldiers commandeered him at six o'clock to build barracks in the forest, if that's true," Mutti answered my question. "We'll have to stay here, so he'll find us when he comes back."

If he comes back.

After two weeks, he returned, grimy and exhausted. "We constructed five buildings before they let us go. I don't want to be rounded up again. We'll have to move on. Now!"

*   *   *

A FEW DAYS after arriving at the Lehmann farm and taking domicile in the chicken coop, we read a note posted on the barn door, clumsily handwritten in German:

All persons living at this property
Are to report to the Bürgermeister's office
Tomorrow at 10:00 a.m.
To be inoculated against typhoid fever.

108

Who is giving the shots in a village? Haven't heard of any doctors or nurses here.

As Mutti, Vati and I neared the mayor's office, we noticed military vehicles parked in front of it. Right away the "iron ring" around my neck tightened. *Russians administering the serum?*

We joined the waiting crowd in the mayor's reception room.

"They're Soviet women doctors in the army who will prick us," an earlier arrival reported her observations.

"They are big, too." A man rolled his eyes.

When the door to the office opened, a group of residents came out to be replaced by another eight people. Soon it was our turn. A soldier admitted us and five other people. He directed us to line up facing the windows and to take off our clothes from the waist up; men, women and children.

One of the physicians prepared the syringes, the other approached our row with a big cotton ball soaked in rubbing alcohol, in her left and the largest syringe I have ever seen in a doctor's hand in her right fist. As she passed from one resident to the next, she wiped the cotton ball over the area of a person's chest where she aimed the syringe like an ice pick; one cotton ball, two syringes.

I guess I'll share the bacteria and bacilli of at least the five people to my left.

Vati and I suffered headaches and sore muscles for a few days after the injection. Mutti became quite ill. I stayed at her side, fighting her high temperature with cold compresses on her forehead and wrapped around her legs. Vati and I felt so helpless without a family doctor's support but succeeded in helping her to recuperate. The three of us were spared from being infected. Months later, Vati learned that his sister and one of her two daughters died of typhoid fever that summer.

Venereal diseases also spread among the population. As soon as German physicians and nurses could organize clinics, they urged men, women and children to visit them for examinations.

Surprisingly, reopened pharmacies had sufficient supplies of antibiotics.

To reach the clinics in larger communities like Neukloster or Warin, we needed transportation. Although our own bikes were taken and probably discarded by Ivan, on different days we picked up three unclaimed bicycles from among the many articles strewn around in the ditches. Every time we used the bikes we worried about the rightful owners recognizing their property and demanding them back. Nobody claimed them, however. Later we were able to use these bicycles on the first leg of our journey to West Germany.

It would have been ideal to drive our Peter, but we could not believe our eyes when we saw Soviet troops using our car for their loud joyrides in Neukloster and environs.

"Did you see Peter today?" Mutti asked Vati and me. "The spare tire was missing from his mount on the trunk. Wires were sticking up in the air."

"Was his license plate still attached?" I asked.

"Yes, barely," Mutti said.

We saw our car three times that summer. Once, we noticed deep dents on its left side. *What became of you?* Vati had always treated the Adler like a family member.

I thought back to happy outings and our family's weekend tours; or the day we wanted to bury our canary, Hansi, in the forest. Vati had put the burial box on the roof of the car while we stowed a picnic lunch and took our seats.

After a few kilometers, Mutti asked, "Who has Hansi?"

None of us had remembered to take our canary off the roof before leaving. We had lost him.

*   *   *

F R O M 1939 T O 1945, the warring participants inflicted and suffered many losses. In September 1945, my parents and I took a big step and risk to give our lives meaning again: to act, and no longer react to deplorable conditions.

Throughout the time we lived under the heel of the Soviets, one thought, a quote by Goethe, dominated my waking hours: *Hilf dir selbst, und Gott hilft dir weiter.* God helps those who help themselves.

Onkel Riko had written that advice in my *Poesie-Album,* a memory book German girls treasure. As young teens, they ask their friends and relatives to write a few lines in their album to remember them by.

Helping myself in the summer of 1945 meant to close this dreaded chapter of World War II by, at last, reaching the Golden West before the Soviets barricaded the border.

WE KEPT OUR PLANS SECRET. In preparation of the escape, Mutti visited the Kellers and retrieved our buried treasures. To convey her jewelry safely to West Germany, we ripped up the hem of my only dress, stitched the precious bijouterie inside of it and neatly refastened the hem again.

Thanks to the bell-shaped skirt, we had an ample hem to hide trinkets in. From the deep-blue material with red and yellow stripes, woven by Frau Barnheim, Mutti had sewn the dress. It featured a round collar, short sleeves and a fitted bodice, joined at the waist by the wide skirt.

I was happy that my Sonnenkind survived its burial. I wrapped it in underwear before placing it in the field pack. Vati carried our reliable iron ration, Mutti's freshly baked Printen, in the haversack at his belt.

"I am relieved that you see the need for our move out of this dead-end life," I said to Vati. "Certainly, we'll face danger and inconvenience, but we've been doing that for years, especially during the last months."

" Here, people now suffer physical deprivations. And what politics will a German government be allowed to pursue under Bolshevik occupation?" Mutti added to my comments. "We must leave. Together we will succeed."

"Hmm, things would probably be worse only in a Gulag," Vati mused. "Let's go!"

O N   S E P T E M B E R 27, 1945, early in the morning of a clear fall day, we secured our bags on the bicycles. In our best clothes—I wore my dress—we rode the well-known road less than ten kilometers to catch the train in Neukloster.

At the railroad station, we left our bikes at the racks and bought our tickets to Berlin. We reached the city in the early evening after many transfers.

What devastation! Looking for lodging, we rode a streetcar and passed huge areas in *Trümmer:* ruins as far as the eye could see. Streets had been cleared and signs with the street names erected. In front of their former apartments women in drab clothing with kerchiefs knotted under their chins sat on stacks of cleaned bricks, hammering and chiseling mortar from each brick. So that these could be used again for new construction, the city paid the women. They were the *Trümmerfrauen,* an expression later used for all German women who had children to raise during and following the war until the early 1950s. They received small pensions for their hardships.

We found a *Pension,* a bed-and-breakfast, where the owner lived in the smallest room of her apartment and rented out the other rooms to earn a livelihood. She shared with us a meager supper of boiled potatoes and rutabaga; and recounted post-war stories as experienced in Germany's capital city before the Allies established their Berlin zones.

In the fall of 1945, people could cross freely from one sector to another, being reminded on big boards that "You are now leaving the British Zone of Occupation," or U.S., French or Soviet zone, respectively. We saw their troops sight-seeing in all the zones. Berliners, with their famous spirit, began to restore their city, opening shops and greenmarkets. We were amazed to see the life-affirming activities. The atmosphere gave Vati confidence; he even recalled some events from his student days at Berlin's university.

For the following two days we visited the British, American and French consulates because we had heard that they ferried German passengers to West Germany on the return flights of their cargo planes. Although we had relatives who would take us in, we learned that only nuclear kin qualified, not sisters, as in Mutti's case.

Our alternate plan was to take a train as close to Helmstedt as possible, from where we could cross the border on foot.

In Berlin-Zehlendorf, in the U.S. sector, we had no problems obtaining tickets to our chosen destination on September 29.

"Look at all those people," I exclaimed as we walked onto the *Bahnsteig*. The platform had little room for walking; waiting passengers and their bundles took up most of the space.

"Do all of them want to leave the Soviet zone?" Mutti asked.

"How many cars are required to absorb these masses?" Vati wondered. "Will we make it into one of the compartments?"

"The aisle is fine. Just as long as we make it inside," I said.

As the empty train backed into the station, several young people jumped on the running boards.

"Fools!" a woman standing next to me yelled. "You want to end up under the wheels?"

The danger of falling off the platform was as great when the train had come to a stop. Amid the shoving of bodies and baggage, children cried for their mothers as they became separated.

"Hold on to me," Vati said.

"I can't," Mutti wailed.

"Just get on!" I pushed both of them.

"Oh, no! My suitcase..." An old man looked down at the track.

"You want to get in or what?" The impatient question came from the rear. "Move it!"

Chaos again. I certainly learned the meaning of it.

My parents and I were thrust forward into a compartment; Mutti and I had seats.

When the train left Zehlendorf I saw through a small opening of the boarded-up window that a handful of people remained on the platform, some of them waving goodbye to relatives. *It seems, not all passengers could hold on to their luggage, abandoned bags and bedrolls.*

Ours was not an express train but stopped at every station. Few riders left along the way. Occasionally, the two locomotives needed their water tenders refilled. At those times we could leave the cars and walk alongside the train to breathe fresh air and exercise our cramped legs. Then passengers exchanged seats.

"Look there," I said to Vati, "What are Soviet troops doing here?"

"That's curious. They certainly have better transportation than these sardine cans."

Back on the train, the smell of sweaty bodies in their unwashed clothes was suffocating, eased only during the night when cooler air entered through the open squares of the "plywood windows". Every passenger was nervous, stoically sitting or standing, deep in thoughts. *Will we make it to the border? And across it?*

Suddenly, unrest befell the passengers in the dark: they swayed and wiggled, moving aside to let others pass. No one spoke when searching hands touched fingers and wrists or stripped a person of jacket, shirt or pants in exchange for their own. The Soviet soldiers we had noticed before, took people's rings and watches, and secured civilian clothes for themselves.

They are fleeing just like us!

In the morning, on another walk outside the train, I looked for the soldiers. They did not want to be noticed but were easily recognized by their shorn heads, and the many rings on their fingers and watches on their arms as they reached for the handles beside the doors when reentering the railroad cars. *Is their loot supposed to pay for their new life in the West? Will they be accepted as political refugees?*

We passed Brandenburg and Magdeburg. Around noon the next day we felt the train stop again.

"Alle aussteigen! Endstation!" a railroad employee called out after gaining attention with his shrill whistle.

People tumbled out of the cars, looking around, fearing that Soviet troops were present.

"This is not even a station," I said to Vati.

"No, but look at the bumpers. This is the end of the line."

Such an eerie place. No houses; no people working the fields that lay fallow. "It's too quiet. Where are the Soviets?" I asked.

"Let's not wait for them. Quick! Shoulder the field pack. I'll take the two bags. Mutti'll hang on to the haversack and the satchel with our documents."

If the scene at the Endstation were depicted in a painting, it would be aptly titled "Flight of the Masses and Classes."

Under overcast skies, the former passengers of the train hurried west, the once rich and the poor, young and old; mothers pushing strollers, children holding on to both; war veterans with canes, and grandmothers in *Handwagen,* resembling small versions of Conestoga wagons.

The able-bodied and less-encumbered refugees distanced themselves steadily from the slower-moving people and soon reached the cover of the forest, the Lappwald, covering a mountain range.

Vati, Mutti and I were breathing heavily as we tried to keep up a steady trot. The wet fallen leaves made progress difficult and treacherous. Sweat ran down our faces and backs. In the distance, we heard shots being fired.

"Are we already in no man's land?" Mutti wondered.

"I don't know," Vati said. "Didn't see any line of demarcation."

"How deep is such a territory?" I asked.

"That varies. On the train I heard that the British zone begins six kilometers from the Endstation."

"We must have covered half that distance, don't you think? If the terrain were only less hilly," I sighed. "Where are the other people? I don't see anybody. Are we going in the right direction?"

"No need to panic. We probably ran faster than most. See the setting sun's rays penetrating the forest, guiding us west?"

In our arduous attempt, running to leave life under Soviet rule behind us, I didn't notice under the roof of the tall deciduous trees that the skies had cleared.

"This is a good omen," Mutti exclaimed. "The sun shines golden upon the West."

With renewed effort, we ran toward the sun.

In late afternoon we were slipping and sliding downhill, right into a hollow, about six meters wide. Exhausted refugees following us fell or stumbled into it. Uniformed men helped them to sit up and rest, pulling strollers safely down; handing candy to children.

"Those are not British uniforms," I said fearfully.

"No. Look at the patches sewn on their sleeves: Belgian colors. During the war, partisans formed resistance groups in France, Belgium, Holland and Poland. Émigrés set up provisional governments in London," Vati explained under short, heavy breaths. "So, the liberated West European countries must have reestablished armies and taken their places in concert with the Western Allies."

I must overcome this paranoia, my angst of uniforms. The Soviet heel is behind me.

ProvisionaryID and proof of non-membership in Nazi party. Aug./Sept. 1945

CHAPTER 9

Testing our Mettle

A S W E P A U S E D in the shallow depression at the British side of the no man's land, we observed new arrivals trickling in continuously, alone or in groups of two to four. *Were all these people on the train with us? How many trains stopped daily at our Endstation? They are draining East Germany. The Soviets will not allow this flood for long. Am I glad we made it across the border! What's next?*

From time to time, Belgian soldiers gathered weary escapees, including us, and led them out of the forest to a waiting bus. After a second bus arrived, the first one transported its passengers to a former aboveground air-raid shelter in Braunschweig.

"This is a processing center for non-residents of the British Zone of Occupation. Have your IDs ready for inspection. As you enter the building, you will find directions posted for your information," the driver announced.

On the ground floor of the shelter we showed our primitive, typewritten pieces of paper with old snapshots stapled on them, our IDs from Mecklenburg. Now we received registration cards, valid for transit in the Western Allied zones until we obtained resident cards at our eventual domicile.

"We are legal," Vati sighed. "Life can only improve from here on."

Oh ja? Well, at least, we are no longer under Soviet domination; and out of the chicken coop. But this place is depressing, too.

I forgot how many floors of accommodations the shelter contained, but they were filled. After the sign-in procedures, we were free to find a niche to spend the unforgettable night.

We left the elevator repeatedly in search of a bunk or two to stretch out on, but they were all taken.

"How many people can this shelter hold?" I asked Mutti.

"You would have to ask the caretakers. Remember that Braunschweig is a city with more inhabitants than Stettin. Many sought safety here."

"We have tried to find room at the uppermost stories to no avail. Let's take the elevator down to one of the lower levels. It doesn't matter where we spend the night sitting on our bags. In the morning, however, we will be closer to the exit," Vati suggested.

When we thought we had settled down, we noticed how some denizens kept looking at the ceiling, others checked their clothing and that of their family members.

"Ach, du lieber Himmel!" Good heavens. "Watch out for those bedbugs marching in columns." Vati warned, "See that they don't settle on us. We'll have to examine each other's backs and bags. Most of all cover your hair."

Just as Mutti and I did during the firestorms; then came the fleas in the chicken coop, now these parasites.

AFTER THAT LONG NIGHT, we telephoned Mutti's aunt and godmother, Tante Klara, in Bad Hersfeld on the Fulda River in Hessen, Hesse. We needed to establish a residence. Did she have any advice for us?

"Why don't you come here? Our home survived the air raids with minor damage. Consequently, many air-raid victims were assigned to our big house. But I have a room for you."

What I remembered from earlier visits to Hersfeld were its healing springs. They had attracted people since the seventeenth century when noblemen and their ladies came to "take the cure." Hersfeld became a spa, as the *Bad* before its name indicates.

Bad Hersfeld suffered great damage during air raids in World War II, thus limiting available dwellings. Moreover, U.S. Armed Forces established a considerable presence in the town and required housing. We were grateful to my grandfather's sister for offering us shelter.

With our transit passes, we were able to cross into the U.S. zone. Passengers on the train identified us as refugees by our exhausted and rumpled appearances.

"Where are you from?" was the question we had to answer often.

"From Stettin originally. On our flight, the Soviets overtook us in Mecklenburg."

"Are they really as bad as refugees tell us?"

These people can't imagine what they hear and read about the ordeals East Germans endured. They don't believe us...

"It depends on how much the victims reveal. Perhaps they suffered worse at the hands of the Red Army than they can talk about," Vati said.

This answer and similar evasive ones stopped most inquiries about the first nine months in the Russian and Polish areas of administration in Germany.

WHEN WE ARRIVED AT HER HOUSE in the afternoon on a pleasant October day, Tante Klara, a widow, greeted us. She noticed the strained expression on our faces as they mirrored the exertion of the previous week.

In her patrician manner she said, *"Guten Tag!* You must want to freshen up. I shall show you the bathroom we will share and the room where you can rest and recuperate from your odysseys. Meanwhile I shall prepare tea and toast."

Tante Klara had been able to keep her library from occupation by assigned tenants. Now this spacious room with tall windows and an alcove became our place of respite. For my parents, Tante Klara had two beds placed in the alcove. My cot was near the book-laden shelves. *Heaven! Books! I get to sleep—sleep?—in a library. I haven't read a book this year…*

W E   T R I E D   T O   L O O K as presentable as possible when we entered the dining room a short time later.

"Sit down and have a snack. Dinner will be at eight."

I was so tired and would have preferred sleep to food.

Tante Klara apportioned a plate with two slices of buttered toast and currant jelly for each of us. She had carved out this refreshment from her meager ration. For that reason she "restricted" us to the quantity served.

"This treat looks so appetizing, but I don't think I can eat it all," Mutti said. "Please take one slice off my plate."

Our diet had consisted of *Printen* since we left Berlin three days before, and a little water in Braunschweig. *You have to eat and drink. See how much you can get down.*

I nibbled. With determination, and two cups of herbal tea, I finished one slice of the delicious toast; my stomach had shrunk too much to accept more.

Tante Klara could not understand our involuntary refusal of her offerings. While most adult Germans lost weight during the war, they could find room for two slices of toast.

Mutti assured her aunt that our appetite would normalize.

"Please, don't be offended. We are thankful for your hospitality. We need time to adjust."

Finding the rhythm of West Germany was our first challenge. We endeavored to meet Tante Klara's high social standards after having lived in subhuman existence for months.

T H A T   E V E N I N G, we met thirty-year-old Ursula, our aunt's youngest daughter, who was spending her vacation at home. Ursula was quite tall, a shapely woman. Inquiring, deep-lake-blue eyes accentuated her delicate facial features. Her general demeanor expected an equal sense of purpose in her vis-à-vis that she displayed. At the *Landfrauenschule Wittgenstein* in Birkelbach, Westfalen, or Westphalia, Ursula taught animal science to daughters of well-to-do farmers and other families attending this finishing school after years of typically European academic schooling.

Ursula's older sister, Hedwig, and her husband, Robert, joined us after dinner to extend their welcome to us. They owned a modern farm at the edge of Bad Hersfeld where they carried out research on animals, soil and crops in conjunction with the University of Marburg.

Not having seen each other for years, we exchanged "East and West" stories with our cousins, answering questions about relatives who were not present.

"And what are your plans after you catch up with yourselves?" Ursula asked.

"I want to finish school," I blurted out.

"For that to happen, we have to establish residence. That means I have to find a job," Vati said. "As soon as possible, I have to go to *Münsterlager,* where the British have established a camp for former German soldiers and prisoners of war who don't have valid separation papers. The process will take three days."

"I have an idea," Ursula said. "Let me make some inquiries."

WE TRIED NOT TO BE A BURDEN to Tante Klara during the following days. Vati secured a temporary *Aufenthaltsgenehmigung,* or residence permit, which qualified us to receive ration cards. Now we could contribute to the meals we shared with Mutti's aunt and cousin Ursula who were glad we lent them a hand doing household chores.

The answers to the inquiries Ursula made assured my life's stability for a year. The director of the Landfrauenschule accepted me as a student. I was grateful and relieved. *It will be a challenge.*

For Vati, Ursula had been promised a job at the sawmill in Birkelbach.

"Oh, Ursula, how kind of you to want to help us but we can't afford the tuition for Almut," Mutti said sadly.

"I made that clear to the director, Gräfin von Grewe. She assured me that the school had scholarship money to cover the expenses. The countess also expressed delight that her niece, Vicki, would meet another fifteen-year-old refugee. Vicki's family had left a large estate in Ostpreussen, where they had bred horses."

"Thank you for your concern and effort. But Almut does not have the necessary clothes." Mutti continued to list obstacles to my attending the school in Birkelbach.

"Don't worry about that, Cläri. Our students buy uniforms from our alumnae. The scholarship includes all expenses incurred at the school," Ursula reassured Mutti.

"Will I find a room?" Vati asked.

"I am sure. Birkelbach is a village seemingly untouched by the war. At the sawmill, you will make contacts."

*   *   *

THE END OF URSULA'S VACATION signaled the start of the fall semester at the *Landfrauenschule Wittgenstein*. Vati and I traveled with Mutti's cousin by train via Marburg to the next station of our lives' journey.

"Erndtebrück!" the conductor called out at our destination.

Bright sunshine illuminated the pastoral setting of the scattered houses and few farms nestling in the hills above the main road.

How peaceful; a perfect motif for Impressionists and their light-filled landscapes.

We passed the sawmill shortly after leaving the railroad station. "From here, it's just a short distance to our school, Curt," Ursula said. "You'll find your way back easily."

Vati nodded. Looking ahead, he said, "And that cluster of buildings on the hill must be your last stop for a while, Almut."

At the entrance gate to the *Landfrauenschule*, I surveyed my next home with anticipation and a throbbing heart. *Will I, at fifteen, fit in with women eighteen and older? They had graduated from high school and passed the Abitur, the formal written and oral final examinations.*

After the cordial reception by the director and the teachers, Vati left for the sawmill and his search for lodging. Ursula took me to my room in one of the two dormitories.

We ascended to the main entrance of the maize-colored stuccoed building and entered through heavy wooden doors. High windows admitted daylight into the foyer. The sight of the thick dark reddish-brown linoleum reflecting the sun's rays reminded me of magazine ads for *Bohnerwachs. I guess I, too, will be waxing this floor soon.*

"Your room is one flight up," Ursula said. "I don't know whether you'll be the first to arrive." Upstairs, she said. "Go ahead, open the door."

My roommate stayed back in the room, quite nervous with barely a hint of a smile. I walked toward her and extended my hand, *"Ich heisse Almut, und du?"*

"My name is Hilde."

"See, Hilde has chosen this side of the room." Ursula pointed at the made-up bed and the books and pictures on the shelves and desk. "Park your baggage in the closet; then come with me to pick up sheets, a coverlet, towels and your uniform."

I returned to make my bed, hang up my few clothes, freshen up and don my short-sleeved dress with vertical narrow blue and white stripes and a starched white, bibbed apron. Hilde sat at her desk, too shy to help or watch.

What is her problem? It took nearly the entire year we roomed together to learn bits and pieces of nineteen-year-old Hilde's background.

Her father was an industrialist in the Ruhr Valley. Because of the frequent bombardments of that area and the resultant loss of her family's home and factory, Hilde spent six years before coming to Birkelbach in a Roman-Catholic convent school. She moved noiselessly like a nun, head turned down, and hands in front of her. I can't recall Hilde ever initiating a verbal exchange, but she always answered politely.

Was the Landfrauenschule to teach her worldly skills? Oh, what a twosome we make. Who assigns roommates?

Hilde and I did not spend much time together. Our schedules reflected our interests: she took many home economics courses; I was in my element caring for gardens and animals.

Cousin Ursula was the teacher in charge of the three cows, two pigs, and the chickens. She taught us to milk cows, slaughter chickens with a surgical knife, and guided us through all the chores necessary for sanitary conditions in stalls, sties, henhouses and the milk shed.

The animals were housed in one half of the two-story building set back from the dormitories. The hayloft and grain storage were located above the stable. The other half of the building contained Ursula's apartment as well as classrooms.

In the second dormitory, Fräulein Schlatter reigned. She was the instructor in horticulture and botany. This strict and friendly woman inspired me to make a career in landscaping. I never refused to take on weekend duty unless I had promised Ursula I would milk the cows and care for her charges.

I learned to plan crops and their succession, select seeds and make clean cuttings for grafting or rooting. I also did a lot of weeding.

"Be sure you pull the roots of every weed after you loosen the dirt with your hoe. Otherwise you'll have to work the same area again in three days," Fräulein Schlatter advised. I practiced that method as long as I had a plot to clear of creepers and climbers. Our manual work gave us insight in the classroom; theories were no longer abstract.

My dorm was the center of culinary activities. Kitchen, pantry, refrigeration chamber and conference room shared the basement with the heating plant.

Our instructor was a cheerful person who met patiently the anxious questions of her highly academic but *weltfremd,* naive students.

"For today's *Mittagessen,* you'll prepare a vegetable soup, macaroni, and peas with ham."

"No dessert?" one girl asked.

"Yes, you'll complement the starchy main course with a fruit compote. You have cooked the vegetable soup once before; so follow your recipe. To cook the macaroni, bring the measured water to a boil and drop the pasta in. Stir to separate the 'macs'. Reduce the heat. Don't overcook your creation."

"How do I know when the water is boiling?" one girl named Rita asked.

"You'll see the change that occurs in the pot. Bubbles will rise to the top."

Every student scurried to secure the ingredients needed for her assignment. When the time came to boil water for the macaroni, Rita watched her pot intently. After a while, she took a teaspoon, dipped it in the pot and scooped out one spoonful of water. Excited, she ran to Fräulein Nehring, "Now is the water boiling?"

O N O N E W I N T R Y O C C A S I O N, Fräulein Nehring instructed us in the dairy how to make cheese. We boiled milk in large cooking pots, added enzymes for fermentation and were told to set the pots on the parapet of the wide descending cement stairs. There, we were to cool the contents to a certain temperature by stirring them before the next step.

"Stirring them?" one brainy girl cried. "By stirring you create friction; friction creates heat. How can you cool anything down by stirring?"

Has she never had a hot drink that she wanted to cool by stirring so she would not burn her lips?

Besides those classmates who seemed to have lived between pages of books, there were also interesting individuals.

Lisa was beautiful and the oldest at twenty-four years old. During the war, she had been assigned to work for her Rhenish city's disaster team, a dangerous job. Because she was engaged to marry a fighter pilot, she applied to the *Landfrauenschule* during the previous year to acquire household skills.

Shortly before the end of the war, her fiancé's plane was shot down; he was killed. As Lisa had been accepted by the school, she hoped to overcome her grief by delving into new activities in the circle of young women.

Her intelligence placed Lisa at the head of the class but her heart was not in her practical work. Instead, she wrote poignant poetry in memory of her beloved.

Lisa and I became friends. During our free time we listened to her records of classical music and discussed German literature, writers and philosophers. In her presence, I realized how much I had to learn. But when Lisa had weekend duty in the gardens or the stables, I was the one to lead her through the chores.

What I had in common with Countess von Grewe's niece, Vicki, was our youth, our backgrounds, and our likes and dislikes. We missed our *Heimat*, our home states on the Baltic Sea with their endless fields and forests, the freedom we had to roam, remembering the good life and forgetting the politics that brought us to this oasis of peace, security, and food.

Neither Vicki nor I were fond of polishing silver. Coming from the Soviet zone, we could not understand how occupation troops, in this case the British, did not plunder this school so rich in inventory and comfort.

"At our home, the cook's helpers took care of the silverware, serving dishes, tea and coffee sets, Father's trophies from his student days, and his hunting prizes," Vicki said. "I didn't know there was so much effort and finger strength involved to achieve this gleam."

"I don't like this assignment either, never have," I sighed. "My mother made me help her put the shine on our silver. She was hard to please. That was years ago. Because of the air raids we stored much of our valuables in bank vaults or in attics on the farms my father supervised. I liked using chromeware. You didn't have to clean the blades of those knives by rubbing wet *Ata,* or similar cleansers, with a cork after every meal, especially after serving red cabbage."

"Ja, or eggs... Who's using our silver now?" Vicki wondered.

"East German farmers would be welcome to it, though I'm sure the Soviet troops found the treasures stored in peoples' attics. They took their booty back to the Soviet Union," I said.

"Many cherished possessions remained in the Polish territory of East Pomerania and Silesia when the residents fled. And a lot of property burned in the ravages of war."

"Let's think of tomorrow," I said, changing the subject. "I'm nervous about my assignment for next week."

"Why?" she asked.

"It's my turn to listen to the evening news on the radio in the administration building and report the information to those assembled at the *Mittagessen.*"

"Oh, I see. I'd be nervous, too."

"Well, the Nuremberg Trials take up most of the newscasts." I paused.

The hearings revealed atrocities carried out by the Nazis and their henchmen in concentration camps that I had not been aware of.

When and why does a human being decide to torture another? How can I be appalled at the brutality of air raids and conquering armies?

"Can't we change? Must there always be wars?" I mused.

"I suppose, people have to individually resolve those questions," Vicki pondered.

"Ja, besser machen. At any rate, I want to relay the findings truthfully."

"You will. We are certainly living history, aren't we? Will future leaders learn from the politics and government actions of the warring parties?"

"I doubt it. Did anyone learn from the fall of Rome, or Napoleon?"

"Listen to us," Vicki said. "Does polishing silver generate deep thought?"

"What better way to forget the fleeting usefulness of this activity?"

"Now, now! We're here to restore our civility. I say, what better way to do some edifying thinking. Besides, I like the smell of the polish."

Vicki and I sat in the serving area next to the dining hall to render the silver back to its sparkle. In this anteroom, glassware, cups, plates, serving dishes and cutlery were stored. A dumb-waiter delivered the food from the basement kitchen.

The class, which had prepared the meal, was divided into three groups before the time of serving. One-third of the students set the tables thirty minutes ahead of mealtime. Then they received the filled serving dishes from the kitchen, served the food and replenished emptied tureens, bowls and platters.

Students in the second group kept sending refills from the kitchen via the dumb-waiter. The third group started washing the cooking utensils as they became available.

The best part came last: All of us cooks, servers, and dishwashers ate together in the downstairs conference room after clearing the dishes from the dining hall and its anteroom. Now we enjoyed the aroma and taste of our morning's endeavors in a happy atmosphere.

Annemarie was in my cooking class and occupied a room near mine. Soon after she arrived in the fall, I asked her, "Were you in Sellin in the *Kinderlandverschickung*?"

"Yes, how did you know?"

"Your school was quartered in the hotel across the street from ours. You know how younger students always recognize the older ones but rarely vice versa. Also, you came from the Rheinland, a famous but distant place, whereas we *Stettiner* were still in our home state. So we noticed you old ladies, but especially you with your peroxide hair."

We worried about the consequences for bleaching her hair as a member of the BDM, *Bund Deutscher Mädchen,* the group of fourteen-to-eighteen-year-old girls in the Hitler Youth.

"Ja, I defied the rule of the natural look with my hair and makeup. Who would have dared take us on after escaping death untold times during years of air raids?"

"When did you leave Rügen?"

"Our city called us back when the evacuations began in Ostpreussen. At our age we were assigned to social services to help the elderly and young families without fathers."

"And now?"

"I need time to think and decide where I might fit in the new Germany."

W E, T H E   C L A S S   O F 1946, spent a memorable year at the *Landfrauenschule* and felt swept from the hardships of the previous time of war and its immediate aftermath into an era of promise. Most of our country and families still struggled daily with insufficient shelter, clothing, food, and the uncertainty about their men in foreign prisoner-of-war camps, or those missing in action. More than three million German soldiers lost their lives during and after World War II.

Vati had returned from *Münsterlager* with documents certifying that he was, indeed, who he said he was. With this verification, he could begin to climb out of anonymity and doubt.

"All refugees say they were landowners or owned businesses, or they claim nobility. Why should we believe them?" many West Germans argued. They were not familiar with the vast agricultural holdings in the eastern part of the country, which complimented the West German industrial centers. And who were the noblemen? Landholders who had supported their rulers for centuries but during the Third Reich initiated the resistance.

The flow of refugees into West Germany, devastated during warfare from the air and on land, became a burden to the West's strenuous efforts of economic recovery. We brought poverty with us but skills as well.

In the sawmill, Vati was a laborer's assistant, handing the wood to the man at the saw. For that job Vati needed no great skills. From his meager income he paid his rent, bought food, toiletries, stationery and postage stamps.

Months went by without answers to his mailed résumés or employment inquiries. When we were able to make contact with Mutti's sister Felicitas, called Felix, in Bad Kreuznach, she, too, helped with the search for a job for Vati in her area.

FOR EASTER VACATION, Ursula and I went back to Bad Hersfeld. I had not seen Mutti since Christmas.

"You have grown and filled out," she said when she hugged me.

"We can wait to buy clothes with my *Kleiderkarte* until I finish my year in Birkelbach because I wear my uniform."

"Yes, but you'll have to use up your ration points while you live in the British zone. Don't let them go to waste."

The question of fitting clothes came up again during my visit, when Tante Klara insisted I be confirmed in the Protestant church on Palm Sunday.

"I have not even had any *Konfirmandenunterricht*," I objected, pointing out my lack of religious instruction.

"It's too late for that. At age sixteen you have a last chance to be confirmed. I have made arrangements with our *Pastor*."

"Does Mutti know about this?"

"Yes. She agrees."

I bet she doesn't have any choice because of her gratitude to Tante Klara and Ursula for providing her with shelter and Vati and me with opportunities.

"I don't have a dress and shoes for church," I said hopefully.

"You can wear my black dress for the occasion and Ursula's shoes."

Tante Klara was taller than I, so Mutti brought the hem up on our aunt's dress. She attached a white lace collar to the neckline and cuffs to the sleeves.

I'll be the only seventy-year-old Konfirmand.

131

In the church, I sat with the legitimate confirmands who stared at me and wondered who I was. At the time of benediction I followed my neighbors' actions. *This is not right. I have not prepared for this sacred act. I am here so my great-aunt can feel better.*

After the service we returned to Tante Klara's house. Immediately she said, "You can take my dress off now before it will be stained."

Mutti and I went to her room, lowered the hem of the dress, removed collar and cuffs, ironed the dress and returned it with my thanks.

We shared the *Mittagessen* as usual. No one made any reference to the church service and its special meaning. Tante Klara was convinced of her good deed: She had saved my soul. No need to dwell on it.

*   *   *

BEFORE THE END OF MY YEAR at the *Landfrauenschule,* Vati had secured a position at the *Landratsamt,* or regional office of the Department of Agriculture, in Bad Kreuznach.

"Great!" I said when he gave me the good news. "Now you'll be living in the French zone, Mutti in the American and I in the British zone."

"Not for long. As the head of our family I will establish residency and bring Mutti and you to Kreuznach. That will not be easy because the French zone has the least agricultural resources in Germany to feed its inhabitants. So, authorities are reluctant to admit refugees into their zone."

"Will you find an apartment for us? Felix wrote that the town has a housing shortage."

"I am going to Kreuznach next week to secure the necessary permits for our relocation, proof of employment from the *Landratsamt* and agreement from the mayor's office to assist us in finding lodging."

"Do you think you'll earn enough so I may finish high school?"

"We'll see; if not immediately, then next year."

"If they put me in the *Untertertia* where I left off in Stargard in my life before the *Flucht* and Soviet occupation, I'll be seventeen and in classes with fourteen- and fifteen-year olds," I protested. "Perhaps I can work during the summer, after leaving the *Landfrauenschule*, and save some money."

"First, we have to move there. Then we'll tackle one problem at a time… beginning with obtaining household articles."

*   *   *

THE FINAL EXAMINATION at the *Landfrauenschule* gave me a taste of those stressful occasions; I "over-prepared," as a professor told me forty-one years later. Because I always was an outsider at these events, I had to show my mettle.

The women with whom I took the academic tests had passed their *Abitur.* They were veteran test takers. Together, Vicki and I crammed the theories of the past year into our minds until we giggled from exhaustion. "We'll show 'em," she said. We did.

"Demonstrating our abilities in garden and stable should be a breeze," I remarked.

"*Ja,* unless you draw one of the lots that designates you to slaughter a chicken."

We carried that dread with us for days, until each of us fished a blank out of Ursula's hat for that task.

"*Gottseidank!*" Thank God!

"What remains is the cooking exam," Vicki worried.

"I'm not afraid of preparing the menu but of the time constraints. How do mothers serve meals on time with toddlers pulling on their aprons, the mailman coming to the door wanting a signature, or a neighbor dropping in with the latest gossip? All I can do in the allotted four hours is follow the steps in my recipes," I fretted.

"*Ja,* and hope my concoctions are edible."

On the morning of our exams, Fräulein Nehring greeted us with a stack of folders, our individual assignments.

"Now listen: If you can read you can cook," she reminded us of her motto.

Didn't our class teach her anything with the "boiling" water on a teaspoon or the "friction" in the dairy? These women can read but their thinking gets in the way of avoiding shortcuts for their recipes.

"Almut, this is for you," Fräulein Nehring said as she handed me my folder. "*Dicke Erbsensuppe und zum Nachtisch Käsetorte.*"

I passed my exam easily. I have cooked split-pea soup with potatoes, carrots, and herbs often in my life but rarely crowned it with a cheesecake.

WHEN IT CAME TIME TO LEAVE the picturesque landscape in the County of Wittgenstein, saying goodbye to my friends, the faculty, and the school's reassuring routines, was difficult. In this safe atmosphere my scarred psyche had healed and I was ready to meet new demands.

*   *   *

VATI AND I WERE ON THE WAY to our new location, Bad Kreuznach, Rheinland-Pfalz, or Rhineland-Palatinate. The train stopped at Remagen, the border station between the British and the French zones. Passengers who wanted to take up residence in the French zone had to leave the train and report to the immigration office.

At the reception desk, a French officer inspected our papers. We proceeded to the waiting room, where we joined several nervous refugees.

"You never know whether they'll be satisfied with your answers in the interview," one woman said fearfully. "My sister…"

The door to the interview room opened. After a young family exited, a uniformed customs inspector called our names.

"Your birth certificate," a woman clerk demanded of Vati.

"I have not yet been able to obtain a copy," Vati said. "My separation papers from *Münsterlager* are valid in the four zones of occupation and guarantee the veracity of my personal data."

"How do we know you were born?"

She means, "You were born on the stated date", doesn't she?

"Well, here I am," Vati shot back.

Oh no! She won't let us in!

"And you?" she turned to me.

"I am his daughter."

"I can see that. Are you Catholic or Protestant?"

"Protestant."

"Another one," she snapped.

The woman stamped our entry permits and pointed at the door. *"Sie können gehen,"* she said, dismissing us.

Back on the train, Vati shook his head. "This incident reminds me of the jokes people told in the Soviet zone."

"You're thinking of the untrained clerks who were ordered to run government offices? They weren't used to reading and writing and didn't volunteer for those jobs, did they?"

"Nor did they have basic office materials, like unsoiled files, forms, stamps, or furniture. Their make-shift operation left them open to ridicule."

"But a year after the war ended they can't find competent people to work at border points?"

"Don't forget how many lives have been lost. It takes time to rebuild a country and its society. All German adults have to undergo denazification procedures. Before they are found innocent of crimes and prove that they were only *Mitläufer*, rather than leaders in the Nazi party, they cannot fill responsible positions. It will get better."

"I am glad that you are cleared. With more people passing the scrutiny of investigations, looking for jobs might become more difficult, especially in agriculture in the Rhein- and wine land."

"Yes, I have much to learn about this climate and its effect on soil, crops and their diseases, as well as insects and other plagues."

"I can't believe we are going to live in the Rheinland. I thought of it as an exotic place with charm and unfamiliar sights and customs."

Leaning forward in my window seat, I marveled at the landscape, so different from the Northeast. The sun shone brightly on the fast-flowing *Vater Rhein* and mountains: the Westerwald on the right bank and the Eifel on our side, the left bank.

The train followed the contour of the river upstream, going in the southerly direction. At times, the highway flanked the Rhein near the water before crossing the tracks. Most of the way, fertile parcels of land bordered the river; land on which the residents of the small towns we passed planted their fruit and vegetable gardens, using all available precious land between river and mountains.

I alternated from side to side in our compartment, determined not to miss any of the new sights. "Look at those vineyards, Vati. How steep they are; working them must be hard."

Passengers in our car smiled at my awe and asked unavoidably, "Where are you from?" Several of them had been on *Hamstertouren* to the farms in the Eifel, where they had bartered bottles of wine for flour, bread, butter or lard to supplement their meager rations. Every time the doors to the compartment opened to admit another passenger or the conductor came to check tickets, the *Hamsterers* worried about government agents looking for smuggled food articles.

Our fellow passengers' anxiety sent a strong message: My year of enjoying four balanced meals a day was over. Vati and I would have to be creative to satisfy our stomachs again with foods obtained through ration cards. *We'll manage.*

Whenever the train stopped and the conductor or the station's intercom announced the names of the larger towns, Andernach, Koblenz, Boppard, I became aware of the reality of these places. *Until now, they were just dots and names in my atlas.*

I noticed the ruins, fire-blackened façades, craters, and destroyed bridges all along the route. Battles had raged in the Rhine Valley, the most famous one at Remagen.

"The next station will be Koblenz," Vati said. "You will see the confluence of Mosel and Rhein that gave the city its name. The Mosel separates the Eifel from the Hunsrück. A short distance south from here, near Oberlahnstein, the Lahn empties into the Rhein on the right bank, flanked by the Westerwald and Taunus mountain ranges."

I looked across the river and observed for much of the ride a mirror image of the landscape we passed through: Above the retaining wall were a federal highway, railroad tracks and vineyard-covered mountains. But often, when our train followed the curvature of the Rhein, scrubs covered entire tracts of arable slopes.

"Why aren't those slopes tilled?" I asked Vati.

"I am not a vintner but I assume that vines need to have southern exposure to benefit from the sun's rays as much as possible. Or, if the *Reblaus,* a plant louse, attacks the vines, the affected vineyard is quarantined for a number of years so that the pest will be eradicated.

"Look, we are approaching the *Loreley.*" Vati pointed at the cliff on the right bank of the Rhein, around which the river bent in a sharp curve. "Navigating the Rhein is dangerous. Submerged boulders can cause severe damage to ships and barges, if the crews aren't careful."

"Yes, I know. Folklore says, boatmen were distracted by the splendid sight of the setting sun caressing the gently swaying treetops on the Loreley cliff. Inattention left the boats running aground, inspiring Heinrich Heine, to pen his famous lyrics about the *Lore-Ley.*

'Ich weiss nicht, was soll es bedeuten,   I don't know what makes it so
Dass ich so traurig bin;   That I feel this very sad.
Ein Märchen aus uralten Zeiten,   A fairy tale long ago
Das kommt mir nicht aus dem Sinn.'   Sowed the memory I've had.

"We had to memorize Heine's five stanzas about an old fable that he could not forget. It was about a desirable young maiden the mariner envisioned atop the mountain, combing her golden hair, reflecting the sun's bright rays.

"I think I'll always remember this view. We, too, are passing the Loreley in the best light... with Heine's *Lied* on my mind."

To emphasize the hidden dangers on this part of the river, a cluster of rocks in the middle of the Rhein appeared around the bend: *Die Sieben Jungfrauen,* the Seven Virgins.

IN LESS THAN AN HOUR, we had to change trains in Bingerbrück. In this major railroad switching station all buildings lay in ruins, temporary structures replacing them.

"It's remarkable what the management has achieved in its efforts to repair the tracks since the war's end only sixteen months ago," Vati marveled.

"Wirklich!" Really. "But see the ruins of the apartment blocks beyond the station? That's what Stettin looked like when we left it. You remember our hometown in better shape because you departed earlier for the Ostfront, don't you?"

"I suppose so."

On the last leg of our trip, the train skirted another tributary of the Rhein, the Nahe, which joins the mighty river between Bingen and Bingerbrück.

The Nahe Valley is situated at the foot of the Hunsrück. As the land flattened out, I saw farms and villages amid fields and meadows, small in comparison to the Northeast.

"Now I believe that you have a future in Bad Kreuznach," I said. "But there are vineyards here, too."

"Nahe wine is well known and appreciated by connoisseurs who prefer a wine lighter than *Rheinwein* or less sweet than that of the Mosel region. Farther up the river, the landscape turns more hilly and mountainous so that the location of vineyards becomes a factor again."

"I can see the silhouette of Bad Kreuznach."

I like the scenery. Will the people be friendly or resent us like the woman in Remagen?

FELIX, MY THIRTY-YEAR-OLD AUNT, greeted us at the *Bahnhof.* I had not seen her since her last visit with us in Stettin years ago when she came for a short respite from the air raids on *Köln,* Cologne, where she lived. I had forgotten about her nervosity, so I was shocked to notice her head shake slightly in continuous motion.

By the end of the war, Köln was fifty-eight percent destroyed. Felix lost her living quarters four times. For saving seven lives under fire, she was awarded the *Kriegsverdienstkreuz ohne Schwerter,* a medal for heroic service by civilians in times of war.

These actions characterized her life: always helping others. Now we were the recipients of her kindness.

"I brought a *Handwagen* for your baggage. Although you don't have much, it would be too cumbersome to carry your bags for the distance to my friends' house, where you can stay until you find your own rooms."

At dusk, we walked through the streets of the wounded and marred county seat. *It's not only the lack of agricultural resources that makes this state's government restrict immigration; it can't keep up with the demand for housing.*

The pock-marked villas in the *Kurviertel,* or spa district, had to accommodate many renters, as Tante Klara had. Officers of the French occupation troops and their families shared several of the large residences with German owners.

We arrived in darkness at the next way station of our odysseys. Frau Warner welcomed us and showed us our room. The kitchen and the bathroom she would share with us. My cot stood in the living room. *I am so sick of inconveniencing kind strangers. When will it end?*

W I T H I N   A   W E E K, the local housing authority allotted a furnished room to Vati and me downtown. Frau Warner gave us a spare bed sheet, which we installed as a divider mid-room. On a hotplate, we heated water and simple meals. The bathroom down the hall was shared by the owners of the apartment, another tenant, and us... a busy place every morning.

Vati's work was vital to the community and county. He had the unenviable job of securing cattle and hogs for slaughter and subsequent consumption by the regional population, as well as French troops.

For once, being an outsider was an advantage: County administrators chose Vati for this position because he was impartial, not having family or other ties to the farmers whose animals he had to requisition. Initially, some farmers tried to bribe Vati.

"Today a man came to my office with two pounds of butter. He wanted me to skip him on the rotation."

"What did you do?" I asked.

"I wrote him a receipt, told him to sign my copy and assured him that the hospital would be grateful for his donation."

Despite the antagonistic role Vati played in these situations, he did not make enemies among the providers or his employers.

A S   T H E   S C H O O L   Y E A R was well underway, we made an appointment with the principal of the Kreuznacher Lyzeum, the girls' high school.

"Did you bring your last *Zeugnis?*" He asked for my last report card.

"No, we retrieved few of our documents that Soviet troops scattered."

"In which level do you think you could succeed?"

"I left the *Untertertia* in December 1944."

"Try to finish that fourth class, then."

After sharing the class with fourteen-year-old children I was bored with the lessons. *I can't tell the principal I had all this material in Pomerania nearly three years ago. He'll be insulted and not believe me.*

"Vati, please help me skip to the next class."

We visited the principal again; he was prepared for our request.

"Teachers have assured me Almut can do the work in the *Obertertia.*" He turned to me, "But what about French? You started it only a week ago."

"We will engage a tutor," Vati said. "Can you recommend one?"

I began my private lessons with Fräulein Dupuis, meeting twice a week at her apartment. Her love of the French language and culture was infectious and inspiring.

My class still did not teach me anything new. I asked a teacher to accompany me to the principal's office to recommend my moving up another class.

"Very well... under one condition: You catch up with the *Untersekunda's* level of achievement in French by Christmas," the principal said.

I agreed. Every day after school I studied, either with Fräulein Dupuis or in our room. By now, my favorite subjects, the sciences and math, presented challenges to me. I had little time for a social life. I made one good friend, though: Inge Lenz.

Inge had lived through the air raids in Darmstadt, Hessen, with her parents, younger sister and brother. Herr Lenz had been an engineer for Merck Pharmaceutical. He was not allowed to seek employment until after his political past was investigated. The Lenz family was relegated to a make-shift apartment in the attic of their own building in the city.

In order to reduce the strain on the household as well as on Herr Lenz's heart condition, Inge moved in with her mother's parents in Bad Kreuznach.

WHEREAS I WORKED QUIETLY and purposefully in class—*I have to get out of here*—Inge argued with teachers and classmates if she felt her point of view was threatened.

"I don't care what they think of me. These people in the hinterland are so provincial," Inge said.

My friend was a petite sixteen-year-old beauty. Dark blonde, naturally wavy hair framed her expressive face. With big blue eyes she looked attentively at an interlocutor but also could send icy glances. In a more peaceful time, her figure could have taken her to runways at fashion shows.

"This quarter I will introduce you to the wonder of sewing machines," our sewing teacher, Fräulein Fischer, said one day.

"During the next class, let me know what material you can round up and what you want to create with it. The time we could individually work on the same project has yet to come. If anyone among you can help out a classmate with a donation of material, we would appreciate that."

I received blue cotton material for a blouse.

"Thank goodness, there isn't enough for sleeves," I said to Inge. "I don't think I could attach them correctly. What are you going to sew?"

"A bikini."

"A bikini? What's that?"

Inge smiled and said, "I found a pattern for this bathing suit. Here, look!"

"Hmm, there isn't much to sew, is there? And it doesn't require much material. Wearing your bikini will certainly attract attention at the swimming pool. No one else will have one."

"They'll be *le dernier cri*, the latest fashion. French girls are wearing them already."

"Good luck with Fräulein Fischer...and the class."

BOTH INGE AND I were outsiders, more mature. Our classmates thought Inge was a snob; they found me a grind and strange. *"Richtige Wanzen."*

"Why did they call us real bedbugs?" I asked Felix one day.

"The native residents of Bad Kreuznach label newcomers to their town 'bedbugs', comparing them to the vermin that threatens people's comfort. After fifteen years, you'll be accepted by the local population, or so they tell you."

"Fifteen years? I doubt I'll be here that long."

My goal was to leave school at the end of the academic year in 1947 after the *Mittlere Reifeprüfung,* a preliminary exam two years before the *Abitur.* I had nothing in common with the sheltered children in my class but the shared curriculum.

"Time to look for a *Lehrstelle* with a local gardener," I told Vati. "Before applying to the *Gartenbauschule* in Geisenheim I have to serve two years as apprentice and one year as journeyman, as Fräulein Schlatter advised me in the *Landfrauenschule.*"

"What field of study will you choose?"

"Landscape design."

Landfrauenschule Wittgenstein.

Students at the Landfrauenschule, 1946
Second row, left: Almut
Second row, right: Hilde

CHAPTER 10

My Freely Chosen Task

DURING THE MIDDLE of the twentieth century, German women made careers or held jobs in many fields that only men had previously pursued. In times of war, women filled positions, such as streetcar drivers, that had been vacated by men who were called into military service.

When I tried to find an apprenticeship as a gardener, however, I encountered hesitancy among the owners of landscaping firms and nurseries. Although they employed female laborers in their businesses, the *Meister* who were certified to teach apprentices had not accepted girls before. Their attitude was based less on gender bias than on the belief that women could not carry out the heavy tasks, could not endure prolonged spading or lifting filled seed crates and rooted bushes and trees.

A potential *Meister* saw only my recent departure from the local *Lyzeum;* he could not imagine my labors in the fields of Mecklenburg. Eventually, Konrad Bretz, a quiet man in his seventies, relented to sign my contract.

From October 1947 to April 1949 I rode my bicycle to and from work at the *Versandgärtnerei* Konrad Bretz on Neufelder Weg in Bad Kreuznach. The specialty of Meister Bretz's firm was growing seedlings for potted plants and vegetables for sale to nurseries and farms throughout West Germany.

At Bretz's, I entered the world of the Guild system. Apprenticeships in most trades take three years to complete, except for trainees with a high school background who continue their academic studies later. They work for two years. In my experience, a new apprentice took his orders not only from the owner but also from the hierarchy: the second- and third-year apprentices and the journeymen. The latter had passed their exams as apprentices and were working for seven years if they wanted to achieve the *Meister* status. They received their designation after their journeys through other areas and countries to study diverse approaches and techniques in their field.

Some journeymen establish their own enterprises after a few years; others take their *Meister* exams in order to be able to accept apprentices.

In 1947, a first-year apprentice received a weekly allowance of five Reichsmark. During the second year he or she "earned" seven marks and fifty pfennig; in the third year, ten marks. This pin money was based on the old custom when apprentices lived in the household of their *Meister* and had few expenses. Herr Bretz had no live-in apprentices and thus enjoyed the benefit of two inexpensive laborers.

Most young people learning a trade had finished their eighth-grade elementary education at age fourteen. Fifteen-year-old Chris, my superior by one year of employment, was commuting to Bad Kreuznach. For his parents, the price of their oldest son's train ticket presented a hardship.

Chris introduced me, the novice, to my duties.

"For the next six weeks, you're responsible for keeping the place clean. The broom will be your sidearm. There'll be cuttings, leaves and potsherds wherever people are working here. Clean it up."

The boy grinned, clearly enjoying his new role as the second-year apprentice. Chris was always cheerful, happy to be alive. The bluish hue to his skin color was a reminder of his stopped heartbeat at birth. It was restored by the midwife.

As I observed the routine of the workers, I thought of ways to eliminate wasted time. I placed receptacles for the refuse near their working stations and I emptied them as they filled up.

The employees complained to Herr Bretz about my innovation. He turned to me and said, "Stop making new work rules. Don't you know you don't belong?"

With that question, my *Meister* vented his frustration at the changing world: girls in academic pursuit capably engaged in manual labor.

Herr Bretz opened my eyes to the old class system, slow to die even after the devastating war we had lived through together. I had to adapt to my workplace. From that incident on, I became more communicative, asking people if they would object to my suggestions for innovations.

After I was trusted with a gardener's chores, I was happy. In my daily log, I recorded the weather conditions as well as the cultivation of all varieties of plants we grew at Bretz's in hothouses, hotbeds and the open air. In one August-1948 entry I wrote,

30. VIII.	30 August.
Chrysanthemen ausgebrochen und angebunden."Rayonnant," "Monument."	All but top Chrysanthemum buds removed, tied plants to stakes. Varieties "Rayonant," "Monument."
31. VIII.	31 August.
Stiefmütterchen, Vergissmeinicht, Tausendschön ins Freiland ausgesetzt.	Pansies, forget-me-nots, daisies planted outside
1. IX.	1 September.
Pelargonien eingetopft.	Geraniums potted.

The most delicate job was the initial care of cyclamen. Their seeds resemble dark powder. At the time of planting the tiny seedlings into bigger seed crates we needed clear eyes and had to gently apply tweezers to separate each specimen from the clusters.

One day during *Mardi Gras*—always celebrated with abandon in the Rheinland—Chris came to work with a hangover.

"This morning you transfer the cyclamen we sowed in December, Chris and Almut," the foreman said and left.

"Oh no! I can't even see the seedlings. How am I going to plant them in exact distances and in straight rows?" Chris whined.

For hours, he suffered bleary-eyed over his task, bending over to look at his rows from side to side. "Are they in line?" he asked me.

I LIKED MY CHOSEN PATH to the future. The work was always interesting, from sowing to harvesting. The atmosphere at Bretz's, though, was often difficult to endure. When I was not receptive to the advances of young Mr. Bretz, the owner's nephew, he also blamed my refusal on my "not belonging." I learned to bear the needling, reminding myself that I was not sorry to have taken this route in fulfillment of a prerequisite for admission to the *Gartenbauschule,* or landscaping academy.

During their training years, apprentices were required to attend a *Berufsschule,* or trade school, one day a week. There they learned the technical aspects of their trade. Subjects dealt with fertilizers and pest control, as well as geological and business topics.

I was glad to find an alter ego in my class. Gisela Fussel had passed her *Abitur* the previous year. Now she was completing her apprenticeship before attending a university to study architecture.

Sitting side by side in class, Gisela and I finished our assignment about chemical substances and other theoretical problems quickly and were allowed to read horticultural magazines and architectural digests while instructors taught the rest of the class.

DURING THE EIGHTEEN MONTHS of my apprenticeship, I was free most evenings and three out of four weekends. I realized I missed the contact with the French language and culture after my earlier concentrated study of both.

You need to practice what you've learned if you want to study roses in Paris, formal gardens in England, and trees and shrubs in America.

The local *Volkshochschule,* or evening classes for the population, offered courses in French. French military units were stationed in the barracks formerly occupied by German troops. Their families lived in requisitioned apartments and houses in Bad Kreuznach. The children attended schools for dependents.

One of the French high school teachers taught my evening class. The young, heavy-set teacher was exasperated because she could not read the handwritings of her German students. One of her comments on my homework was *"L'écriture française est plus ronde!"* as she compared the more straight up-and-down strokes Germans use to the smoother, rounded ones commonly practiced by the French. She repeated this reminder to us every week in her melodious voice.

I A L S O   E N J O Y E D exploring Bad Kreuznach on foot or bicycle.

On one of my strolls on a Saturday afternoon, I walked along the *Salinenstrasse* toward the center of the town. A few people did some last-minute shopping before stores closed early for the weekend. Suddenly my eyes felt drawn to the opposite side of the street where a young man held my stare. He crossed over and stopped in front of me. "Excuse me, are you Almut?" he asked.

"Yes, and you are Gerhard Steindorf."

We laughed in disbelief that Friedeberger schoolmates should run into each other after five years apart, hundreds of kilometers from our old school and the potato fields.

"Even though we've changed, I thought I recognized you," said Stein, as we called him.

"And I you. Where do you live? How is your family?"

"At long last, my father found a teaching job at the elementary school in Rüdesheim, near Kreuznach. Our family survived all hardships since leaving Friedeberg. My brother and I ride our bikes to the *Gymnasium* here. It's my last year."

"And then?"

"The *Johannes-Gutenberg-Universität* in Mainz. I want to study education. But what about you and your parents?"

"Wait. Do you have to be some place?"

"No," Stein said, "I just needed a break from cramming for the *Abitur*."

"Want to walk to the Kurpark? We could sit on a bench there and catch up with our histories."

In the following month, I invited Stein to our living quarters.

G O T T E S   M Ü H L E N   M A H L E N   L A N G S A M , a German proverb states. God's mills grind slowly.

A year after Vati and I moved into our one room with a curtain down the middle, the authority of Bad Kreuznach allocated a room and a kitchen for us so that Mutti could leave Tante Klara's house in the American zone and join us in the French zone.

Our next accommodations were located at the western outskirts of the town. Due to the severe housing shortage, our widowed landlady, Frau Eichner, and her cat were restricted to the largest room on the first floor. My family and I occupied the other room and the kitchen. Again, we shared the lavatory.

Over time, we were able to buy used furniture. Mutti created a living room with two beds that we converted to couches during the daytime and a large desk that also served as a dresser, as well as a sideboard when we entertained. Two chairs were pushed under it from each side.

In the cramped kitchen stood our round table with two old chairs; a third one we borrowed from the living room when we sat down for our meals. My mattress leaned upright against the wall.

150

How I hated to move the furniture aside to make my bed every night—and pick it up in the mornings.

A small cabinet for dishes, pots and pans had its place beside the window. The sink, in which we washed dishes, laundry, and took our sponge baths, was installed against the third wall. Vati had built shelving for our two-burner gas counter stove; curtains hid a pail and wash bowl underneath.

A sergeant of the French military, with his wife and two young children, lived upstairs in two rooms plus a kitchen and a full bath.

The three parties reached their rooms via the foyer inside the same front door. We all listened to the French radio programs heard clearly through the open doors above.

In this environment we entertained our visitors, including Gerhard Steindorf. I lost contact with Gerhard after that visit, when we both left town in the spring.

THEN CAME THE DAY IN JUNE 1948 that West Germans had been waiting for: a return to normalcy, when we could make purchases without ration cards, when stores again offered choices and our money had value.

Announcements on radio and in the newspapers informed the population that for each member of the family, the heads of households could collect forty *Deutsche Mark* (DM) at the local precinct offices.

On the day of the *Währungsreform,* or currency reform, Vati, Mutti and I walked down the hill on *Mannheimer-Strasse* into the center of Bad Kreuznach in bright sunshine. People emerged from houses and side streets.

"Everyone is smiling," I said.

"Guten Morgen," we answered the greeting of a stranger.

The joyous mood of the adults carried over to the children, who hopped and skipped ahead of their parents.

"How long was this monetary conversion planned?" Mutti wondered. "And how could the authorities keep this event secret?"

"I don't have precise answers," Vati said. "But last year the Americans introduced the Marshall Plan, with the idea that the United States would help European countries by infusing huge grants into their economies if the populations would help themselves."

"What do you mean by 'help themselves'?" I asked.

"Basically, we are to do what we always do: work for our livelihoods. The difference will be that the participants in the Marshall Plan can engage in international trade. It's a new beginning for West Germany, and for that we need untainted currency. With forty *Deutsche Mark* per person everyone will have an equal start."

"How can businesses and factories operate on such a small amount?"

"They'll receive special allotments."

AFTER SIGNING THE RECEIPT for DM 120.00 for our family, Vati handed me *zwei Mark,* two marks. "Tomorrow you can go into town and buy something you like. Check out the new prices."

"Oh, thank you. I know I want a decent piece of soap. Will the stores be stocked so quickly with goods we have done without and missed for years?"

I barely remembered the fragrant *4711* cakes of soap Mutti used long ago. We had to use abrasive kinds to wash our hands. With ration cards, we could buy one or two small softer pieces of *Schwimmseife* per month, a soap so light it would float if dropped in water. I tried to avoid that because every slight contact with water diminished the size of the cake immediately.

The next morning I went downtown, hoping to satisfy my longing for a creamy, mild luxury bar at the drugstore opposite the busy market square.

Look at that! Farmers did not waste any time bringing their produce and poultry to market.

No longer would citizens come to the farmer and beg for eggs, butter, milk, or meat in exchange for silverware, paintings, rugs, or other valuables. After years of bartering, city dwellers grumbled facetiously about the walls of pig sties being decorated with Persian carpets.

On that morning, however, with their regained power to choose from among the producers' supplies, the many shoppers' comments combined in the air, resembling the buzzing of bee swarms.

Like magnets, the luscious early fruits and vegetables attracted me before I reached the drugstore. With the two marks in my pocket, I did not know whether to splurge on the strawberries that enticed me not only with their deep-red color and meaty plumpness but also, and especially, with their aroma. Compared to vegetables, though, they were too expensive for my limited funds. I settled for a generous bunch of freshly washed carrots with their greens on top and took a big bite of one after I had paid.

"Aren't they sweet?" a voice behind me asked.

"*Guten Tag, Ulla!*" I said as my former classmate stepped beside me. "You bought some, too?"

"*Ja,* we live over there in the green building." Ulla pointed across the square. "This morning my family watched the traders set up their stalls and display their wares. When my mother saw the oven-ready chickens being strung under the roofs of some stalls, she gave me five marks for a chicken, new potatoes, peas and carrots. Of course, I had to taste the vegetables," she said, smiling.

"Are you buying anything but food?" I asked.

"Not now. My mother and I want to look around this afternoon to decide who needs what most in our family. Purchases will probably have to wait until paychecks come in D-Marks."

"I am going to buy soap for myself." Pointing at the carrots in my hand, I said, "These'll probably be gone by the time I get home."

"Have fun. *Auf Wiedersehen!*"

"*Tschüss,*" I said and waved goodbye.

A S   I   L O O K E D   A T   T H E   W I N D O W   D I S P L A Y of the drugstore, I was astonished to see Lux and Palmolive soap displayed along with toothpaste and hand cream.

In the store, too, showcases exhibited toiletries we had lacked for years. Confidently, I approached the counter behind which Frau Löffler waited to serve me.

"I would like a bar of Lux soap, please."

"Gladly." She even had a bag to drop my soap in; until then, customers brought their own *Netze,* nets, or *Einkaufstaschen,* shopping bags sewn of linen or braided straw.

Munching carrots, and occasionally enjoying the scent of the soap, I walked home on a day that is etched in my memory, when civilized life was reborn.

*   *   *

I N   J A N U A R Y 1949, I began my preparations for the *Lehrlingsprüfung,* the exam after the completion of my apprenticeship in the spring. The examining board accepted my year spent at the *Landfrauenschule* as part of the required two years' training.

Why did I save the chore of copying my daily log into a respectable book until three months before I had to hand it in? Procrastination cost me many nights of sleep. On weekends I paced, measured and recorded the entire area of Bretz's grounds, placing buildings, trees, shrubs and compost heaps into the site plan I had to present.

I also developed people skills in addition to learning the practical work for my future profession. Before being told I did not belong, I naively believed that if I met people openly and fairly they would react in kind toward me. Now I became aware and more tolerant of the individuals' accumulated experiences that formed their views on life and their fellow human beings.

Despite this insight, I had to summon self-control whenever the Bretz nursery had a sale on potted plants. Forgetting that nature's products are not perfect, customers took their time choosing the plant they would buy.

"If this Gloxinia with its colorful blossoms had as many buds as that one and the rich foliage of the one in the second row, I would pick it... Well, let me see...I guess I'll take it."

THE RECOMMENDATION by the *Berufsschule,* along with my log and the site plan, excused me from an oral examination.

As a *Gehilfin,* or journeywoman, I aimed to fulfill the next requirement for admission to the *Gartenbauschule.* In April, I left Bad Kreuznach to work at one of West Germany's large growers of perennials, Kayser & Seibert, in Rossdorf near Darmstadt, Hessen.

The area necessary to cultivate plants for landscaping is by necessity much larger than that needed by growers of potted plants and seedlings. I was filled with happiness at the sight of the wide spaces and long beds planted with perennials of varied dimensions and stages. *This is where I want to be, one step closer to my goal.*

"Welcome to Rossdorf," Herr and Frau Seibert said as I entered their manor. "Please join us for lunch. After the meal we will show you where you'll stay while you are working with us."

Besides the difference of the size of this business compared to Bretz's, I realized that I would *belong.* Herr Seibert, a lanky, dark-haired man, looked at me with steel-blue eyes as he explained some of my duties over lunch.

"We had many rainy days this month but were able to plant most of our rooted cuttings. I hope you brought rubber boots and rain gear."

"Yes, I came prepared," I assured him.

On the way to another building, I felt dwarfed next to Frau Seibert. She guided me along a row of scentful *Iris pumilia,* Dwarf Iris, which displayed their early blue-and-purple blossoms.

"From your résumé we learned you're familiar with work in the soil. You will like your fellow *Gehilfen.* Anna Kuhn comes from Kaiserslautern. She is your roommate. Arndt Behrens's hometown is Hamburg. He is a boarder at our house.

"Here we are at one of the storage buildings," Frau Seibert said. "Let me show you the upstairs."

At the top of the staircase was my living quarters for the next six months. Frau Seibert opened the door to my room.

"You see where Anna has staked out her side," Frau Seibert said.

"Yes, I'll unpack my belongings in this half of the room. Thank you."

"The bathroom is across the platform. If you have forgotten anything, let me know. We can probably help."

I was pleased with this airy room, large enough for bed, desk and chair as well as desk lamps for each occupant on opposite sides. A table with two chairs in the middle and a built-in closet at the foot of my bed completed the arrangement.

Anna came running upstairs, eager to meet me.

"Guten Abend! Did you find us readily? This is a great-looking nursery, isn't it? The boss and the workers are friendly as long as you can keep up with them."

I learned about work tempo in the potato fields of Friedeberg.

"As soon as I wash my hands and change out of my muddy clothes, we'll take a bike ride into the village. Before the stores close, we can buy some groceries. The Seiberts are feeding us the hot noon meals in the common room, except on weekends," Anna said.

"Do we have dishes?" I asked.

"Oh ja. Look in the lower part of your nightstand," Anna replied.

"Okay."

I made my bed and observed Anna's smooth and efficient movements. Taller than I, she had a proud bearing and held her head high. Shoulder-length wavy hair softened the chiseled lines of Anna's face and the expression of her deep-blue eyes.

"I'm ready. Are you?" she asked. I nodded.

On our excursion into Rossdorf, I noticed the post office near the railroad station: two life lines to the outside world.

"Is our mail delivered to Kayser & Seibert (K&S) or do we have to pick it up here?" I asked.

"It comes to the office."

I could barely make out Anna's answer before the deep drone of the huge low-flying airplane overhead temporarily smothered all other sounds.

"You'll get used to the presence of the American cargo planes," Anna said during a lull. "In their holding pattern for the Rhein-Main Air Base in Frankfurt they cross over our area. The noise seldom stops."

The U.S. and U.K. governments established the Berlin Airlift when the Soviets halted road and rail traffic between the West and Berlin. In a continuous stream, planes provided the population of West Berlin with food, coal and various other supplies around the clock via the airlift.

Another plane interrupted our exchange.

"The Soviets didn't think their blockade of the city could be broken," I shouted.

The West German population knew of the heroic actions of the Berlin Airlift crews. During their "Easter Parade" of April 15th and 16th, they landed one plane with precious cargo per minute.

In addition to setting "birds" on the tarmac, British seaplanes came from Hamburg and landed on the Havel River, delivering salt. Only seaplanes were built to withstand the corrosive effects of this mineral.

I resumed our conversation. "Did you hear about the Candy Bomber?"

"Of course. Most of us in the American and British zones, and especially Berliners, remember his name, Gail Halvorsen. He made it his mission to drop candy to the waiting children of Berlin before he landed his heavily loaded plane," Anna said.

"The Western Allies have ended World War II. The Soviets seem to keep it going; or are they eager for World War III?" I asked.

Anna shrugged. Looking straight ahead she replied, "Oh no! We need peace. There's been enough killing during six years of war."

In time, the Soviets realized that the Western Allies were determined to keep the Berlin Airlift operational for the duration of the blockade. Americans paid a high price. They lost thirty-one lives during their fifteen-month effort to keep a life line open to the West Berliners.

AT THE GROCERY STORE, we bought mostly non-perishable food because we lacked refrigeration. For our first meal together, though, we picked up milk, cold cuts and tomatoes.

Over supper, we told each other about our backgrounds. Anna never spoke as much again as on our first day. Though she was always polite and communicative, she was reserved and liked her privacy. *A perfect roommate.*

I appreciated Anna's tendency to keep eye contact when talking with me. Her face mirrored the full attention she gave to our conversation.

"Herr Seibert suggested I spend an hour tomorrow morning to show you the premises before our work assignments."

"It's going to rain, according to the forecast," I said.

APRIL, APRIL! Macht was er will!

"This fickle month does as it pleases," Anna remarked as we toured the meticulously kept fields of spring-green plants; several species showed early blossoms.

"We look more like sailors than gardeners in our slickers," I quipped. "I'm ready to go to work, though."

At the packing plant, Herr Seibert instructed the foreman about the orders to be filled. "And you two can select twenty *Dicentra spectabilis.* You know where they are, Anna, don't you?"

"Yes," she answered.

On the way to the beds planted with the requested bleeding heart, Anna explained, "You'll see how advanced the buds are.

158

That calls for careful packing. But it's what the customer wants—perhaps for a newly designed garden or park."

I WAS PLEASED with my new environment. As the days and weeks passed, I observed the growth and change of the perennials. I learned about the soil, space, and care they needed in Rossdorf's and similar zones' climate.

Despite the established routines we followed, the work was varied and never boring. The practical application of our lessons came when we *Gehilfen* each took our turn at caring for K&S's designed and planted garden area at the SÜWEGA LANDAU/Pfalz, 1949, the southwest garden show in Landau, Palatinate.

This assignment was one of the highlights of my experiences as a *Gehilfin*. During the one-week stay in Landau, I weeded the borders daily, watered the lawn and plants as necessary, and replaced spring bloomers with later-maturing species.

When Vati and Mutti came to visit, they perceived immediately how appropriate my choice of occupation was. As I guided them through K&S's display, Vati asked, "You are in your element, aren't you?"

"Definitely. It was worth overcoming the rough spots at Bretz's as well as labor in inclement weather. Whenever I need to bolster my resolve, I recall the opening of this folk song:

'Mein Handwerk fällt mir schwer,   My craft seems a hard chore,
D'rum lieb' ich's noch viel mehr'... "   So I love it even more...

"I am glad to hear that," Mutti said. "Have you found any new favorites besides the poppies and bachelor buttons you liked since childhood?"

"Yes," I said, laughing. "Then, flowers had to be red or blue, or smile at me like pansies or daisies. Now I would add Delphinium, or larkspurs, in different colors as background plants to my garden. Also, I might place Scabiosa with their pale purple,

159

blue or white blossoms on long stems near red and yellow primroses."

"I favor Scabiosa, too," Mutti said. "They bloom throughout the summer."

"Exactly. And do you remember the Reseda the Barnheim grandmother used for borders of their flower beds? I would definitely plant those."

When in bloom, the spiky, greenish-white Reseda emit a calming fragrance.

M U T T I A N D V A T I were not my only visitors at the garden show. Inge Lenz and her fiancé, Odward Schlamp, made an afternoon excursion to Landau, where I showed them my accommodations at a bed-and-breakfast—*how far I've come from the chicken coop*—and my place of work for a week.

Odward was an engineering student at the *Technische Hochschule* in Darmstadt. For his hobby, photography, Odward found the perfect setting at the garden exhibition in which to place Inge, thus capturing the beauty of both his bride-to-be and the colorful garden.

The SÜWEGA attracted a steady flow of admirers daily, weather permitting. As a representative of my employer, I was able to answer many horticulture-related questions.

"I like edelweiss but don't see any in your garden," a woman said. "Is Landau's climate not conducive to their culture?"

"It is less the climate that prevents edelweiss from thriving in this zone than the rich soil and fertilizer, which our plants prefer. Edelweiss require dry, meager soil to produce the characteristic white fuzz on leaves and flowers."

"Don't you like Dahlia?" a young boy asked me. "My mother has a lot of them."

"Dahlia are attractive. But what you see in this show are the products that each grower specializes in. As you walk from one display to another, you will recognize plots featuring annuals, such as Cosmos and Zinnia; they are arranged by seed growers.

Companies cultivating tubers and bulbs sell Dahlia, lilies and many of our early spring flowers, such as tulips," I said.

"Oh… thank you."

"You are welcome. I am glad you asked. Do you see any plants here that you like?"

"*Ja*, those dark-red marguerites over there."

"They certainly look like marguerites, but they're of the Pyrethrum family."

"Next January, he will want to order from my catalogues," the boy's mother said and smiled in parting.

AFTER MY RETURN TO K&S, Herr Seibert had a new assignment for me. "I need someone to fight the mouse infestation before the pests fatten themselves on any more juicy roots. Are you willing to do that?"

"What does the job involve?" I asked, hesitating.

"Setting out traps, checking them twice every day, and burying the dead vermin."

"On this property, that's a full-time mission."

"Precisely. By the end of a week the survivors will have fled. This action has to be taken annually in order to prevent greater damage to our plants."

"All right, where do I start?"

"In the barn. The foreman can show you the traps."

My fall from the gardens of Landau. Most rays of sunshine create a shadow. Now I am the hunter, not the hunted. Life involves death.

Bewildered, I carried out my agreed-to chore. *Mein Handwerk…*

AS HERR SEIBERT had predicted, I could return to regular work after several days.

Although Anna, Arndt, and I seldom received the same assignments, it became obvious that blond, curly-haired Arndt found reasons, or excuses, to work near me. He was a serious, goal-oriented young man, three years older than I. Soon enough, mutual attraction led to romance.

When neither one of us was on weekend duty, Arndt and I explored the area on our bikes, or took trains to visit Bad Kreuznach or Darmstadt. At the time, we felt we had a future together: absolving our academic studies and, subsequently, building a landscape design business. But, as Vati used to say, jokingly, *"Erstens kommt es anders, und, zweitens, als man denkt."* How right he was: First, plans develop differently, and second, from what people think.

I left K&S in October; Arndt stayed through the winter until he returned to Hamburg to begin his studies. Not long after my departure, the man of my future found another love interest.

To calm my broken heart, I buried myself in studies at the Private Interpreters' College in Bad Kreuznach, where I had enrolled for the winter semester. My courses in English and French were to prepare me for qualification as a business correspondent. I also took basic Spanish. Successful completion of these courses would enable me to apply to study abroad.

Always planning ahead.

Page from apprenticeship journal Dec. 1947.
Signed by Meister Bretz

Kayser & Seibert garden design at Süwega/Landau 1949

CHAPTER 11

A Twist in the Road

THE INTRODUCTION OF THE DEUTSCHE MARK brought changes for many West Germans, including my family. The free market eliminated government-run procurement and distribution of consumer goods.

Vati was ready to establish his own business, a *Viehagentur.* In his livestock agency he bought cattle, hogs and sheep from farmers and sold them to butchers. He had become familiar with the area through his previous employment by the county's department of agriculture and had won the trust of the producers. But to the competition, he was still the outsider, the *Wanze.* His knowledge, fairness, and drive enabled him to operate debt-free after two years.

During my stay in Rossdorf, Vati and Mutti found an apartment in Bad Kreuznach. Frau Dietz, the elderly owner of the three-family house was widowed. Because of the housing shortage, she was forced to live in the attic apartment. At first a French couple resided on the second floor. After the creation of the North Atlantic Treaty Organization, certain French and U.S. troops received orders to exchange locales. So, French troops were stationed east of the Rhein and U.S. units were posted in the French zone. Therefore, when I returned to Bad Kreuznach, an American sergeant and his wife occupied the second-floor apartment.

Our flat on the ground floor was divided into the master bedroom with space for Vati's desk and bookcase, the living room with my convertible bed, a full bathroom—a first for us after five years—and a spacious, well-equipped kitchen with balcony.

Behind the house, Frau Dietz's garden stretched out. Apple and pear trees shaded the small lawn. Rows of strawberry plants abutted the weed-free beds of leek, onions, carrots and cabbage.

"This is a wonderful place," I said when I inspected the apartment and stepped out on the balcony. "Who is the happy gardener?"

"Frau Dietz asked us whether we wanted to use the plot. She is too old and invalid. We share our harvest with her," Mutti said. "You'll have to meet her."

"Of course. I can take her mail upstairs tomorrow."

When I rang her doorbell the next day, I called out, "I have your newspaper and letters from your mailbox, Frau Dietz. I am Almut, the Fingers' daughter."

From behind her front door, I could hear Frau Dietz shuffle slowly to greet me.

"Guten Tag, Almut," she said. A welcoming smile wrinkled her full face. "I am glad to meet you. I heard you're going back to school?"

"Yes, this afternoon I'll enroll at the *Private Dolmetscher-Schule.*"

"But you don't want to become an interpreter, do you?"

"No. I have six months to fill before I can enter the *Gartenbauschule* in Geisenheim to study landscape design. I plan to use this time to improve my foreign language skills so I learn about horticultural practices in other countries."

"I see. Good luck to you. And thank you for bringing my mail."

"You're welcome. Is there anything else I can do for you?"

"Not today. I am trying to get out to the bakery. I need to walk."

"Well, so long. Be sure to let us know when you need help."

THAT AFTERNOON I took placement tests. Classes began the following day. Three students had enrolled in my Spanish course; in French eight, and twelve students registered in the English class.

The woman who taught Spanish made no permanent impression on me. In contrast to our English and French instructor, Joe Stedronsky. The patient gentleman displayed a ready smile, sometimes sardonic, other times in humorous reaction to our ignorant attempts at the languages he had mastered. Then his brown eyes twinkled behind spectacles and his brow lifted in quizzical amusement, "Are you sure that's what you want to say? 'The grocer sold his favors'? "

Herr Stedronsky spoke not only the target languages but also many of their regional dialects, which he demonstrated to us. For most of his students who brought only book knowledge to class, it was difficult to carry on conversations in the languages we studied. Our assignments included news reports by the British Broadcasting Corporation, BBC, the American Forces Network, AFN, and Radio Luxembourg. With my background, I was comfortable with BBC but felt challenged by AFN—true to the general perception by Germans that to speak English you had to have one hot potato in your mouth and two for American pronunciation.

Our English class was more enjoyable than my French and Spanish courses. The greater enrollment and the students' varied purposes made this class interesting. From the butcher's son who wanted to serve his American customers to the young female secretary aiming to seek employment with international companies; from the girl with aspirations in the travel industry to another planning to work as a nanny in England. They, and others, thought the knowledge of several languages gave them flexibility in their chosen fields.

And then there was this handsome young man, a former prisoner of war in America as well as in England. During breaks in our class, Bert Metzroth and Herr Stedronsky merrily discussed topics of their choice, mostly in American English, which left the rest of us gaping.

Twenty-three years old, Bert sat diagonally in front of me so that I saw more of the back of his head, and of his hands as he raised them to respond to questions. I was attracted to both physical features but was still emotionally attached to Arndt.

At social functions at the college, I realized what a wonderful dancer Bert was. He let me know how he enjoyed my company but respected my feelings for Arndt—until he learned of our final breakup.

"I am not ready for new disappointments," I said. "Arndt and I have so many memories…"

"We'll make new memories," Bert said. His serious face exuded confidence. In pursuit of his goal to win me over, he created many memorable opportunities.

FOR OUR FIRST OUTING, Bert picked me up in a Jeep he had bought at a war surplus yard. We wanted to spend the afternoon near the scenic Rhein. Barely out of Bad Kreuznach, his vehicle emitted clouds of steam. The engine was overheating. Bert had come prepared, however. He always put two Jerry cans of water behind his seat for an emergency like this one.

Are we making memories?

After quenching his Jeep's thirst, Bert climbed in again, smiled victoriously and said, "Come on, Prancer, you know the way home."

Bert's lighthearted remark brought to mind the many times Vati and I had patted the necks of the horses we rode or gently tapped the reins of a team and said those very words, save for the names of our steeds.

I felt wondrously touched. It seemed so right to have my past connect with this Sunday drive.

In bright sunshine, the wind in our hair, we passed the fields and villages of the Nahe Valley alongside its river to where the stream emptied into *Vater Rhein* at Bingerbrück.

My date pointed out historical sights or ruins and spoke of their fabled bygone days. I saw the *Drususbrücke,* the bridge Romans built across the Nahe as they penetrated Germania under Drusus and Tiberius in 9 BCE.

"The bridge was destroyed and rebuilt during nearly twenty centuries of warfare, but its pilings are the original ones."

"That is difficult to fathom, Bert, considering the frequency of battles fought in Europe's history."

"Often, conflicts arose over border disputes between France and Germany. Can you see the *Germania* high above the vineyards on the eastern bank of the Rhein?"

"Yes, I have not yet visited the site but I'm familiar with its story," I said.

After the French lost the war of 1870-71, their reparations included the cost of the monument the Germans built and erected on land between Rüdesheim and Assmannshausen.

"Wait until you are in front of the colossal pedestal on which she, the embodiment of Germania, the country, stands facing west. One of her arms is raised, holding in her hand a seven-meter-long sword in defiance of the opponent."

"No wonder we can recognize her from this side of the river. As for paying reparations, it's the consequence of losing a war. We learned about that twice in this century, didn't we?"

"Indeed. What is nowadays laid down in treaties used to be carried out by pillaging," Bert said.

"My experience has been that governments enforce treaties after their troops engage in ravaging countries, populations and properties," I remarked.

"Let's leave gloomy history behind and not spoil this beautiful day, Almut."

"Will you tell me about all these castles, though?" I asked, pointing at three to the left of our road.

"I'll do that when we check them out. Being there will transport you into the time robber knights and noblemen resided in their strongholds.

"The next village is Trechtingshausen, where I was born and where my family has lived for five generations."

"Will I meet your parents?"

"Yes, and probably my sister, Ina. She, her husband and their two children occupy the second floor of our house. My grandmother lives with my mother and father downstairs."

"And you?"

"I have a room on my sister's floor but still partake in Mother's cooking."

Until Bert parked his Jeep in front of the Metzroth residence, I thought about everything I had discovered about him in the past hour, away from the *Dolmetscher-Schule*. When a contagious smile brightened Bert's handsome face with its healthy color and his brown eyes sparkled in full attention to me, I melted. His knowledge of and pride in his native surroundings and family was endearing.

"What are you dreaming about? Hop out and come into the house to say hello to everyone who wants to meet you."

"Oh, what a big garden."

"Uh-huh, you can admire that later. We'll go inside first."

The Jeep had announced our arrival. Herr and Frau Metzroth greeted us at their door, "Welcome to our house. Bert has told us that you are in his English course," his mother said.

Oh, and what else, I wonder?

"Thank you. Bert is the star. No one else in our class has used English in conversation with native speakers. We are trying to catch up."

"Will you have some *Kaffee und Kuchen* with us?" Bert's mother asked.

"Or a glass of our wine?" Herr Metzroth offered.

"Maybe all three?" Bert suggested impishly.

Frau Metzroth had already set the table in the dining room.

"It's still too chilly to sit on the balcony but you have a view of the river and the vineyards through the glass doors."

"Yes. You live in a spectacular area of our country. During my childhood I read about it and knew vineyards only from pictures."

"They are a lot of work," Bert's father, a practical man, remarked.

"But taste the final product." Bert lifted his glass, swiveled the wine, sniffed it and took a sip. "It is worth all the sweat."

"The men have already switched to wine," Bert's mother said. "Would you like another piece of *Apfelkuchen* and some more coffee?"

"Thank you. Your apple cake is delicious and moist but I can't eat any more. I held out my cup. "I'd like a refill, though. We are lucky to again have *Bohnenkaffee* instead of ersatz to drink with our pastries," I noted.

Bert became restless at the table. "It's so quiet in the house. Where are Ina, Walter and the kids?" he asked.

"They went to visit Walter's sister and may not be back before evening," Frau Metzroth said.

"Well you wanted to see our garden." Bert looked at me. "Are you ready?"

"Yes, I am."

Turning to his parents, he grinned. "As I told you, Almut likes to dig in the dirt."

About two meters behind the house, a border of natural stones, set in cement as high as the three steps leading into the garden, dammed in the soil. Attracting my immediate attention was the stone wall separating the Metzroths' property from their neighbor's.

"Who built that barrier?" I asked.

"You are looking at the remnant of a medieval fortification surrounding this settlement," Bert answered.

"Unbelievable. First the *Drususbrücke* and now medieval ruins. In the Northeast, we had few ruins dating back centuries. Invading hordes set fires along their paths, causing total destruction."

"Well, you recognize the difference between eastern and western cultures," Bert smiled as he teased me. "The Romans civilized us. They planted vineyards so we might drink wine whereas you lived with your animals under one roof into the nineteenth century."

"Not in every province. Besides, who supplied the wheat, rye, meat and dairy products so you may eat?"

W E H A D A T E R R I F I C T I M E on our first excursion. Dating Bert became too time-consuming for me to keep up with the study of three languages: I decided to drop Spanish.

Vati and Mutti realized where my relationship with Bert was headed.

"What about the *Gartenbauschule?"*

"I don't know. I'll postpone it and stay with languages for now."

B E R T C O N T E M P L A T E D the future, too. He had filed papers for emigration to the United States fifteen months earlier. Thomas B. Bunch was his sponsor. This former sergeant in charge of a detail guarding German prisoners of war on the Liberty ship *William Yancy* befriended Bert on the transport from Italy to the U.S. in 1944.

Anticipating his visa in good time, Bert talked to me about the employment Tom Bunch offered him in his furniture store in North Carolina.

One evening, about three months after our first date, we sat in his sister's living room. I wore a ruby-colored, two-piece creation my mother had sewn. Light-blue rolled silk accented the neckline and the long sleeves.

During our conversation regarding Bert's plans I alluded jokingly to Germans' desire to have a rich uncle in America. "You can send me a CARE package."

Bert took my hand, his eyes held mine. "Wouldn't you like to come with me?"

Shaking, I stuttered, "Is that a proposal?"

"Yes. Do you want me on my knee?" There was that smelting smile again.

"No... I mean, no, you don't have to kneel. And, yes, I'll go wherever you go."

H O W   W A S   I   G O I N G   T O   T E L L Mutti and Vati that their only child planned to leave them, the country, and even the continent? Bert and I kept our secret until he found an opportunity two months later to ask Vati for my hand.

My parents had invited us to join them on a Saturday drive to Wiesbaden where we visited the spa's beautiful gardens on that late spring day.

"Bert and I will enjoy a *Kännchen Kaffee* in the Park-Café until you return from your survey of local stores," Vati suggested.

"A small pot of coffee sounds good to me, too," Mutti said. "We'll have it later. First, let's do some window-shopping, Almut."

"*Bis später!*" I waved a see-you-later to Vati and gave Bert a crossed-fingers sign behind my father's back as I turned to follow Mutti.

As Bert related to me afterwards, Vati's immediate reaction to our request was, "You are so young."

"But Almut said you and Frau Finger were the same age when you married. Moreover, consider the experiences behind us: They helped us mature beyond our years."

"I can't argue that," Vati said, nodding in agreement and stroking his chin. He added, "My wife and I are aware of our daughter's happiness. Are you still determined to go to America?"

"Yes. That's why we need to marry soon, so that Almut can accompany me as my wife."

"There is a lot to think about. Let's hear what strategy our ladies advise for achieving your proximate goal."

While Bert in his quest faced my father, I gently prepared my mother, "Mutti, Bert and I want to marry."

"I was afraid of that, because I can't think of you living 4,500 kilometers away; across an ocean, yet."

"*Kommt Zeit, kommt Rat.* In time we'll find ways to visit each other. Travel is no longer as difficult as it was one hundred years ago when Bert's great-grandfather went to America."

"What happened?" Mutti looked wide-eyed at me and placed her right hand anxiously over her heart.

"I'll let Bert tell you. The gist of the story is, we don't want to be separated."

In late afternoon, we returned to the Park-Café where all tables were taken; people hoped that the out-of-doors season had begun.

"I see our men," Mutti said and smiled at me as she emphasized *our men.*

"Oh, good! Bert looks happy," I surmised. We couldn't tell the outcome of their deliberation by Vati's mien.

"Your leaving will be hard on him." Mutti bravely deflected her own worries.

Vati looked at Mutti, "Bert and Almut turned our little excursion into a fateful event. I assume you know about their plans?"

"Yes. Our daughter broke the news an hour ago. Please order us some refreshments. My nerves need to be quieted."

"Hmm, the coffee aroma is enticing." Sitting down beside Bert, I asked, "How bad was it?"

Vati was able to laugh by now, "We are still talking to each other."

"Almut mentioned your great-grandfather's emigration to America. What was his fate?" Mutti had waited impatiently to have Bert answer her question.

"Like you," Bert smiled at Vati and Mutti, "my parents are concerned about my, and now our, well-being in the New World. By recounting the tale of his grandfather's hope to take his family to America, my father implies that we could always return home if our plans did not work out."

"Perhaps you could proceed on that basis," Mutti said, full of hope.

"No, that's what we must avoid. My great-grandfather, Nikolaus, was married at the time and had a son, Anton. When Nick suggested to his wife that they could probably make a better living in America, her response was, 'You go ahead and establish yourself. Then come back to help us move.'

"So, in 1856, Nick left Trechtingshausen with his cousin to make their fortune in the States. As a skilled cobbler, Nick founded a shoe factory in Louisville, Kentucky. His success in this endeavor rested on the Army's great demand for boots during the Civil War."

"That reassured your great-grandmother, didn't it?" Vati asked.

"Again, no. Great-Grandma refused to leave her native land. Nick sold his establishment and returned to Germany. My great-grandparents had more children. With the proceeds from the factory sale, they sent all their offspring to college, except, my grandfather and namesake. He had already learned the cobbler's trade."

"Now you understand our haste to be married, don't you?" I asked my parents. "I am not going to let Bert go alone. I can be a help in carving out our future."

"So, what is your agenda?" Mutti wanted to know.

"I thought we should finish our courses at the Dolmetscher-Schule, followed by our wedding," Bert said.

"Hmm, ja. There is another problem…for others; not for us," I hemmed.

"What's that?" Vati and Mutti asked together.

"Bert's family is Catholic. His father's cousin is an auxiliary bishop in Trier…"

"What do you *want* to do?" my parents wondered.

"We have to be married at a *Standesamt,* anyway. After the formalities at the magistrate's office, Bert has agreed to a service in the Protestant Peterskirche in Bacharach with only you and Herr and Frau Metzroth in attendance," I said.

"I believe I can persuade them to participate. They approve of Almut," Bert said, beaming a smile at me.

"It is obvious, you have been working on your intentions for a while," Vati commented. "Let us know your parents' reaction, Bert. Perhaps we can meet them soon and decide how to share the news with family and friends."

"The sun is disappearing behind the city's tall buildings; I feel chilly," Mutti said, crossing her arms tightly in front of her for warmth. "If all of you have finished your coffee, we could return home. I'll promise you *Heringssalat und frische Brötchen* for supper."

"*Ja*, we prepared the salad this morning," I explained. "The rolls we can pick up at the corner bakery."

V A T E R U N D M U T T E R M E T Z R O T H consented graciously to our marriage. As planned, Bert and I studied for our exams. We had learned to write and answer business letters to become "foreign correspondents." Bert was fluent in English, so he felt no anxiety in anticipation of our finals.

"You're too confident to worry about the grammar, aren't you?" I teased him.

"Not really," he said. "What about you?"

"I can't say I'm not nervous. With the written part I should do all right. Grammatical rules were drilled into me at the several high schools I attended. It's conversation I'm worried about."

The day before our oral examination, Herr Stedronsky sternly warned us to not laugh when facing the five examiners. "The local superintendent has a poor sense of humor. You must be serious about your demeanor and your answers."

Six of us filed into the examination hall, my former French classroom. Its three high windows allowed daylight to emphasize the dismal color of the wall paint. During class, I had not noticed the dinginess of this room, but now—a *foreboding?* We sat down on the wooden chairs lined up opposite the tables behind which five members of the examination board of Rheinland-Pfalz sat. We were well-prepared.

"Fräulein Finger, please translate this sentence: *Die Glocke hat geläutet.*"

Aha! Irregular verbs, I thought, to ring, rang, rung.

"The rang bell," was my confident response.

"Ahem," the superintendent cleared his voice. "Do you want to think that over?"

I puzzled over his request. What was wrong with my answer that still seemed to hang in the air? *Oh no!* I burst out laughing at my mistake. Smiling, I said, "The bell rang."

One or the other of my fellow students froze in his chair, Bert slid uncomfortably from side to side on his.

Why did I laugh after what Joe Stedronsky had drummed into us?

When our group was dismissed, the superintendent called for a recess during which he vehemently informed our instructor and the four other examinants that I did not qualify to pass the finals. Herr Stedronsky pointed out the high grade on my written exam. He was excused and returned to our group in the hallway. His brow was lifted, his eyes wide open: Our instructor looked worried. Shaking his head, he said, "Didn't I caution you about that man's inferiority complex, Almut?"

"Yes, I didn't laugh at him, but at my unintended answer. Could I be flunked for that?"

The examiners convinced their colleague that my original response had the right components and was the result of tension.

Bert and I passed at the top of the class, but he received a higher mark in grammatical proficiency, a fact my partner plays like a trump whenever he needs to poke fun at me.

AT THE CONCLUSION of the winter semester, Bert enrolled in the course for *Dolmetscher und Übersetzer.* As an official interpreter and translator he intended to look for employment with the American Forces while waiting for our immigration permits.

My job during that time was to procure documents about my legitimate existence. The briefcase Mutti and I had affixed to the frame of my bicycle on our flight was lost. It had contained our important records. I was reminded of the customs clerk at Remagen who asked Vati to prove that he was born. Where should

I turn to obtain my parents' marriage license, my birth certificate, and other documents the U.S. Consulate demanded, such as affidavits by witnesses to our past, certifying our Stettin address, vouching that Fingers had not been Nazis? Where were our former neighbors five years after the war?

Evacuation of people and archives could take place only upon official notification. For Stettin, this proclamation was not issued because the declared fortress was not expected to fall into enemy hands. To my surprise and relief, I learned that some wise and brave authorities had, against orders, relocated personal records of the residents of my hometown to western areas. Thus I was able to secure various papers and addresses from Hamburg and others from Berlin. Our marriage license, dated August 12, 1950, completed the *Papierkrieg,* red tape.

We made few preparations for our small wedding party. On that glorious August day, Bert took the train to Bad Kreuznach to join Vati, Mutti and me for the ride in Vati's 1938 BMW to Bacharach for the civil and religious ceremonies.

Bert had brought my bouquet of yellow roses and our wedding bands. True to German tradition, he slipped mine onto the ring finger of the left hand, indicating engagement.

At the appointed time, we met Vater and Mutter Metzroth in front of the *Peterskirche* in Bacharach. As we entered the church through the portal, the organist began to play sacred music. All six of us stepped up to the altar. During the ceremony Bert and I changed each other's wedding bands from the left to the right hand. We were now married.

The organ's mighty sound had attracted passers-by and tourists who filled the pews. After the rites were completed, the many strangers became our well-wishers.

B A C H A R A C H   T A K E S   I T S   N A M E from Bacchus, the god of wine and merriment in Greek and Roman mythology. The picturesque town lives up to the god's reputation. Backed by steep vineyards, the settlement is nestled on the left bank of the Rhein and attracts visitors throughout the year to wine festivals and the many restaurants and hotels.

Vati led our party from the *Peterskirche* to one of those splendid dining establishments, *Zum Kranentor,* a reference to the gate in the medieval wall leading to the crane that serviced ships on the river. After crossing cobblestoned streets, we climbed steps to the ancient sentry walk and the restaurant.

"So romantic," I marveled. "How did you find this place, Vati?"

"Mutti and I spent an afternoon selecting the spot that would contribute to the festive atmosphere of this day. Come inside and see the medieval motif carried over into the dining room."

The minister who had performed our nuptials joined us for the feast. His anecdotes about Bacharach's history were informative and interesting.

When seated, Vati said to Bert's father, "Nikolaus, you are the connoisseur. We arranged for the menu but left instructions that you would select the wines at the table. Does that agree with you?"

"Of course. I'll study the wine list."

Bert's mother, an excellent cook, read the menu card printed for this occasion. Vati had asked Bert, Mutti and me to each select a favorite for the three-course meal: *Ochsenschwanzsuppe, gebratenes Hähnchen, Aal in Blau.* "I can tell that Bert chose Oxtail Soup, Cläri the grilled Cornish Hen, and Almut Eel Boiled, which brings out the blue color of the fish's skin."

"Ja, und Eisbombe zum Nachtisch," Mutti added. "Everyone likes rich Italian ice cream for dessert, I trust."

"If we still have room," Bert cautioned.

"We can walk off the heavy feeling in our stomachs in the *Rheinanlagen* after the meal," I suggested.

"You will have to excuse me after this very fine meal," the pastor said. "I have to polish my Sunday sermon."

THE PARK ALONG THE RIVER was designed beautifully. On our stroll, we inhaled the fragrance of the colorful roses, continuous to beds of showy Cosmos, Coreopsis and Dahlia.

Against this bright background we took snapshots to preserve the momentous event. Our parents, Bert and I alternated posing in our finery. Since we expected to leave for America in the near future, we had kept expenses low and eliminated traditional wedding frills. Our happiness was not based on bridal gown or tuxedos. Instead, I had chosen a fashionable but conservative dress of soft magenta wool with three-quarter open sleeves. The front of the bodice was sewn in a quilted pattern and featured buttons covered with the dress material. They secured the opening from the left shoulder to the front of the waistline. An A-line skirt and a belt of the same material completed my wedding dress that I wore for years to festive occasions, along with my black suede pumps.

My husband looked dapper in his new dark blue suit, white shirt, blue tie sprinkled with tiny white dots, and his black shoes. Our parents, too, honored our day with gala-worthy outfits, especially Mutti, who could again afford custom-made clothes. The light-lilac crepe-de-Chïne dress with black-lace appliqué emphasized her svelte figure and attracted attention whenever she wore it.

BERT AND I SPENT the next two nights in a hotel in Bad Kreuznach so that we could be present for Mutti's fortieth birthday on August 13. The following day we took a *D-Zug,* a fast train, to Konstanz *am Bodensee,* the city on Lake Constance. This lake is also called Lake Überlingen and borders on Germany, Switzerland and Austria.

"There is so much to see and do. I have wanted to come here for a long time." I was so happy; my feet did not seem to touch the ground. Yet, we did a lot of sightseeing. Fascinating was our visit to the *Insel Mainau,* the tropical island in Lake Constance. "Did you know bananas grew on German soil?" I asked.

"This island belongs to the Swedish Lord Bernadotte. Consequently, it is Swedish territory. To say that you are looking at Swedish bananas is even stranger, isn't it?"

"*Wirklich.*" Really. Look at all the tropical plants. Some of the orchids have sweet scents. Oh, would you take a picture of this gorgeous white hibiscus blossom with pink stripes?"

"We'll be out of film soon," Bert announced.

"Before returning to our *Pension* we can buy more."

"All right. It's time to catch the boat back to Konstanz. I am hungry, and you?"

"I'm hot. The air on the island is truly humid, tropical. Yes, let's leave. Where shall we dine tonight?" I asked.

"Listen, I hear the ship's bell. We don't want to miss the ride back. To answer your question: Hotel Barbarossa is reported to have an extensive menu. Do you want to try it?"

"Can we afford it?"

"Not every night, if we want to stay within our savings plan," Bert said. "The passage to America does not come cheap." Most evenings we made sandwiches in our hotel after a day spent at the beach or exploring the old city and its historic sites.

As we toured the bustling center of Konstanz, Bert and I noticed the varied styles of architecture the residents had chosen for their buildings over the past two thousand years.

With our visitors' annotated city plan in hand, we walked on grounds where Roman conquerors under Claudius are said to have fortified Celtic dwellings in the first century.

"Around AD 300, Constantinus Chlorus, who gave the city its name, built a small Roman fort," I read to Bert. "At the end of the sixth century, the diocese Konstanz became a spiritual and intellectual center, which in turn attracted mercantile interests."

"And there are signs of the steady evolution of this community and its residents all around us. Let's enter the *Münster Unserer Lieben Frau,* dedicated to the Virgin Mary in 1089," Bert said. "By the spacious layout of this cathedral you can still recognize the formerly pure Roman basilica. At the time of the *Konstanzer Konzil* the Church renovated this building. You saw the ribbed vaulting, pointed arches, and steep roofs on the outside, the characteristics of Gothic architecture in the inner sanctum. The brochure mentions "areas of classical as well as baroque styles."

"Oh, look at the magnificent Renaissance organ and the ornate woodworkings in the choir loft," I said.

"The details are remarkable. About the *Konstanzer Konzil:* The religious leadership of the diocese hosted the only Vatican Council ever held on German soil; it took place from 1414-1418," Bert explained.

"Wasn't that the time Johann Hus was burned at the stake?"

"Exactly," Bert said. "The *Konzil* and the reformer's death served to unify the Church. With peace in the land, Konstanz developed into the city of practical trades and commerce. But that's enough culture for one day. Interested in lunch at a sidewalk restaurant?"

"Ja, and the beach this afternoon."

Over our mouth-watering lunch of *Rheinsalm, Röstkartoffeln und junge Erbsen,* we consulted our city plan again.

"What do you want to do tomorrow?" I asked.

"First, let us savor this meal."

"You're right. The salmon is tender and well seasoned with lemon zest."

"Uh-huh. I am also fond of roasted potatoes and baby peas," Bert said.

"I'll have to remember that. As for tomorrow?"

Bert suggested a visit to the *Haus zur Kunkel.* "There we can view frescos painted around 1300. They depict scenes of silk and linen weavings. These paintings are the earliest examples of *Profanmalerei* in Germany; profane art portrays secular subjects."

"Hmm, I'm getting quite an education on our honeymoon," I said, grinning at Bert.

WE LEFT KONSTANZ two days early, having exhausted our allotted financial resources. From the train we again enjoyed looking at the bountiful countryside as we passed through Baden-

182

Württemberg into Rheinland-Pfalz and headed to our new domicile, the Metzroth house in Trechtingshausen.

Almut and Bert, Trechtingshausen, 1950

Preparing the soil for planting,
Trechtingshausen, 1951

CHAPTER 12

Waiting to Emigrate

B E R T' S   R O O M became our temporary quarters until our visas arrived. At least, that's what we thought. "You take my bed," my husband said, "we will make the chaise longue into a bed for me at night. During the day it will be our couch. It doesn't have a back but a headrest at one end. Some day, we'll have *Ehebetten* like most German couples. There is no space for side by side twin beds anyway."

"I know, but I am good at *Bettenbauen,* setting up bed. Remember my mattress leaning against the wall in my parents' kitchen from morning to evening? We'll not have to live long in this make-shift arrangement."

"Let's hope so."

The washbasin with running cold water was installed at the north side of the room, next to the door. Behind the opened door stood a dresser, joined by a table and two chairs against the south wall. Through the good-sized window facing east, we had the same view of the Rhein and vineyards that I had marveled at from the downstairs dining room when I first visited Bert's family. To the right of the window stood my bed; the couch had its place under the north window, two feet from the basin.

"We need a *Schrank* in which to hang up our clothes," I said.

"*Stimmt,*" Bert agreed. "We'll buy one and place it where the table and chairs are. Those we can move into the middle."

"We won't have room to dance, will we, Bert?"

"Not for a tango but how about some slow dancing?"

"Bertus! Almut! Dinner is served," Mutter called from downstairs.

"Oh, weh. I wanted to help in the kitchen or at least set the table."

"Well, just don't slip up again," Bert kidded.

THUS BEGAN OUR WAITING PERIOD. Two weeks after we returned from our honeymoon, Vati and Mutti gave a reception for us. They had sent out invitations to our relatives and friends, naming the date of the administered church rites. By receiving guests in a secular setting, the *Rhein-Hotel* between Bingerbrück and Trechtingshausen, we hoped to avoid qualms some guests might feel attending services at a Protestant church. The exuberant atmosphere confirmed our judiciousness.

After the party, we focused on the productive side of life. Bert helped his parents bring in the grape harvest before applying for jobs as an interpreter and translator. Agricultural authorities determined the beginning of the harvest, depending on the maturity and sugar contents of the grapes.

I was excited to be picking grapes, an activity I had not previously experienced. It was cold on those October mornings in the vineyards, just as it had been in the flat potato fields in Friedeberg. Instead of the even rows of unearthed tubers, I now looked for grapes on vines planted on steep inclines from the river valley. The rows of vines were one meter apart. The foliage, covered with hoar-frost, hid some of the grapes. When brushing the leaves aside to cut the grapes with my shears, my hands turned numb quickly. I tried gloves. They did not help. They soaked up the moisture and became stiff, adding to the discomfort. As the sun rose over the eastern hills, sending its warming rays to the upper part of the opposite mountain first, I looked for the sun's ascent to warm me up. Well before noon, the pickers shed their jackets and sweaters in climbing temperatures.

As the line of hired hands and I harvested the fruit, I was again the novice, remembering my efforts at keeping up with workers who labored for a living in potato fields and horticulture. Moving uphill, I maintained my place in the line, despite being pregnant.

Bert was the *Leejelsdrejer.* With a thirty-pound wooden *Leejel* on his back he collected the grapes we had gathered in our baskets. His container held about fifty-five kilos, one hundred and twenty pounds, of tightly packed grapes. This load Bert carried halfway down the mountain to the big vat on a parked cart. There he stepped on a crate so that his hip leaned against the edge of the vat. Grabbing hold on that edge, he bent sideways to empty the *leejel.* From morning to dusk Bert performed this task countless times until workers helped him pull and push the cart to the collection site at quitting time.

A gunshot signaled the end of that day's harvesting, as one had announced the start in the morning. Field wardens thus indicated the working hours and protected the areas' vineyards from theft.

Vater oversaw the work in his vineyards and the transport of the grapes by truck to the press-house. Although anxious but happy to bring the precious harvest in, he always had encouraging words for his crew. "Don't forget to whistle while you work," he reminded us with a wink. Whistling, we could not sample too many grapes.

IN LATE AUTUMN, Bert sought and found employment as a German civilian with the U.S. Air Force in Wiesbaden, Hessen. Although we had practiced shorthand at the *Dolmetscherschule,* we had no typing skills. Bert overcame this deficiency in a course at USAF Headquarters where he subsequently worked as an interviewer of German POWs returning from the Soviet Union.

His job required him to leave Trechtingshausen on the six-o'clock train to Mainz and continue by bus to Wiesbaden. He returned home thirteen hours later.

My contribution to our livelihood and savings plan came from part-time work. I kept my father's books for his business. Every Monday morning, I registered at the slaughterhouse the arrival of the livestock Vati had bought during the past week. He knew each butcher's preference: fat, lean, or marbled meat. The competition was intense. Monday afternoon, Vati gave me his sales list which I entered into the log. Tuesdays, all the facts came in from the scales manager and the meat inspectors. Now I could tabulate the costs to the butchers and write out their bills.

Each week, after my two-day stay, Mutti drove me back to Trechtingshausen where I returned to my knitting and other preparations for the birth of our child.

THAT EVENT WAS HASTENED by an accident. On a Tuesday afternoon in February, Vati and I finished our paperwork at my parents' apartment, sharing *Kaffee und Kuchen*. To keep the coffee hot in the china pot, Mutti placed it in a cooking pot with water on top of the iron heater before going shopping.

"Would you like me to pour you a second cup, Vati?"

"Ja, bitte."

I lifted the *Kaffeekanne* out of the water and turned towards the table. Suddenly the bottom of the pot fell out and the coffee with grounds saturated the woolen stocking of my right leg from the knee to the foot, scalding my leg.

Shocked and in excruciating pain, I let out a steady scream at the top of my lungs. Only when Vati said, "Almut, stop it!" was I able to do so. With shaking hands, I dug a hole with my right thumbnail into the softened flesh, trying to take my hand-knitted stocking off. Until Mutti returned from her errands, Vati fanned a newspaper over my elevated leg.

"Was ist passiert?" she asked. What happened?

Evaluating the wound, Mutti said, "I don't have that much gauze and ointment, Curt. I'll make a list of what we need from the pharmacy. Hurry, before they close."

For a week, my mother treated my burns. I could not stand up by myself. To lower my leg from a lying position caused me indescribable pain. Yet, I had to keep moving because of my pregnancy. On our walks, Vati and Mutti supported me on each side; Bert helped out on the weekend.

"Take me to the hospital," I said to Mutti one late evening when I saw no improvement in my wounds.

At the *Diakonissenhospital,* administered by Sisters of a Protestant order, the emergency nurse said, "You better stay with us. We'll admit you. A doctor will evaluate your condition."

To my surprise, I found myself wheeled to a room on the maternity ward. Three young mothers welcomed me. *What am I doing here?* Mutti stayed with me until ten o'clock, hoping to meet the doctor who never came; no one treated my burn.

"I'll call you tomorrow morning," Mutti said.

A sister checked me every hour. At eleven she advised me to get some sleep. I would probably give birth before long. I was exhausted and welcomed Sister's suggestion. But I thought, *Give birth soon? Without breaking water? Or labor pains?* The constant pain in my leg masked the contractions. At four in the morning on February 20, 1951, two Sisters took me to the delivery room. Veit was born an hour later, weighing eight pounds.

"Is he all right? Not hurt by our traumatic week?" I asked.

"Here is your beautiful boy. You can examine him yourself."

"Veitlein! We came through this mishap," I said to my crying little boy. "With God's guidance we'll weather future storms." I stroked his black hair. Calming down, he opened his blue eyes and put his red fist to his mouth before Sister took him in her arms.

"He is yours. You'll have him from now on. Let me bundle him up and put him in his crib," she said. "Then I'll treat your leg. The burns will heal quickly after your baby's birth. The body can take care of only one thing at a time. Your pain will diminish, too. You have less weight to put on your leg."

After ten days, Veit was baptized in the hospital chapel before we were discharged. Bert and my parents attended the rite. Edzard, his godfather, held him during the ceremony. Suddenly

Edzard grimaced, shifting his hands. I reached to take Veit from Mutti's brother. *Oh, he is wet through his diapers, plastic protection and his lovely baptismal gown.*

Years later, Edzard told his godson how he had "baptized" his great-uncle.

W E W E R E S T I L L W A I T I N G for our visas for America nearly two years after our wedding. Bert kept our sponsor, Tom Bunch, informed about our growing family. Was Tom interested in bringing three people to the States? A sponsor agreed to guarantee employment for the sponsored parties or vouched financial assistance so the immigrant did not become a burden to the U.S. government.

Bert's letters to Tom remained unanswered. Inquiries at the U.S. Consulate in Frankfurt apprised us of Tom's service in the military in Korea. Since sponsors by definition are responsible for the welfare of their invited newcomers, our applications rested; in their absence, military personnel can not assure the immigrants' independence.

"Our waiting period might take years if we have to wait for the end of the war," Bert said. "I'll try to find a job closer by."

Thanks to his résumé, Bert was hired as a medical clerk and official interpreter by the 57th Field Hospital in Bad Kreuznach. He shortened his commuting time on trains by half.

"We have to get out of these cramped quarters," I said. "Besides, I would like to do my own cooking and have a bathroom for ourselves. If we had an apartment in Kreuznach, we could relieve your parents from their—certainly loving—daily care for us; we could spend more time with each other every day and avoid Veit's and my overnight stays at my parents' when I work for my father."

"Ja," Bert agreed. "But Veit will miss all the attention he is receiving in this house."

"Especially from his cousins, his favorite playmates," I said. "Being eight years old, Reiner is kind to have a toddler clutch his hand and expect the big boy to allow him to tag along. And three-year-old Iris wants to 'mother' Veit, the crown prince."

IN BAD KREUZNACH, we moved into one of the new four-story tenement blocks *Auf der Steinkaut,* situated on a plateau above the city. From our second-floor apartment we had a striking view far into the Nahe River valley towards Bingen. Through the opposite windows we saw the street where Bert walked to and from work. The 57th sat at the edge of a cliff above the Nahe, facing the Hunsrück Mountains.

"You realized in Konstanz how fascinated I am by the elements that shape a community, such as geography, climate and natural resources, history and the inhabitants' skills. During my school and apprenticeship years I didn't have the time to explore Bad Kreuznach," I said to Bert one morning. "Today I will take Veit to the *Altstadt.*"

"That's a good idea. On Saturday we can visit the *Salinen.*"

"*Ja,* the weatherman predicts good weather."

As I pushed Veit in his stroller through the old part of the town and its cobblestoned streets, his little bag of apple slices held greater interest for him than architecture or the *Nahebrücke,* the bridge built in medieval times. It was constructed with eight arches. Midway, two *Brückenhäuser,* small buildings supported by bracings provided apartments and stores. A Swedish cannon ball was embedded in the front of one house during the War of Reformation, 1618-48.

On our way home, I guided Veit's carriage along the Nahe through the *Kurviertel,* the cultural heart of a *Bad* or spa, with its concert hall, drinking fountains and hotels.

SOON, VEIT WANTED TO WALK with us rather than look at the world from his stroller. Along the way he pushed his nose into flowers to smell them, or he picked up sticks and "beautiful" stones to show those to me. He greeted every dog. Who was scared of potential aggressors? Not Veit; I was.

We often went to meet Bert after work. When he saw his *Papi,* as he first called his dad, as many young German children do because it is easier to pronounce than *Vater,* Veit ran toward Bert, stretched out his arms and asked, *"Papi, kannst du mich tragen?"* He was tired and wanted his daddy to carry him.

On one of those late afternoons, Bert lifted Veit on his shoulders and said to me, "I have mentioned Dr. Ingraham to you, haven't I? He is the psychiatrist at the hospital."

"Ja, has his wife arrived from the States?" I asked.

"That's why I bring his name up. Peg is kind of lost when Merle and his colleagues are at work. She has met only a few wives who seem to be busy with their children. Peg is afraid to venture into town because she does not speak German. Shall we invite them for dinner so they'll get to know a German family?"

"Sure, that would be fun," I said. "Will my English be sufficient?"

"Time to find out," my smiling husband said. "Don't you think so?"

"Yeah," I answered in American. "I'll prepare a German meal.How about *Sauerbraten mit Rotkohl undKartoffelklössen?"*

"If you must. Marinated beef is not one of my favorites," Bert said. "Red cabbage and potato dumplings are fine."

"Okay, pork roast then."

"And *Rumtopf* for dessert." Bert suggested.

"Will they like rum-soaked fruit?" I asked. "I'll have a cheese platter in reserve."

Bert licked his lips. "Sounds good. Afterwards we can stretch our legs near the *Salinen."*

G E S A G T, G E T A N. As said and planned, our getting-acquainted visit with Merle and Peg went well.

On our stroll through the park in which the evaporation structure stood, Peg wanted to know the significance of *Bad* before the names of some German towns or cities.

"It indicates that local natural springs, rich in minerals, are harnessed for medicinal purposes. Romans realized centuries ago the value of hot and cold springs in which they took baths, and drank the water from fountains because of its healing qualities," Bert said.

"We know these spas as resorts," Merle explained. "In Europe, physicians often prescribe medical treatments at specific spas, depending on the patient's ailment and the required mineral. Bad Kreuznach is known for its *Salinen* and their relief in cases of respiratory disorders."

"This wall of twigs and branches must be twenty feet high," Peg marveled.

"*Husch-Husch,*" choo-choo, Veit said, pointing at the water-wheel-powered pumps. They reminded him of the wheels on a steam locomotive.

"Watch the pumps force the spring water to the top of the woven sprigs and limbs from where it trickles down into catch basins before being recirculated. The released saline vapors permeate the air," Merle said.

"I can see that with the sun shining on the salt-coated *Salinen,*" Peg observed. "Can we, too, sit down for a while?"

In the peaceful setting, many people rested on benches facing the beneficial structures. They took deep breaths while reading, writing or solving puzzles. They were "taking the cure."

S O B E G A N O U R L A S T I N G F R I E N D S H I P with Peg and Merle; fate had sent them to us. Before completing his assignment in Germany, Merle said, "No matter who is discharged from the service first, Tom Bunch or I, we'll get you over there!"

In August 1952, Jaimye Sue Ingraham was born in Bad Kreuznach, Veit's hometown. Our friends departed soon after that happy event. Merle established his private general practice in Greenfield, Massachusetts. Six months later, we received the entire package of their required paperwork as sponsors.

"Oh, this is so gracious of them and so embarrassing to us," I said after looking through Ingrahams' affidavit, bank statements and disclosures of various assets.

"Well, their government wants proof that we will not need financial support from the public. Will our application with a new sponsor go to the bottom of the pile or be attached to Tom's file?" Bert wondered.

"At any rate, it will add time to our waiting."

"Let's make some changes," Bert suggested.

We were happy with our life in Bad Kreuznach but knew that Bert had no chance of advancement at the 57th Field Hospital; nor were there any other opportunities for him in that town.

"I have to look in major cities reachable from Trechtingshausen with our Volkswagen. Vater offered to help me build an apartment on the top floor of my parents' house. What do you think?"

"How long will that take?" I asked.

"Two months. I'll order the material we need during the week. On weekends, Vater and I can work on the project which he will advance Mondays through Fridays while I earn our keep at the 57th."

WE RELOCATED to Trechtingshausen in the spring of 1953. I liked our nest under the roof of Vater and Mutter's house. A flight of stairs from the second floor led to our entrance. Inside we stepped into the unfinished hallway; but the walls were up. The kitchen, living and bedrooms smelled of new paint; gleaming electrical appliances waited for me to use them; full-size windows invited bright daylight into our apartment and afforded us scenic views up and down the Rhein.

Through the three windows that spanned the east wall of the living room, Veit watched the endless activity of barges, tankers, excursion ships of the *Köln-Düsseldorfer Line,* a few pleasure boats—often American—and the *Nachen* of the *Trexheiser Flotte.* Men rowed the work boats of the local fleet across the swift river to tend their *Wingert,* vineyards on the right bank. In his high chair, Veit imitated the horns blown by ships, the whistles of the trains passing on both banks, and with his arms he signaled clear passage for all traffic.

194

Work on the completion of our bathroom progressed slowly over the summer because cultivating vineyards and gardens took precedence. Fruits that are rare in Pomerania, such as peaches and apricots, thrive in Trechtingshausen's climate. But Oma and Opa, as the grandchildren called Bert's parents, had not planted raspberries. "You need those to take the tartness out of currant jelly," I said to Bert. "Will you help me prepare the ground for the plants?"

"What do you mean? Turn the soil?"

"*Ja,* but we have to go three spades deep for those beds. In the first row we take out three layers and pile them up separately along the side. The soil from the second row we turn over layer by layer to fill the first row, top soil on the bottom. We follow this pattern for the entire bed. Into the last cavity we transfer the soil from the first row in the right order."

"*Muss das sein, Gärtnerin?* " Bert asked.

"Is that necessary? Yes, because raspberry plants' deep roots need broken-up ground to facilitate growth, the gardener tells you. Also, water and fertilizer have leached from the top soil to the layers beneath, storing nutrition. By turning the ground we renew the process."

"If I didn't love you, I might not agree to sign up for this weekend labor." Bert took me in his arms. "Besides, I like raspberries."

INA WAS NOT ONLY BERT'S OLDER SISTER but also became mine when we shared the same house. She was the smallest person in her family but had the most cheerful and kind personality. Ina was always ready to help. In conversation she showed her undivided interest. Our shared pastimes included reading, knitting and *Pflaumenkuchen.*

When plums were ripe for picking, many German housewives baked the traditional cake. The lightly sugar-coated fruit bubbled in the oven, juice spilling over the dough and burning to a crisp on the outside of the pans, the grates and over the bottom. Cleaning this mess often took longer than the preparation of the universally-liked dessert.

But in Trechtingshausen, *Bäcker Kloos* came to the rescue. The baker and his workers mixed the yeast dough, let it rise and spread it out on large baking sheets. Customers readied the plums at home: washed and drained them, cut open one side of each fruit, removed the stone, and carved four slits on the top of the unfolded plum. The slits prevented the fruit from curling up. Then Ina and I took our heaped bowls to the bakery. In a work room we joined other women who had made reservations. The baker handed us sheets with dough on which we placed our plums in neat rows. After sprinkling sugar over them, *Meister Kloos* shoved several sheets at a time into his brick ovens and told us the pick-up time. For a fee we avoided the smell of burned food in our kitchens.

I admired Ina's many talents. As Mutter had been a seamstress, she taught Ina to sew for herself and her children. When knitting machines for personal use came on the market, Ina mastered styles and stitches. Soon she developed a home industry. Our children benefited the most from her talents.

"V A T E R, M U T E R, I N A! Listen to this letter," I called out as I took our mail from the postman one morning in the spring of 1954. Bert and Walter, Ina's husband, were at work. "The American Consulate has scheduled physicals for Bert, Veit, and me in Frankfurt."

Our parents did not mind that we chose to live in limbo for years but wondered whether we should not forget about America and move aggressively toward a goal in Germany. "You still want to leave us?" Vater asked.

"Yes," I said. "We know that you hate to see us leave, especially Veit and the baby on the way. But Bert is right; we have greater opportunities in the States than in a country that requires certificates or diplomas at every step of achievement before persons are deemed worthy of a job they are capable of performing."

"Are you saying you're sorry to have spent years learning your trade to qualify for academic studies in the pursuit of your objective?" Mutter wondered.

"Not at all. I learned skills for life. But think about Bert: He came home years after the war ended. Programs to integrate veterans into the work force or enable them to finish their schooling were discontinued. In America, Bert will be able to build on his skills and talents," I said, adding, "Just like your grandfather had done, Vater."

"Wish we hadn't grown so fond of you," Ina said, turning away.

BERT REACTED TO THE NOTIFICATION from the Consulate with emotions. "I now realize I had given up on our emigration and was ready to accept the position with the Government of Rheinland-Pfalz in Koblenz. Are you still willing to go?"

"Yes, although I question the timing," I said. "We'll have to find out when we can expect our visas. I don't want to give birth on the way."

We passed our physicals and interviews. In August, we received our precious documents that enabled us to establish a timetable. Bert booked our passage for December on the *Gripsholm,* the first German passenger ship after WWII, owned by the *Norddeutscher Lloyd.* During the war, she had sailed in the service of the International Red Cross under a Swedish flag.

After four years of waiting, five for Bert, the three months preparing our farewell from family, friends, and country seemed too short to accomplish the necessary tasks.

"I'll make you an oversized locker for your linens, blankets, towels, and other big items."

"Thank you, Vater," Bert said. "We have the footlocker and two suitcases; they will set the limit of what we can take."

"Of clothes, yes," I agreed. "What about our china, glasses and cooking utensils? We can't buy those right away in America.

We'll need to pay for food, furniture, as well as medical and hospital bills until we are insured again."

"All right. I can build you a crate, too," Vater offered.

"And our books? Especially Veit's; we want him to remember his German—and learn more—so he can speak with his relatives when we see them again; have him hear familiar sounds when we read to him," I pleaded.

"We'll ship those to you when you have settled," Vati said. "Right now, Veit needs to learn to respond in English in case he gets lost."

Veit met our efforts at teaching him survival language with questions in his big blue eyes. Why did his parents talk in tongues that no one else in his little world used? As we practiced phrases in repeated demonstrations, Veit caught the meaning of the words and gave us perfect translations. "What's your name?" we asked.

"Wie heisst du?" he responded.

"Where do you live?"

"Wo wohnst du?"

"Let's not give up," I said. "Perhaps he'll store the correct responses in his memory and bring them up when needed."

The sorting and packing of belongings added to Veit's confusion. People came to our apartment to look over the furniture and appliances for sale, sometimes walking away with an item. Then Veit protested; pointing a finger at the offender, he screamed, *"Mammi! Das ist mein!"*

How will he accustom himself to all the abrupt changes in the next six months? I worried. *How will I? But I have been uprooted repeatedly. Repotting makes a plant grow strong.*

F R I E N D S   A N D   R E L A T I V E S come to say goodbye and wish us well.

"Don't forget us now! Send us your address right away."

"Keep in touch."

Inge and Odward brought Veit a teddy bear to remember them by. A letter from Jutta arrived in the midst of our preparations. She had located my whereabouts with the help of the

Red Cross ten years after our summer on Rügen. At our reunion visit, which was also an adieu, Jutta presented Veit with a little sack of chocolate money wrapped in gold foil for his voyage.

IMPATIENCE AND UNCERTAINTY were constant companions in the course of our final weeks in Germany. Planning and decision-making put great pressure on the mind. *Will these headaches ever stop?* The thoughts of a last time when I looked out of our windows, shook hands with acquaintances, shopped in the village, or worked for Vati, filled my senses. *Leaving Germany is what you want. Now look forward. You are not alone; you will have Bert, Veit, and the expected baby with you.*

Ruminations such as these sustained me on the day of saying goodbye to Vater, Mutter, alte Oma, Ina and family.

While I was getting dressed and Bert loaded our luggage into Vati's Volkswagen—we had shipped the large containers to the *Gripsholm*—Reiner and Iris played with Veit downstairs until I entered the room.

"I guess, this is it," Vater said. We exchanged hugs with our loved ones, fighting tears.

"Where is Reiner?" Bert asked.

Our calling, "Reiner!" indoors and outside did not produce Bert's godson. We learned later that Reiner was too broken up to see us leave.

Vati and Mutti drove Bert, Veit and me the 470 kilometers—272 miles—to Hamburg for a farewell visit with Tante Doktor. During our two-day stay we received dental care, reminisced about Vati's and her student days in Berlin, about our beloved Stettin, and our friendship. Bert heard a few episodes that had not reached his ears before.

On November 22, 1954, on our way to the *Gripsholm* via Bremen, we parted from Veit's Omi, Opi, and godmother at the Hamburg Hauptbahnhof. Watching their tear-stained faces and their handkerchief-waving hands from the moving train, I embraced Bert and Veit. "It is harder for those left behind to say goodbye than for people who travel toward new challenges, don't you think?"

"Not always," Bert said. "The hearts of soldiers going to the front are as heavy as those of their families."

"Separation is part of modern life, isn't it?" I mused. "Today, sons and daughters settle less often in the same environment in which their elders and forefathers toiled."

"For so long, our parents worried about our surviving the turbulent times of the war and post-war years. Will they think we are ungrateful?" Bert asked.

"I don't believe so. But Vater often questioned aloud, 'Who will tend the vineyards?' Remember, he objected to your occasional drinking of Coca-Cola, asking, 'Who will drink our wine if our youths prefer soft drinks?'"

With similar conversations and thoughts we tried to bridge our past to our future. Veit could only wonder what came next after the emotional past weeks. He busied himself with the few toys he had selected and been allowed to take in his hand luggage.

WE STEPPED OFF THE TRAIN in Bremen where we checked into a hotel before doing some sight-seeing. Exercising our legs a bit before the ten-day voyage will be good for us. I love to look at building styles of the Middle Ages as found in Hanseatic cities. Bremen has a long prosperous history in trading."

"Seaports are the gates to their countries and were established before most inland settlements," Bert said.

"I know. This city was also a center in the quest for freedom from the dominance of religious rulers. The *Marktplatz,* where we can observe the influence of commerce and religion on architecture, is near our hotel," I suggested. "If we go before sunset we won't feel the dampness of a gray November evening."

Standing on the market square in front of the statue of the legendary Roland, little Veit said, *"Ein grosser Mann."*

"Yes, it is a big statue of a man," Bert explained.

"On our next-to-last day in Germany, I can satisfy my long-held desire to see this six-hundred-year-old symbol of the local citizens' independence from theocracy," I remarked.

"The statue is six-hundred years old," Bert agreed, "proof that the people for whose freedom he fought never forgot him. Roland, though, is believed to have died fighting the Saracens, Moslems invading Spain, in the late eighth century."

"Sieh mal die Tiere!" Veit pointed at the famous monument depicting a wolf standing on a donkey, a cat atop the wolf, and, crowing from the back of the cat, a rooster.

"Yes, you remember the fairy tale of the *Bremer Stadtmusikanten,* don't you?" I asked. "Before you go to sleep tonight, I will tell you again how they wanted to go to Bremen and give concerts, each singing in its own voice, braying, howling, meowing and crowing."

"Oh, ja." Veit clapped his hands and practiced the animals' sounds.

B E R T   A N D   I   W E R E   A W A R E of the finality of our decision: a last dinner in Germany; a last night on German soil. We were excited and had no regrets.

The following morning, we three took the train to Bremerhaven, forty-five kilometers north of Bremen, where we boarded the *Gripsholm.* Our luggage awaited us in cabin 327 on C-deck. While freshening up, we heard a knock on the door. Herbert, Bert's friend during their captivity as POWs in Scotland, wanted to wish us a safe voyage. He was the captain of a tanker and had tied up near the *Gripsholm.*

When visitors had to exit the ship and the crew prepared for departure, a band on the dock played a medley of German folk songs, notably the well-known farewell melody *Muss i denn, muss i denn zum Städtele hinaus,* do I have to leave this town? We watched the proceedings from the top deck. "I see Herbert," Bert said, "he is standing to the right of the tuba."

"A true friend," I said. "Let's wave. Perhaps he'll recognize us, too, at this distance; he's looking into the sun, though."

As we began our voyage we watched our native country and our past fade into dusk. "We have each other," Bert said, "we are going to make it!" He embraced us.

"Providence willing, we'll succeed."

With Veit between us, holding his hands, we went to dinner.

IN OUR SPACIOUS SPARKLING CABIN, we spread out the ship's *Kabinenplan,* which indicated the location of the cabins but also all areas of interest to the traveler, such as dining rooms, nursery, offices, verandas and promenades. My bunk was wide enough to display the detailed plan and mark the layout of the ship.

"If we go on an inspection tour now, while we are in protected waters, we will know our respective destinations in inclement weather," Bert said.

"What do you mean?" I asked the man who was on his third Atlantic crossing.

"Well, you might be preoccupied with your balance and holding on to railings, but you will know where you want to go."

"That sounds ominous."

THE *GRIPSHOLM* entered the Strait of Dover on our second day aboard. After breakfast at our assigned table in the dining room, we took Veit to the kindergarten. Two friendly nurses greeted the arrivals and showed them around the large room furnished with big and small toys and bolted-down children's furniture. *"Womit möchtest du spielen?"* one attendant asked Veit. He chose a wooden train that he could lead around the spotless floor.

"We'll come back in a little while and see whether you want to stay longer or walk around with us," I assured Veit.

"Gut," he replied over his shoulder, strolling toward the train set. Veit's ease in meeting people, particularly children, helped him adapt to new situations.

Bert and I went on deck to walk in the brisk air and to check what land we could see.

He said, "This is the narrowest point of the Strait." Pointing across starboard, he added, "Those are the White Cliffs of Dover."

"Hmm," I reflected, "they remind me of the *Wissower Klinken* on Rügen. I told you about our class trip."

"Yes. Both of us have memories of white cliffs, don't we?" Bert said. "I look at these and remember working as a POW in the gardens of Dover Castle."

"Let's go portside," I suggested. "It's a clear day; perhaps we can spot the continent. We are abeam of Calais."

After taking a last look at the Old World, Bert and I went below to check on Veit. He was busy coloring a paper hat he had learned to fold. When he saw us, Veit waved us off.

"We'll come back before the noon meal," I said.

T H E   M E A L   P L A N on the *"Gripsholm"* followed the German eating pattern: *Frühstück,* breakfast, *Mittagessen,* the dinner in the middle of the day, *Kaffee und Kuchen* in mid-afternoon, and *Abendbrot,* supper, when sandwiches and salads were served. We attended the first sitting, glad to have a table to ourselves so we could give Veit our undivided attention.

During the first two days, we toured the different decks and laid down on deck chairs after the meals, wrapped in blankets with only our faces sticking out. The ship glided through the swells, forerunners of ocean waves. Clouds hung low in the gray skies.

"Möwen," Veit said as we watched errant seagulls accompany us for a while.

"We might not see any more birds until we'll have crossed the Atlantic," I said.

"Then they'll all be American birds?" Veit asked.

I laughed. "I never thought about seagulls' nationalities; but why not? We'll probably find species with differences between their European and American members."

"Such as squirrels," Bert said. "They have gray fur in America and are reddish-brown in Europe."

Through Veit's innocent questions, we realized that he, too, was thinking about the changes we would undergo in our chosen country. *Too much time to contemplate; too little to do after months of hectic activity.*

THE SEA BECAME ROUGHER on the third day aboard the *Gripsholm*. The crew worked with zeal to secure the ship before its encounter with the forecasted hurricane, just at the end of the hurricane season. Veit had enjoyed watching the waves through the porthole. Standing on my bunk, he saw them roll by just below eye level. Now, safety measures included shutting all portholes, stringing lines around the glassed-in deck, and lifelines in all open spaces.

Stewards wet the white linens on the table surfaces in the dining rooms to prevent plates, silverware, and serving dishes from sliding into our laps.

During the storm, one-third of the crew and many passengers became seasick, Bert and Veit included. Although seven months pregnant, I was the gofer for my family. My two men did not make many demands and wanted to suffer in their bunks. With a little coaxing, the dry toast and tea the steward supplied, Bert and Veit got up to practice our new skills: Whether we stood in front of our sink to brush our teeth, or tried to master stairs to reach the kindergarten or dining room, we moved with the pitch of the vessel. We timed when to rinse our mouth—bending backward—and when to spit—bending over. Going up stairs, we took three quick steps as the bow descended and held on until the next cycle. *Was this what Bert referred to on our first evening on board when he spoke of being occupied with holding onto railings?*

We smelled the kindergarten from a distance. Fewer children attended; of those, many vomited. Only one nurse was present, spending more time on cleaning with antiseptics than on guiding children in their activities. Veit developed an ear infection, tonsillitis and bronchitis. The ship's doctor brought the maladies under control, but Veit lost all appetite.

Our table steward, a father himself, enticed Veit with buttered *Zwieback* and chicken broth, "If you can eat this now, I'll have vanilla pudding and raspberry syrup for you for supper."

"Schokoladenpudding und Vanillesosse?" Veit bargained.

"Abgemacht!" the steward laughed, it's a deal.

The food on the ship was attractive in the word's truest sense. Our choices at every meal were scrumptious, healthy, and colorful. Passengers refrained from indulging, though, as they and the ship were tossed by the angry sea and wind. Our dining room was often sparsely visited.

Once the hurricane had passed, the pitching of the vessel became less violent. The bow did no longer burrow and disappear into the sea—a scary sight that the ship's brave—or reckless—photographer captured with his camera as he was tied to the crow's nest.

The sky cleared after five days; the sun shone benevolently upon our ark. A tanker, the only vessel we saw cross the path of the *Gripsholm* during our ten days aboard, was working the boiling sea.

Late in the afternoon of December 2 our ship put into Halifax, Nova Scotia, for a short stop. Goods were unloaded, others taken aboard. Family members of an American passenger who had died during the crossing came to escort the body to the States.

From the upper deck, we looked at the city spreading out before us, its lights replacing the golden sunset. The lack of motion by the vessel was a welcome change from the recent sharp dips up and down.

"Is this America? Can we get off here?" Veit asked.

"The country before us is Canada. We'll get underway shortly. In two days we'll be in America," Bert explained to our little son.

During the following night, another storm accompanied us for most of the last leg of our voyage. Few passengers, however, were ill-effected by it: They had grown sea legs.

In bright sunshine the *Gripsholm* entered New York City's harbor. When she passed the Statue of Liberty, she leaned slightly towards it because every immigrant on board wanted to greet this symbol of freedom. We stared in awe at the skyscrapers.

At one o'clock in the afternoon on December 4, 1954, the *Gripsholm*, which would be known as the *Berlin* from that day on, tied up. Some passengers we had noticed at the beginning of our voyage reappeared, pale and gaunt, on this day.

For us, the tedious immigration procedures began; tedious because we had to stand in long lines while customs officials waded through all the documents that the applicants had provided. What took the consulates years to process, these officials tried to check and verify in minutes. When we reached the table, the officer pointed at the two thick files in front of him and asked, "So, where are you going, to North Carolina or to Massachusetts?"

Stunned for a moment, we assumed that Tom Bunch must have returned from Korea and could resume his sponsorship; thus the two files. Quickly Bert answered, "Massachussetts."

"Okay," the officer said, "Welcome to the United States of America."

"Thank you."

With our registrations in hand, Bert, Veit, and I disembarked. We located our luggage among the multitude of unloaded crates, suitcases, and bags on the pier.

Nearing the exit gates, we searched for the Ingrahams. Merle's familiar broad grin greeted us from afar. We still had sea legs and walked haltingly toward him. Merle picked Veit up and said, *"Da bist du ja!"* Here you are. Bert and me he greeted with "Welcome to America!"

M.S. Gripsholm *entering N.Y. harbor, 4 Dec. 1954*

Luggage tag.

Bow of M.S. Gripsholm *during hurricane, Nov. 1954*

Veit-Thomas Metzroth at nursery aboard M.S. Gripsholm, *Nov. 1954*

CHAPTER 13

Making the Transition

MERLE GUIDED US through the throng of people at the dock, expectant relatives and sponsors as well as new arrivals. Many tip-toed, heads high, in their search to spot their parties. Veit felt threatened by the people rushing around him, and the strange sounds they made. *"Papi, kannst du mich tragen?"*

"I'll take your suitcase, Bert," Merle offered, "so you can carry Veit. He's afraid of being squashed, poor boy."

"Almut, why don't you wait here with Veit while Merle and I take the luggage to his car. You can sit on a bench, away from the traffic."

Veit wanted to take toys out of his bag. "Wait until we are at the hotel," I said. "You might lose some if you bring them out now."

A young woman shared the bench with us and overheard our conversation. "Here is something for you." She smiled and handed Veit a spring-loaded stuffed rabbit. "I was going to give it to my nephew, but I have other presents for him."

Veit did not know whether he was allowed to accept the toy and looked at me. I was hesitant, too.

"It's a welcome gift," the woman said.

We thanked her. *Is that an omen? Americans are glad to have us?*

"MY CAR IS JUST OUTSIDE the hall," Merle said to Bert. "Peg is waiting at the Hotel Taft on Seventh Avenue, where I have reserved rooms for all of us."

"Thanks. Almut and Veit need a rest. Our bodies still think they have to move with the pitching of the boat."

Veit remarked about the many cars in New York City. *"Wo sind die Opel, Mercedes und VauWes?"* In Germany he knew most of the brands, now he missed the familiar cars, mostly our VW.

Peg met us in the lobby. "You made it! How was your crossing?"

"Interesting," Bert said.

"Ich gehe nie wieder auf ein Schiff," Veit volunteered. This opinion, never to go on a ship again, he kept for eight years, indicating how frightful the experience had been for him.

"We don't have to worry about another voyage today," I assured Veit.

"Right," Merle said. "Why don't you relax a bit in your room. Later we can go for a stroll."

While Veit and I stretched out on our beds to read, Bert heaved the Manhattan phone directory into his lap. "I wonder whether any Metzroths live in this city." After a while he said, "Bertha's number is listed, and Charlie's, the undertaker's. Could they be mother and son?"

"You don't want to call them, do you?" I asked.

"Nah," Bert laughed, "just kidding."

PEG AND MERLE picked us up in late afternoon. The mid-day crowds had thinned out in the streets. Looking at window displays, I became concerned at the prices. *How can we afford furniture? Will Bert find a job soon?*

"Das Haus brennt!" Veit called our attention to the smoke emanating from an upper story's *hole* in the building near us.

"No, the house is not burning. Look closely, Veit. The super-sized figure is blowing smoke. It is an advertisement for Camel cigarettes," Merle explained and we translated.

210

"Are you hungry?" Peg asked. "Have you ever been to an Automat to eat? I did not see any in Europe."

"No," Bert said, "we only read about them."

"Let's go inside," Peg suggested.

"We'll show you how to help yourself to the food you like. Take a tray and slide it along the shelf in front of the recessed rows of small glass doors. As you choose your item, drop a nickel into the slot next to the individual door, open it and remove your selection to put it on your tray," Merle explained.

The food looked inviting. The offerings we did not recognize, we avoided. *I'm sure, we'll learn what they are in time.*

"Will this table at the window be all right? From here Veit can observe the goings-on in the Automat as well as on the street and we can catch up with family news and plans," Merle suggested.

"Perfect," I said. "How is Jaimye Sue, the Bad Kreuznach native?"

"Jaimye is fine. Merle's parents are taking care of her in our absence."

"Is your practice doing well?" Bert asked Merle.

"Yes, I am fulfilling my five-year requirement in general practice, a prerequisite for the study of psychiatry."

"Will you deliver our baby?" I wanted to know.

"Make an appointment with my secretary." Merle smiled, nodding toward Peg.

"What are my chances of finding work, any work?" Bert wondered.

"The job market is depressed at this time. But we have spread word of your availability and your many talents."

"Do you like the chicken noodle soup?" Peg asked me.

"Yes. I'm glad I found light fare. And Veit enjoys his peanutbutter sandwich with jelly again."

NIGHT HAD FALLEN when we exited the Horn & Hardardt Automat. The lights from stores and neon signs illuminated the avenue. We had never seen such a colorful display in streets.

Discovering differences between life in Germany and America became a constant reminder of the gigantic step we took.

The following morning, Bert paid our hotel bill: $13.00 for the room, $0.60 tax, and $0.16 for an in-house phone call. $13.81 was a big slice out of our resources that we had to exchange at the rate of DM 4,25 for $1.00.

Before leaving New York, we visited the Empire State Building, from whose top floors we looked across the vast city. I was not comfortable at that height in my advanced state of pregnancy, but I did not want to miss the opportunity. *When might I be able to come back here again?*

"Sieh mal die kleinen Menschen auf der Strasse!" our "big" boy remarked, looking down at the small people in the street. Veit showed no fear.

"You saw New York City from above," Merle said in the elevator as we returned from the windy, lofty height to the street level." On our way north we'll drive you through several boroughs before passing through suburbs and the countryside."

My emotions changed with every area through which we traveled. At times I wondered, *Is this America? I don't know whether I want to stay or return to Germany. I would not live in these projects.* By the time we reached Greenwich, Connecticut, and I saw open spaces and one-family homes, I relaxed. "Let's take a break. I'll stop at Howard Johnson's," Merle said.

In the restaurant, we surveyed the menu. I had no idea what I was looking at. My academic studies in the English language had not prepared me for reading and comprehending menus.

Looking for a way out, I asked Peg what she would order.

"We like New England clam chowder. They serve crackers with it."

"I'll have the same," I said. "Veit would like a peanut butter sandwich with jelly. You introduced him to that in Bad Kreuznach."

One ingredient in the chowder was sand. The clams were not cleaned well before meeting the soup. I, of course, thought that sand was an unavoidable by-product of this dish. *I can live without this,* I decided but politely finished my meal.

BRIGHT SUNSHINE ACCOMPANIED US on our ride through Connecticut and Massachusetts on this December day. Where I saw large, plowed fields, I was reminded of Pomerania, in particular when I noticed installations for the cultivation of tobacco in the Connecticut Valley. "This looks familiar," I said, noticing the rolled up shading material. "Tobacco farmers in the Oder valley used the same method to protect the delicate plants in the summer."

At dusk, we reached our destination: Greenfield, Massachusetts. Coming up Bankrow, I glanced ahead, "Alvin and Olga," I read aloud.

"Yes," Merle responded, "the Gebhards own that restaurant. They are of German descent."

Still having things German on your mind, don't you? I chided myself. *Turn the page.*

I LIKED THE SINGLE–FAMILY HOMES I saw on our ride north on Federal Street but was amazed at their exterior. "Are they all built of wood? Isn't that a fire hazard?"

"When we were in Germany, we were just as surprised at the brick and concrete dwellings. We wondered about the building costs," Merle said. "People everywhere make use of their resources. They adjust to their lifestyles."

"Here we are at our abode, a Cape Cod-style house," Peg announced as Merle parked the car in the driveway.

We unloaded the car, freshened up, and joined Peg and Merle in the kitchen. They were preparing supper.

My eyes grew big as I watched Merle "building" sandwiches. In Germany *belegte Brote* were buttered slices of mostly dark bread with cold cuts or cheese arranged atop. Lettuce was served on the side as a salad.

"What would you like to drink? We have milk and sodas: ginger ale, birch or root beer," Peg offered.

Soda is a cleaning agent. Ginger is a spice I use for baking; ale is like beer. Spiced beer? Birch is a tree; it has roots. They make drinks of all that? Was I using the same thinking process girls at the *Landfrauenschule* applied to friction as a cooling agent?

Bert had told me of soft drinks, but they were fruit-flavored, much like German *Orangeade*.

I'll never forget how I enjoyed our first meal at Ingraham's house. *May all transitions be as pleasant to make.*

"W O U L D   Y O U   L I K E to meet my parents and sister, Eleanor?" Merle asked on the following morning. "I am going to pick up Jaimye Sue."

"Gladly," Bert said, including Veit and me in the agreement.

Ray and Blanche Ingraham were a kindly couple with the presence of New Englanders as I had seen pictured in books and magazines. Eleanor, a Julliard graduate and piano teacher, lived with her parents. All three embraced us as family. They became Veit's American grandparents, and aunt.

Jaimye, however, saw competition in Veit. At first, she shied away from him, withdrawing with her toys, not wanting to share. After a while, she realized that Veit was no threat. Both children were curious about the other's playthings, Jaimye's dolls and Veit's Lego blocks; the latter had not yet reached the American market. Jaimye's favorite pastime, though, was to sit in front of her monkey-in-the-box and to wind it re-lent-less-ly. Was it the only toy that communicated with her with its tinny-sounding melody and lyrics?

"All around the cobbler's bench,
The monkey chased the weasel.
The monkey thought t'was all in fun,
Pop! Goes the weasel.

A penny for a spool of thread,

A penny for a needle
That's the way the money goes,
Pop! Goes the weasel."

I could not make any sense of the words. "Why is a monkey chasing a weasel?" I asked Merle one morning.

"This nursery rhyme has undergone many changes in the last hundred years or more. It's said to have originated in London. Tailors took their pressing irons, called weasels, to pawn shops when they ran out of money before payday. 'That's the way the money goes...' "

"And the monkey?" I asked.

"We speak of getting the monkey off our backs, which means to rid ourselves of burdensome problems. The tailors needed to pay their debts in the taverns," Merle said.

"I have much to learn about English nursery rhymes as recorders of history," I mused.

Peg and I cleared the breakfast table. Merle and Bert lingered over a second cup of coffee.

"Here comes the mailman," Jaimye called out.

Merle rose, "I'll get it."

"More pretty Christmas cards for me?"

"Yes, and a telegram for Veit."

"A telegram from Germany?" I asked and worried.

"No. Open it and find out," Merle encouraged me.

"It's from Rudolf, the red-nosed reindeer, assuring Veit that he would guide the other reindeer and Santa's sleigh to Veit's new address."

I read the message without comprehension. Peg laughed and said, "We'll have to go for a ride tonight and show you the Christmas decorations on the roofs of people's homes and in their front yards. Then you'll see more than one red-nosed Rudolph. You probably guessed that Merle's parents sent this wire."

"Such a thoughtful welcome."

How could we explain to Veit the many differences between German and American traditions for the same holiday?

215

Veit's books showed horses pulling the sleigh of the *Weihnachtsmann,* Santa Claus, as they stopped at the front doors. The German Santa was less rotund and jolly than his American image.

Why did Americans display Christmas decorations so early? German families observed the Advent season in the spirit of anticipation of the holy days in December. On the fourth Sunday before Christmas, they lit one candle on their wreath on the dining room table; they burned two, three, and four, respectively, on the following Sundays. The candles and the ribbon around the wreath were red.

"You do not have an Advent wreath custom, do you?" I asked Peg.

"Some churches hang wreaths with purple ribbons from the ceiling in their entrance halls. Three candles are purple; one is pink for Rose Sunday. The color combinations vary between denominations." Turning to Merle, Peg asked, "Will you put up our Christmas tree this weekend? Then I can place presents underneath. We do that earlier than Germans do, as I remember," she said to me.

"Yes, in Germany, parents set up their family's tree behind closed doors on Christmas Eve. Vati inserted white candles into the drop-catching holders..."

Peg interrupted, "Candles on the Christmas tree? Now *I* have to ask you, 'Isn't that a fire hazard?' as you asked us about our houses built of wood."

"I never knew anyone whose tree caught fire in the house. Freshly cut and set in a stand filled with water, trees lasted well during the twelve days of Christmas.

"Besides the white candles, my father decorated our tree with separated silver tinsel, glass-blown colored balls and various Christmas heirlooms. At the same time, my mother arranged Gunhilt's, Edzard's, Vati's and my unwrapped presents in their traditional niches; wrapped gifts from out-of-town relatives she laid alongside. Every family member also received a *Weihnachtsteller,* a deep plate, abounding with home-baked cookies, marzipan, chocolates, and an apple. During the war and for three years afterward, we had few sweets.

"Tell the story of Edzard's advice for Vati," Bert said.

"One year Edzard teased Vati through the closed door, 'Curt, be sure to whistle while you work in there. You don't want to spoil your stomach.' So Edzard added another tradition to our family's Christmas preparations. Remembering his "concern," we even reminded each other in jest to whistle whenever we created delicacies."

"With the same lightheartednes, my father suggested to grape pickers to whistle during the harvesting," Bert recalled.

"Getting back to Christmas, what were the children doing during their parents' secret work?" Merle asked.

"As long as they believed in Santa Claus, they had to take a nap so they would not notice Santa coming to bring their toys. Older children worked to the last moment to finish their hand-made presents, their effort in gratitude for the gifts they would receive. Or they reviewed the memorized Christmas poems and the music they wanted to play on their instruments when their parents opened the door to invite them inside.

"The sight and the fragrance of the tastefully adorned Christmas tree, the candles' warm glow reflected in the shiny tinsel and ornaments, and in the background, the rich sounds of church bells ringing throughout the land created awe every year, and memories for a lifetime," I said.

*   *   *

BERT, VEIT AND I observed our first Christmas in America in two stages. After Peg and Merle returned from church on Christmas Eve, we all sat before their tree. They had trimmed it with tinsel, ornaments, bells, lanterns, garlands of cranberries and popcorn. The reflection of the large colored electric lights shone from the shiny decorations as well as the big blue eyes of our children. Filled with anticipation and excitement, they waited to play with the toys Santa had left under the tree.

Keeping with a German tradition, Veit recited every German child's first poem before receiving presents:

Lieber, guter Weihnachtsmann,	Dear good Santa Claus,
Sieh mich nicht so böse an,	I won't give you pause,
Stecke deine Rute ein,	put your switch away,
Ich will auch immer artig sein.	I promise to obey.

"What's a switch?" Jaimye asked after hearing her dad's translation.

Veit eagerly showed her a picture in his book and said in German, "If you are not good, Santa will bring you not toys but a switch like this one to warn you."

Again Merle translated and Jaimye looked under the tree. She beamed a smile at everyone when she did not see a bundle of twigs, resembling birch-brooms of the past.

"No switch this time, but remember to be good always," Merle reminded Jaimye.

"Santa left gifts for each of us," Peg said as she handed out wrapped and unwrapped presents.

"Will Santa leave toys at Granma and Gramp's, too?" Jaimye wanted to know.

"We'll find out when we go to their house tomorrow," Merle said. "So you best head to bed now. You may take your new doll with you."

"I'll take my truck," Veit said.

"FROHE WEIHNACHT! Merry Christmas!" Eleanor greeted us as she helped to bring our salad, pies and presents from the car into the house. Inside, we met Granma's brothers Allyn and Charles Newcomb, as well as his wife Mabel and daughter Maverette. They lived next door on their farm. Allyn owned a landscaping business. Like the Ingrahams, they were a kindhearted family.

Gramp took our coats and led us to the festively set dinner table. "The turkey is ready. Are you?" Granma asked.

"I don't know about the children," Peg said. "Jaimye is taking a peek at your tree. But I'm looking forward to your Christmas feast."

As our hosts passed bowls and platters laden with familiar and unfamiliar offerings, they were as surprised that we had never eaten glazed yams, boiled onions or corn niblets as we were to taste these for the first time. "The vegetables are delicious," I said. "Would you tell me how to prepare these dishes?"

"We're learning something new every day," Bert declared. "Veit in particular is overwhelmed by the many changes in his daily routines. It will become easier for him when he understands English better. We're working on that."

When none of us could eat another morsel, Granma suggested to the men and children to wait for us women in the living room until we had cleared the table, stored the leftovers, and washed the dishes.

"F I N A L L Y!" Jaimye exclaimed as the enlarged family assembled in front of the Christmas tree. Eleanor sat at the piano, leading us in the singing of Christmas carols, starting with "*O Tannenbaum,* O Christmas Tree," which we, Merle, and Eleanor sang in German. For the Austrian carol "Silent Night," and others that followed, Eleanor gave us song books with English lyrics. The familiar melodies evoked memories and brought me close to tears. *I wonder how Mutti and Vati are spending the holidays without us. Bert's family still had grandchildren to spoil.*

The Ingraham-Newcomb families opened their hearts to us. Veit not only received toys from "Santa" but also American clothes. Among them was a one-piece dark-green snowsuit with matching hat, as well as brown rubber boots that were handed down in our family for years. They became immortalized in our photo albums.

AFTER CHRISTMAS, Bert found a job as the produce man at the local Red & White store. He earned thirty-five dollars a week. We still lived with Peg and Merle, who suggested we wait and look for an apartment after the birth of our baby in the new year.

CHAPTER 14

1955

I N   J A N U A R Y, the weather changed from the dreary and damp conditions of the previous month to cold days with brisk winds, and snowstorms that left several inches or feet of accumulation. *Just like in Pomerania*. When the sun broke through the clouds and made the icy crystals on the snowy landscape glisten like diamonds, children emerged from their homes, happy to build snowmen and forts and have snowball fights.

Veit was eager to meet the neighborhood children. Early contacts were not always successful because of the language barrier. Feeling depressed and rejected, he asked me, *"Was ist stupid?"*

Rather than translate the offensive word, I said, "They wonder why you can't speak with them. They have never met a child who could not speak English as they do. With time you'll learn. We'll help you."

Both Veit and I strove to increase our vocabulary. We read Jaimye's Golden Books and listened to the Children's Hour on the radio. My favorite lessons were a series about the Scarlet Pimpernel.

While Bert worked at his job, I tried to be helpful to our unselfish sponsors. Peg was the receptionist and secretary at Merle's office every Monday, Wednesday, and Friday afternoon. On those days, I played with Jaimye and Veit, read to them, or took them for walks before preparing dinner for our two families.

The Ingrahams enjoyed our German meals but also taught me American recipes, such as pancakes and waffles for breakfast.

"Can you bring the children to the store tomorrow?" Bert asked one day. "Aunt Jemima will be there."

"Who is Aunt Jemima?"

"She is a food producer's representative, demonstrating how to make the perfect pancakes with their mix. Her picture is on the boxes as well as bottles of syrup. After making the pancakes, people spread butter and pour syrup over them."

"We use maple syrup, a sap, tapped and boiled right here in our county and neighboring New England states," Peg said. "In a few weeks, when the sap flows, we'll take you to a sugar house. There you can watch the owners make syrup, and you can eat sugar on snow."

Birch beer; maple syrup; sugar on snow?

Merle laughed. "Your face tells me you're confused. No, we don't sprinkle sugar on snow. Sugar houses store fresh snow in freezers to serve later, topped with their maple syrup. But don't tell Aunt Jemima that."

TIME PASSED QUICKLY, presenting new impressions almost daily. One Saturday in January, I dried the dishes after Peg had washed them. Suddenly, sirens all over Greenfield sounded a familiar alarm; I dropped the plate, trembled with fear, and had to lean against the counter.

Bert and Merle led me to a chair and gave me some water. "Once a month, the sirens are activated to test their readiness," Merle explained. "I'm sorry we didn't warn you, knowing that you carry horrible memories. You can't afford severe shocks days before giving birth."

"Well, now I know. I'll mark the first Saturday of every month on the calendar."

I counted the days to delivery. "I feel I have to tell you a secret." Bert hesitated as he spoke to me. "American women like to surprise their pregnant sisters or friends. They give them baby showers."

"Baby rain? What's that?" I asked.

"Parties to which they invite many friends and relatives who will shower the expecting mother with gifts for her and the baby. Your shower is this afternoon at Granma's. I waited until now but don't want you to be so surprised that you go into labor." He stroked my hair. "Just be surprised."

In the afternoon, Peg asked me whether I wanted to come along to pick up Eleanor to go shopping. "Yes, I'd like to join you," I said. Bert, who had the afternoon off, agreed to entertain Veit and Jaimye. He made a motion indicating to seal my lips, as Peg turned toward the door

Peg drove us from Cooke Street via Washburn Avenue and Silver Street to the Senior Ingraham's house on Leyden Road.

"They must have company," Peg said as she parked the car next to others in the driveway. "I'll fetch Eleanor."

A moment later, Eleanor waved me inside. "Come in, Almut, I'm almost ready."

I labored my heavy self up the snow-free steps into the house. "Surprise, surprise," the chorus of gathered Ingraham relatives and friends called out. *I am glad Bert warned me.*

"Hello, my name is …"

"How are you? I am pleased to meet you."

"Welcome to America."

Eleanor took my wraps and led me to the place of honor, an armchair decorated with baby-blue, pink, and yellow ribbons. Streamers hung from the lamps and curtain rods of the living room. Next to my chair stood a bassinette filled with gaily-wrapped presents. The guests sat on a couch and chairs arranged in a circle that included me.

"I'll start the coffee," Granma said, looking at me. "Why don't you open the packages?"

The kindness of the people, whom I had not known even a few weeks before, astonished me. Their presents met a baby's needs for several months. *How can I ever thank these women? By returning their sentiments, helping those in need.*

*   *   *

NICORD MERLE FELIX was born on January 20, 1955, the day we expected him. I was not conscious at the moment of his birth. When Merle Ingraham detected difficulties, he immediately called for an anesthetic.

Hours later, I awoke in the recovery room. Merle was at my bedside. "Almut, your little Nicord came into this world with an open spine, a condition called spina bifida. An infection has caused his temperature to rise. I have called a pediatrician to evaluate him and to direct immediate treatment. Rest for now. We'll give you regular reports on Nicord's condition."

I was devastated and confused. *What did I do wrong? What kind of life would Nicord have?*

Late that afternoon, a tall, heavy-set man supported himself on crutches as he struggled toward my bed in the room I shared with another woman.

"I am Dr. Card, Nicord's doctor. His condition has not stabilized. We are treating the infection, but he is not responding. I know I am not bringing you good news. When we encounter crises in our lives we tend to ask, 'why me?' Never, 'why not me?' Please know, we'll do everything to help your baby. Do you have any questions I might answer for you?"

"Yes, what causes spina bifida?"

"Mostly, a genetic defect, we tend to believe. Less often it's drugs a mother takes during the first trimester of pregnancy."

"My doctor in Germany prescribed Thalidomide, a sedative to curb the morning sickness, which, in my case, expressed itself in incessant vomiting for months."

"That drug is now under investigation. We have been seeing a number of unusual birth defects lately, noticeably in babies of women in Europe, including American dependents of our troops." Turning to leave, Dr. Card added, "Dr. Ingraham will be in touch with you."

I feared for our baby's life and health. After leaving the womb, our little boy fought to cope with a strange environment and I could not even hold and protect him.

What irony to hear this severely afflicted man show his concern for Nicord. How those questions 'why me,' and 'why not me' pierce the mind spoken by him. I will never forget this meeting.

After Dr. Card had left, my roommate turned to me and said, "The doctor was stricken with polio when he treated his young patients. This town loves him."

"H E L L O , A L M U T , do you feel like going for a walk along the corridor with me?" Merle asked as he visited me the following morning.

"Yes, how is Nicord, and is Bert with Veit?"

"I'll answer all your questions on the way." Moments later he explained to me the efforts the medical staff and nurses had made to try to stabilize Nicord's condition. "But his little body succumbed to the infection. I know how devastating this loss is to you. Believe that Providence has saved him from a life of operations and paralysis, and you from desperate feelings of helplessness. You will grieve, and with you, Bert and Veit. In time, you will heal. Your family needs you. Our family and friends are sorry for your loss and will stand by you."

"Does Veit know?"

"Bert told him that Nicord was an angel, and that you would come home in two days."

I was bewildered, too stunned for tears. A nurse had let my roommate know of our loss. "I am sorry, Almut. But you are young and can have more children. Concentrate on getting well now."

The tears came when I put the baby clothes in our suitcases and covered the bassinette with a sheet before storing them in the attic.

S O O N   A F T E R   M Y   D I S C H A R G E from the hospital, we moved to Pond Street into a brand new third-floor apartment the owners of the house had just finished as rental property. At the top of the stairs was a platform where Bert parked his bicycle. Our entrance door opened into the huge kitchen, adjoined on the left by a full bathroom. Beyond the kitchen, a hallway with an alcove connected the rear of the house to the front and our bedroom. Veit's room was opposite the alcove. I liked to sit there to read or sew.

The Ingrahams and their friends had given us a few pieces of furniture; an upholstered rocking chair, a rickety bed for us, a cot for Veit, and an old foot-operated sewing machine. We needed a dinette set, pots and pans, serving dishes, kitchen and cleaning utensils, appliances, and food. Now came the time to learn about installment plans, an unfamiliar way for us to make payments. Every week, we divided Bert's pay into many envelopes with due dates on the front, which left twenty-five cents of spending money. Baby sitting and cooking at Peg and Merle's was an honor for us and done in gratitude; it also helped keep our food bill down.

"Will we buy a fridge?" Veit asked. He was thinking of Ingraham's well-stocked refrigerator, or, more accurately, the ice cream in it.

"Not this month," I said. "We have to pay off the washing machine first. Aren't we lucky Grand Union opened a store last week around the corner on Federal Street?"

"*Ja,* but we have to go there every other day for milk and a stick of butter."

V E I T   M A D E   R A P I D   S T R I D E S in learning English from his neighborhood playmates. For his birthday in February, we bought him a toy farm, fences and animals from a Sears catalog. The Ingrahams gave him figures of Indians and horses, and small tepees. He had them spread out on the floor of his room. Lying in front of his arrangement, "the farmer" negotiated with the Indians in English as I entered Veit's room.

"Now remember, when we are among ourselves, we speak German so we won't forget it before seeing our relatives again. When we have company, we speak English," I said.

Veit turned to look at me in all seriousness, "Well, did the Indians speak German?"

I laughed out loud. In less than eight weeks of playing with his new friends our son had perfected a four-year-old's conversational English. "No," I said, "Indians spoke their tribe's language until they trusted white men to trade with them; then some learned English."

"That's what my Indians are doing," Veit declared.

*   *   *

WHEN SPRING GRACED NEW ENGLAND with warmer temperatures, the soil smelled of promise; trees blossomed; snowdrops, crocuses and tulips announced the return of Nature's colorful palette. Mothers brought out their little children in strollers and prams.

"Everybody has a baby but us," Veit observed on our way to Wilson's Department Store to price used refrigerators.

"I am sad, too, that we lost Nicord. We will not forget him. Perhaps you will have a brother or sister some day. Now let's see whether we can find a small fridge."

ALLES NEU MACHT DER MAI: May renews everything. One day, Bert scanned the help wanted section in the *Greenfield Recorder,* the local afternoon newspaper.

"Listen to this," he said. "I can do that: proofread at a local printing company." So, Bert composed a job application based on his education at the Private Interpreters College Dittrich and on Langenscheidt's *Handbooks of Commerce Correspondence*:

Gentlemen,

On the strength of your advertisement of the 28th inst., I beg to ask you to enter my name on the list of candidates for proofreader.

For your approval I take the liberty of submitting to you the following detail about myself.

I am a native of Germany and immigrated to the United States of America on the 4th of December 1954,settling in Greenfield.

I have obtained the certificates of Foreign Correspondent as well as Interpreter in Germany and possess a good all-around knowledge of the English language. I am quite prepared to undertake the duties named in your advertisement.

If you will kindly grant me an interview, I can furnish you with further particulars.

Esteeming your favorable reply,
I am, Gentlemen,
Yours respectfully,
Rupert A. Metzroth

Two days later, the company's treasurer was at our door—we could not yet afford a telephone—to take a look at the writer of a British-phrased letter. He approved of the applicant and suggested Bert visit the company for an interview and a tour of the plant. By agreement, Bert started his career in the printing business on 5.5.55, earning fifteen more dollars weekly than as a produce man. We added another envelope to our collection for the old-model refrigerator with the compressor on top, forty dollars in installments of five dollars per week.

IN JUNE, PEG AND MERLE welcomed another daughter, Merlene, to their family, and I was pregnant again. "Try to drink ginger ale and eat saltine crackers and dry toast at the first sign of nausea," Merle suggested.

Although I had to force myself to do that, it worked. Phasing in other foods in increments, I suffered none of the prolonged morning sickness of my two previous pregnancies.

The summer heat, however, became insufferable in our attic apartment. Whenever possible, we went to the public swimming pool after Bert returned home from work. With the skill I acquired in 1945, I loaded beach gear and a picnic supper onto our bike. Bert sat Veit on the saddle and we were off, walking the two miles to the Green River.

Some afternoons, the two daughters of the friendly second-floor tenants invited Veit to watch cartoons on television. The evening their mother, Jean, bid us to dinner, remains in my memory.

Her husband was an uncomplicated man. He fired his questions and opinions like bullets. "You are from Germany, I hear. Were you Nazis?"

Bert explained that we had been too young to be members of the Party.

"Well, then, are you Communists now?"

"No. After years of checking our past, the U.S. Government is surer of our political backgrounds than of those of some U.S. citizens," Bert said.

"All right, Joe, you have your answers. Can we enjoy our pork roast dinner now?" Jean calmed her husband's fighting mood. She explained, "His folks left Lithuania in the 1880s, escaping the threat of being subjugated by Russian cultural dominance. At this time of the McCarthy hearings, Joe is upset with people who, to his mind, don't recognize the threat to freedom Communism poses."

*   *   *

A T   T H E   H E I G H T of the summer heat we heard of the availability of the upstairs apartment in an old brick house two doors from our sweatbox. The owner, a grocery manager at the Red & White store, and his British wife offered to rent it to us. We traded a roomier, friendlier-looking flat for a cooler, more compact tenement with easier access from the main entrance. Elms shaded the front of the house; in the back, a porch outside our kitchen kept the interior from direct exposure. The bricks provided insulation in summer and winter. The focal point of the kitchen was the gas-oil-combination stove that scared me from the day we moved in. *That's the greatest fire hazard I can imagine. I will have a job preventing the children from touching the oil-fed-furnace side of the monster.* And the pilot light of the range and the water heater worried me, too. "We'll have to air out the oil fumes in the winter, Bert."

*   *   *

A T   T H E   P R I N T I N G   C O M P A N Y,   Bert met new challenges. To modernize the plant, his employer ordered offset presses, which accelerated the printing process by four thousand impressions per hour over the production of the letterpresses.

Upon the equipment supplier's recommendation, an employee was to observe the operation of an offset printing company and receive first-hand experience. That employee was Bert.

"I have to go to Boston for a few days," he said to Veit and me. "Will you be all right?"

"Sure. We have friends all around us in case of need."

Bert took the train from Greenfield. On his return, he described the splendor of the fall foliage that had struck him with awe as he traversed most of Massachusetts from west to east and back.

"What did you see?" asked Veit.

"What did you learn?" I was eager to know.

"I saw enough of Boston to want to go there with you some day and explore the historic city, its environs and the harbor. The lessons I received in the preparations for offset printing, typesetting, photography, and plate making, were numerous and challenging. Look at this tome on the subject." The book Bert showed us became his constant companion.

Before long, the former proofreader realized he needed to gain an understanding of layout. "I think I'll enroll in a correspondence course from Art Instruction, Inc." Thus the kitchen table became our most important piece of furniture; it served as dining surface, cutting board for sewing projects, and as easel.

"Can I do my artwork here, too?" Veit asked his father.

"Yes, if you'll stay at your end of the table." *Another artist in the family?*

*   *   *

1955, THE YEAR OF STRENUOUS EFFORTS to build a foundation for our life in America, came to a close on a happy note. Riko Claas Curt, a healthy eight-pound baby came into the world on December 23. Veit had his brother.

CHAPTER 15

The Time of Our Americanization

B E R T' S   S U C C E S S in his new career relieved us from the severe financial restraints of the first years after our immigration. The purchase of a 1947 olive-green Nash enabled us to explore Greenfield, Franklin County and other areas of Massachusetts.

"This car is much bigger than our VW in Germany," Veit said.

"About twice as big. You have ample playroom between the front and back seats, don't you? We can also secure Riko's travel crib there," I noted. "Where are we going today?"

"Let's drive up Rocky Mountain, the eastern boundary of Greenfield, to the Poet's Seat Tower. From its top level, we can overlook the town," Bert suggested.

"I see the high school and Grand Union on Federal Street. Pond Street must be close by," I said. "Interesting, how Greenfield is nestled amid hills. Did the early settlers choose the Connecticut and Green River valleys for protection as much as for the fertile land?"

"We'll have to study Greenfield's history," Bert said. "For now we want to become acquainted with the town's geography, people and opportunities."

W H E N   M U T T I , our sons called their grandmother Omi, visited in the spring of 1956, we took more extensive rides, from the Berkshires and the Mohawk Trail to Cape Cod and the neighboring

New England states. I, the native of Pomerania, found so many similarities between the countryside of my childhood and our new environment.

On Cape Cod, I asked Omi, "Does this summer colony remind you of a place you have been to?"

"Yes, of Rügen," she answered.

Her greatest pleasure and reason for making the trip to America was not the sightseeing but to be with her grandsons. Veit enjoyed the attention Omi paid him by playing board games and going to stores, where he acted as interpreter. Riko became spoiled in her lap as Omi led his hands to clap to *"Backe, backe, Kuchen,"* patty cake, patty cake, and other rhymes. Saying goodbye was so difficult for all of us when Omi had to return to Germany. Peg offered to look after our sons while we took my mother to the *Queen Elizabeth* in New York Harbor.

Omi, Bert and I rose early on July 26 for the drive to New York.

"I'll switch on the radio for the four-o'clock news and weather report," I said. "What happened? Listen to the reporters' excited voices."

After a moment, we were able to discern anxiety from facts: on the previous night, the Italian liner *Andrea Doria* had sailed through Nantucket Sound toward New York in thick fog, when at fifteen minutes before midnight the Europe-bound Swedish-American passenger ship *Stockholm* sliced deep into the starboard side of the *Andrea Doria*. Many fatalities occurred on the Italian ship; passengers and crew were being rescued by the *Stockholm* as well as other ships rushing to the accident scene.

"That isn't news you want to hear before setting out on a trans-Atlantic crossing," Omi said.

"Certainly not. But neither must you fear your passage because of this collision. Keep in mind the many safe voyages made every day," Bert reassured her.

I'm glad we never elaborated on our Gripsholm experiences.

*   *   *

T H E   N E X T   S T E P in our Americanization was Veit's enrollment in kindergarten in September. With some of his Pond Street playmates, he walked confidently the two blocks to the Pierce Street Elementary School that housed the morning and afternoon kindergarten classes and grades one through three. We mothers followed the little group on their first day of school. Because Veit was with friends, he was not afraid to leave me at the classroom door. "Bye," he said and waved with a smile.

"Bye. We'll be back in two hours," I assured our now-big boy and turned Riko's stroller to go home. I felt a lump in my throat, aware that Veit had taken his first step into independence from his mother. Riko did not want to let his brother go either; he leaned forward with outstretched arms and cried. "Veit will play with you after school," I said. "Let's hurry home so you can have your nap and be ready to pick him up." With those words I jogged, pushing Riko in his stroller. He liked our going fast and crowed with pleasure.

A S   V E I T   B E G A N his educational journey, Bert and I worried: Did we have sufficient knowledge about our chosen country, her people and institutions? Would we be able to answer our children's questions as they advanced their learning?

A college student brought a solution to our uncertainty. He hoped to contribute to his tuition by selling encyclopedias door-to-door. *Can we afford another installment purchase? Can we not take the chance?*

Soon *"The People's Encyclopedia"* arrived in several boxes. The volumes supplied us with knowledge, and the containers became make-shift furniture. In our living room, they joined the nineteenth-century sofa, a period piece in ornate carving and red velvet upholstery. I moved four of the heavy-laden cartons into the middle of the room and spread a tablecloth over them; the others I arranged around the table.

234

"Can we sit on them?" Veit asked while Riko pushed a toy car around one. "Yes," I said, "as long as you choose one that is completely filled."

"Vati, what is this?" Veit asked Bert. He pointed at colorful, transparent overlays in one of the volumes.

"Together, the transparencies show you a V-8 engine like you see in a car. When you lift one sheet after the other you recognize the several components of a V-8," Bert explained.

"In another volume, I saw the human body portrayed in layers," I said. "It's a fascinating display that's easy to understand."

THROUGH THE FIRST NATIONAL grocery chain, we added a different set of books to our library. Weekly food purchases over a certain amount enabled us to obtain the books within a year. Bert and I had read some of the classic novels in German, such as *The Count of Monte Cristo* and *Tale of Two Cities,* but we wanted to know more of what our children would read in school.

The first book the store offered of that collection featured Emily Brontë's *Jane Eyre* and *Wuthering Heights.* While I recognized the morals the author meant to stress, I hoped that future volumes would stir me to greater interest. Bert and I had met many life-threatening challenges and could not appreciate Miss Brontë's writings. We were pleased with works by Charles Dickens, Mark Twain, Herman Melville, and others.

AMERICAN POPULAR ART of the 1950s also impacted our boys' growing up. They watched Indian and early-American lore on television. Davy Crockett's raccoon fur cap with the ringed tail was the favorite head gear of young boys. Holster sets completed their outfits for play unless they wore Indian feathers. I was not comfortable with our sons toting toy guns so soon after a devastating war.

"But I have to defend myself," Veit answered my doubts. "I don't want to play dead all the time and be out of the game."

"Well, as the king of the wild frontier you must try to negotiate with your enemies," I encouraged him. "Just like Captain Kangaroo settles differences among his friends every morning."

*　　*　　*

HALF A YEAR AFTER OMI'S VISIT, Bert's father came to check on our welfare. The boys rarely budged from their Opa's side. He drew pictures with Veit and gave Riko rides on his shoulders. When he made a dresser, a bookcase with glass doors, end tables, and toys with his great craftsmanship, the boys watched him in our landlord's cellar workshop. To save money, Opa produced his masterpieces from wood he chose mostly from lumber scrap bins and by using only basic hand tools.

After two months, Opa was ready to return home. "I can tell Oma that you are on your way. Some day, she might come to see for herself," he said.

"That is something to look forward to for all of us," Bert assured him.

*　　*　　*

WE WERE HEALTHY AND HAPPY in America. Bert progressed at the printing company, where he became art director. When we were expecting another child in 1959, we looked for a house.

"Will we have a yard?" Veit asked.

"Can I have a swing and a cat?" Riko begged.

"And a garden for me," I said, adding to the wish list.

Bert laughed. "Anything for me that we should look for?"

"A workshop and a garage," Riko determined.

Glad to be able to satisfy all the "requirements" of our first house in America, we bought a Cape Cod-style house on the northern outskirts of Greenfield. The colors of the outside paint reflected a fad of that time.

"The house was painted recently," Bert said. "The grey coat looks fine, but we'll have to get rid of the pink trim."

"I don't like it either. Changing the trim can wait, though. Think of all the work we have to do inside the house. But it's ours!" I said.

"And the bank's," Bert added. "Yes, I'll finish the upstairs rooms for the boys. Fortunately, they already have a full bathroom. Thanks for reminding us that I needed a workshop, Riko."

"And a garage," Riko said.

Our Cape Cod sat back on a good-size lot with a large front lawn on both sides of the gravel driveway that led to the separate garage. Behind the house, an area of untilled soil, equal in size to the front lawn, stretched to a wooded area. *"Unser Wald,"* our forest, we called it.

The four of us took as much delight in our spacious outdoors as inside the home. Riko found the hallway, which surrounded the closed-off staircase to the upper floor and to the basement, irresistible; round and round he went, singing, "King of the wild frontier."

Through the rear entrance we stepped into a sparkling white kitchen with its metal cabinets and appliances. From the small adjoining dining room we overlooked our garden through a picture window. Next, we entered the living room, which spanned the depth of the house.

"I am pleased the previous owners left the drapes for the picture window and the four regular ones. We need to buy furniture before window treatments," I said.

The master bedroom and the bathroom with shower we reached from the hallway on the opposite side of the living room.

"I like the practical layout of the house and the full dormers to the rear. The looks from the front are deceiving. We have a lot of room," Bert said.

"Living out here, we have to face one fact, however: Our children will be bus students. Time for me to get a driver's license," I concluded.

BERT PICKED UP A BOOKLET and regulations at the Registry of Motor Vehicles for me, which I memorized with ease. Knowing that driving instructors are wife savers, Bert insisted I take lessons from a professional rather than my husband.

On the day of my test, I reported at the registry. *Oh no! I didn't know the employees wore uniforms.* The fear of Soviet troops in their uniforms, which had caused my throat to tighten as if by an iron ring, returned at the sight of my examiner. He became suspicious when, with my excellent vision, I detected early the small mirror that he passed by my head from back to front. In the oral test, I quoted the called-for answers verbatim from the booklet. Surprised, the officer asked me more questions than he had other applicants before me.

By the time we entered the car, I was shaking so severely I could not control my knees, let alone the clutch.

"I think you should practice a little more and come back in a week," the examiner said.

The iron band around my neck remained for several days. I had to live down my failure.

"You'll be all right next time," Bert said. "Now you know about the uniform. Your driving is just fine." He was right.

*   *   *

EITEL YENS WAS BORN on October 14, 1959. Our ten-pound bundle had kept us waiting for three weeks; he looked and acted that age. There was not a wrinkle in his face; for the first two days he cried until exhaustion forced him to nap.

"After a thorough examination of your not-so-little fellow I believe he's demanding more food," Merle said. "Let's add some cereal to his milk. Cut a slightly bigger hole into the nipple of his bottle."

We tried that without success. On the third day, Merle suggested I feed Eitel with a tiny spoon. "We can't increase the quantity; so let's increase the quality."

I was afraid Eitel might choke, but he knew from the first spoonful how to eat and swallow.

*   *   *

IN THE SPRING OF 1960, Bert and I applied for citizenship. We prepared for our test by studying the papers we received from the U.S. Immigration and Naturalization Service. They included basic information about the government and the "Fourteen Do's and Don'ts of the American Flag."

My sample of the reading test was predictive, "At eight o'clock in the morning, I go to school and..." The friendly examiner cut me off, "I see you know English." We passed.

In June, Bert and I became Naturalized Citizens of the United States of America. Veit was included in this procedure with the provision that, when he became of age, he agreed with his parents' action.

The Ingrahams and friends surprised us with a Red White and Blue party at the Yankee Peddler Inn in Northampton, Massachusetts, to celebrate our milestone.

*   *   *

AS U.S. CITIZENS, we could sponsor Mutti and Vati for immigration. The war and post-war efforts to make a living caused Vati immense stress.

"Unless you slow down your current pace and stop smoking cigars, you have two months to live," his physician said at Vati's reluctant office visit.

My parents had expressed a desire to join us in their retirement years. They missed seeing their grandchildren grow up. The doctor's diagnosis, though, was unexpected. Vati hesitated.

"I'm fifty-three. My knowledge of English is minimal. What can I do over there?"

"We'll have to find out what opportunities we may have. While waiting for our visas, I'll take cosmetology courses," Mutti determined. At forty-nine she could expect many years of work.

Many European women practiced routine facial care using cosmetics; some visited salons weekly for treatment by certified cosmetologists. Through exposure to Elizbeth Arden's, German and other well-known beauty products, Mutti assumed that American women equally strove for a wrinkle-free, youthful look. She traveled to leading spas in Baden-Baden, Paris, and Vienna to study and obtain certification as a qualified cosmetologist.

Vati sold his business. Together, he and Mutti closed the German chapter of their lives. In Greenfield, my father joined Bert in the prep department of the printing company.

When Mutti wanted to pursue her occupational plan, she learned of the Massachusetts law, which required cosmetologists to hold certificates as hairdressers. Undaunted, she worked as a laborer for a paper company to earn money for tuition at a hairdresser school. Following that training, Mutti had to apply her acquired skills for one thousand hours in beauty salons.

During these years of preparation, my parents realized they needed to move to a city to attract sufficient clientele for Mutti's business. They bought a house in Holyoke, where Mutti opened "La Belle Femme."

Vati commuted daily north on I-95 to Greenfield, a distance of 30 miles. At night he returned to their home around which he created a showpiece garden.

*　　　*　　　*

I WAS HAPPY IN MY ROLE as a full-time mother and wife. Observing our children's growing interest and discoveries in their surroundings, their eagerness to meet new playmates, and their delight in books and crafts were my reward for doing the daily household chores.

After work and after dinner, Bert spent hours finishing his correspondence course with Art Instruction, Inc. Veit and Riko often sat silently nearby. "We are drawing, too," Riko said. "Cowboys and Indians."

We dedicated weekends to home improvements. The two older boys handed Bert tools as requested and liked to use the measuring tape. I was concerned with steadying the ladder. Eitel made more noise with his wooden hammer as he pounded colorful pegs and squares into his little workbench than the rest of us doing "real" work.

In the garden, too, we worked as a family.

"Today, Vati and I will turn the soil. Do you boys want to have a place where you can dig and operate your construction toys and John Deere equipment?" I asked.

"*Ja*, but can I also plant some flowers?" Veit asked in return.

"Gladly. You can help us prepare the beds later."

"What beds?"

"Beds for the seeds and plants we want to drop in. You measure the width of each bed, allowing for a path between them; then drive in a small stake at each end and fasten a string from one to the other. That will give you straight lines for the beds as well as the paths and rows."

"That's a lot of work," Veit said. He dropped his head, unsure he wanted to give up that much playtime.

"We'll not do it all in one day." I tousled his hair. "We'll call you when we're ready for the first two beds."

ONE SUNNY, WARM DAY in the late spring of 1961 I was feeding twenty-month-old Eitel his noon meal when Bert came home for lunch as he did every weekday.

"Hello, teacher," he said and kissed me. A wide smile lit up his face.

"Daddy, Daddy!" Eitel lifted his arms toward Bert.

"Hi, big boy, I didn't forget you." Bert bent over to take Eitel's hands. "Hmm, your chicken soup looks and smells good. Finish it, and we'll go for a walk."

"What did you call me?" I asked Bert.

"Teacher. I received a call this morning from Larry Cox, a guidance counselor at the high school. He also teaches two sections of German to interested students. Recently he agreed to establish a high school guidance department for the dependents of the U.S. military in Tokyo."

"And?"

"Mr. Cox's assignment is for one year. He asked me if I would consent to your teaching German at Greenfield High School for that time." Bert grinned; he anticipated my reaction.

"He what?" I asked, eyes blazing. "Is anybody going to ask my opinion? Do husbands in America make unilateral decisions about the welfare of their families?"

"Simmer down. I, too, was surprised at his approach and assured Mr.Cox I'd let him know the outcome of our deliberations."

"Daddy, all done." Eitel reminded his father of his promise and clambered out of his converted high chair. By unhinging the top of the chair and folding it over, turning the entire contraption upside down, it became a low seat that faced the platform, which then served as a table.

We, too, had finished our soup and sandwich. Bert thanked me, raised Eitel into his arms and suggested we enjoy a few minutes of sunshine in our budding garden.

AS I LOOKED AT BERT patting Eitel's cheek, and scanned our hard-earned property, I was aware of the drastic changes our family had to make if I were to accept the opportunity to grow personally and to gain insight into the school system that educated our children. *Can we adjust to the upheaval of the boys', Bert's, and my routine without hurting any of us?*

"Do you believe I'm up to the task of teaching teenagers of a culture in which I didn't grow up? Will we understand each other? And how will the professional staff react to my lack of an advanced liberal arts education?"

"If I doubted your capabilities we would not have this discussion. Through Merle, Mr. Cox ascertained information concerning your background; he based his considerations on that," Bert said.

"Will I be able to handle two jobs, household and teaching? We would need a babysitter. And a second car."

"You want to try it then? We have three months before the school year starts in September, time to make the necessary arrangements."

I took a deep breath and asked my enthusiastic partner, "Will you help me keep the family grounded?"

"What a question! Haven't we worked as a team to get this far?" Bert sat Eitel down and hugged me. "And now I have to return to work."

MR. COX INVITED OUR FAMILY for the following Saturday to go on a sight-seeing ride through Franklin County in his spacious convertible. *Was it a Lincoln?* He engaged the children by pointing at and identifying red and green maple trees, cattle breeds grazing in the meadows, and cats guarding their barns.

Merle had prepared us for the encounter with this unassuming, brilliant man who had studied at Duke, Harvard and in China, spoke the two major Chinese dialects, as well as German, French, and Spanish.

In the passenger seat, I curled my arm around Riko. While driving, Larry Cox turned his attention occasionally to me. I noticed how his high brow arched over his discerning, steel-blue eyes. The facial features were nearly symmetrical. With his self-assured but friendly demeanor, he replaced the awe I felt for his achievements with trust in my abilities.

"And here we are at the Indian monument," Mr. Cox said outside Charlemont, on the Mohawk Trail. "Boys, would you like to walk around it and read the different American tribes' names inscribed on the stone plaques? Many tribes send representatives to the annual powwows here."

Veit and Riko each took a hand of Eitel's and led him close to the tall Indian statue. Bert and I strolled alongside Larry Cox through the memorial grounds.

"I'm glad you are willing to fill in at Greenfield High School for me this year," he said. "Your students will welcome a native German teacher. Greenfield's population includes a good number of German immigrants and their descendants. Local schools should reflect in their curriculum the people they are serving."

"Thank you for your confidence in me. I shall do my best to deserve it," I said, looking up at the slender man.

"Could you meet with our acting superintendent Robert Casey on Monday? Upon my recommendation, he will interview you to take the necessary steps for your employment."

"Yes. Mr. Casey can call me."

"You will like his easy and reassuring manner," Larry Cox said. "Now, if your sons are ready to go back, we can leave."

After that meeting, I didn't see the accomplished gentleman for two years.

AT THE SUPERINTENDENT'S OFFICE, I presented my U.S. citizenship certificate and my German diplomas before I filled out a teacher's application form.

"With these documents we can ask for a state waiver for you. Because we could not find a teacher for only one year's employment and were fortunate to have you agree to help us out, the Massachusetts State Department of Education will not deny us," Bob Casey said.

Before school opened in September, the Metzroths had to engage a babysitter, buy a second car and, most importantly, prepare our sons for the impending changes.

A 1955 YELLOW PACKARD with black roof and trim was distinct from other used cars in appearance and quality. The technological improvements over our previous second-hand cars included electric windows and also automatic shift and level adjustment. The black interior was in impeccable condition.

We bought this royal coach and made it available to our friend and former Pond Street neighbor, Honey Peterson, the middle-aged favorite of our children. She volunteered to take care of Eitel during the day and of his brothers after school until we found help who would also prepare dinner. Every school day, Honey took the car to her house after I returned from work. On her arrival in the morning, I drove the Packard to school.

Veit and Riko were excited that Mutti was a teacher. Eitel looked forward to playing with Honey.

ON TUESDAY AFTER LABOR DAY I reported at Greenfield High School, GHS, for my first day of school in America. I was as scared as a five-year old leaving the snug nest of her family. Bob Casey met me at the school's main entrance and introduced me to the principal, Charles Bybee, a man of medium height who appeared ill at ease.

"Hello, welcome to our school," he said. "You come with high recommendations from Larry Cox. Let me guide you to the cafeteria where all staff members of the Greenfield School System are assembled for a meeting with the new superintendent, Dr. Downie.

"Here is a group of high school teachers: Gertrude Studer from the English department, Dora Garbose teaches French, and Eleanor Finnin, business," Mr. Bybee said. "Ladies, please meet Almut Metzroth. She will teach German this year. I will see you all later."

These women look so venerable. Are there any my age?

"Good morning," Mrs. Studer said, putting down her coffee cup. "It's nice to meet you. Would you like to sit with us?" She pulled out a chair to her left. True to the reputation of Germans as handshakers, I extended my hand to my three new colleagues.

"Where did you go to school?" Mrs. Studer asked. "I went to Middlebury."

Uh- oh! That's what I was afraid of: my lack of degrees.

"I studied English in Germany," I said.

From the podium, Bob Casey, asked for our attention. I was saved for the moment from further questions by the venerable three.

"Just in time for the beginning of the 1961-62 academic year, Greenfield has filled all vacant positions on our professional roster. I am pleased to introduce you to Dr.Downie who in turn will ask you to welcome to Greenfield the new additions to our faculty."

"Greenfield's institutional achievements, its proximity to academic institutions, and its healthy economic base attracted me to the town," Dr. Downie said. "These advantages are supported by your excellent teaching staff, which will be enriched by a new class of enthusiastic professionals."

F O L L O W I N G   T H E   M E E T I N G, only the high school teachers remained in the cafeteria and regrouped.

"Hello, Almut, I am Ellen Pierce, the local Roman pedagogue," she said. "Welcome to the foreign language department. Would you like to join me on my march to the coffee urn?"

"Yes, thank you. You must be popular with your students if you conduct classes with humor," I said. "Where I come from, Latin teachers did little to enliven their dead language." Encouraged by Miss Pierce's cheerful disposition, I slipped in the disagreeable adjective.

She smiled. "Watch out! I might just send my legions up the Rhine River to your door! And, call me Ellen."

I knew I had made a friend to whom I could go for assistance. Ellen was one of the five female teachers who were part of the faculty at GHS with between thirty and forty years of service to the school. Only Ellen, besides Margaret Lawler in the English department, reached their students in entertaining ways while drilling them on grammar and exploring literature. No surprise then that they had the largest enrollment despite administrative efforts to even out class sizes.

I was not brought up to call my grey-haired elders, as I perceived these esteemed colleagues to be, by their first names. Foreign language teachers understood my hesitancy from the study of the respective cultures. Others, though, reminded me repeatedly, "You live in America now. We address fellow workers by their given names. Relax!"

Inhaling the aroma of the coffee, I carried my cup, a small danish, and a napkin to an empty seat at the first row of tables, which Ellen had suggested. While she greeted a history teacher, I sat back to look closer at the person whose sparkling eyes behind unframed glasses had welcomed me. Her facial expressions and slightly forward-bent posture assured her interlocutor of her full attention. With slender hands she punctuated her statements.

"Almut, meet Howard Boucher. I hear he lives on your street."

"Good morning, ladies and gentlemen!" Charles Bybee said, interrupting my brief encounter with my neighbor. "I know that you are eager to see your class lists and to prepare your classrooms for tomorrow's invasion. Today, our office staff will assist you whenever possible. By Monday, all of us will have a clearer picture of needed improvements in academic areas as well as the physical plant. I have scheduled a meeting for Monday at three o'clock in the library. Thank you."

Betty Nee, the office factotum in the noblest sense, stood behind a long table at the cafeteria exit and handed each teacher a folder with student roster, both a teacher's and a student's handbook, a list of special seating requirements and samples of various forms.

"Mrs. Metzroth, German, Room 103," I read on my yellow container. *Looks so official.* The doubts I had expressed to Bert returned.

"Deep in thought?" a friendly voice asked as teachers walked along the corridor to their rooms. "I am Ross Burns. I teach Chemistry and Physics. My lab is across the hall from your classroom." We shook hands. My new neighbor smiled, "Holler when you need questions answered."

"Thank you. I'm sure I'll have many of those," I said and raised my eyes to the soft-spoken man. His manner emphasized the sincere offer. "This is a beautiful building; it let's the sunshine in," I added as we passed the glass-enclosed courtyard.

"Yes, the modern design sets it apart from our old high school. We are aware, though, of some disadvantages these ceiling-to-floor glass panels present. In time you'll discover them," Ross said. "Here we are: your classroom on the right and mine on the left. Don't work too hard. Save some energy for tomorrow."

W H E N   I   E N T E R E D the spacious room 103, I counted twenty-eight student desks. They faced mine, behind which a green chalkboard adjoined a bulletin board on the north wall. A second chalkboard and bulletin board covered the length of the wall to the student's right. To their left, a window front from ceiling to counter height admitted daylight. Below the room-length counter were the book stacks, protected by sliding peg-board doors.

I was relieved to see that the textbooks Larry Cox suggested rested in their delivery cartons on top of the rectangular table next to my grey metal desk.

While inserting a book receipt into as many student texts as I needed to hand out according to my class lists, I snuck a peek inside *A First Course in German.* "Oh no!" I said aloud when I realized the German lessons were all printed in *Fraktur,* an ornate type of printed German resembling Gothic lettering. I checked the copyright: 1952, and 1953 for the *Second Course in German.* I shook my head and wondered whether Larry Cox was as detached from post-war development in Germany as his inquiry about my availability indicated. German books had not featured the archaic lettering for years. Knowledge of it abroad is shared mainly by researchers.

I decided to take a copy of each home to prepare my approach to teaching from these books. *Back to work!*

"Hello, Almut. I am Jessie Brown," said the white-haired lady entering my room. "I teach home economics and have taken care of this homeroom in the past. You probably have so many things to learn that the administration spared you this assignment."

"Hello. I am pleased to meet you," I said. "What do you do in homeroom?"

She explained the routine to me. "Most days I take attendance and read a Bible selection. The students also listen to daily announcements on the intercom. Seniors whose last names start the alphabetical order report to Room 101. This order continues in this room and so on down the corridor."

"And on the first day of school?" I asked.

"Tomorrow, students will receive their schedules in homerooms. They copy those on the two cards you placed on their desks, one for the office, one to keep. If we have time left, we look at their handbooks and point out changes from last year, if any."

"During that time, I think I'll take a walk throughout the building to familiarize myself with the location of the departments," I said. "Mrs. Brown, could you tell me what to do with all these new pencils, the reams of paper, and the two boxes of tissues?"

"You put one pencil on each desk and store the others until needed. The paper and the tissues are for the use of the students. I'd place them on the table." Mrs. Brown looked at me, her face a picture in watercolors: sky-blue eyes under a shapely brow, rosy cheeks on a pale canvas, and a full mouth primed with lipstick. "Don't schools in Germany provide those materials?" she asked.

"No, parents supply those for their children. I wondered for a long time why our children never wanted to buy notebooks to use in school."

"They will want some of those in junior high."

With those words and a sneeze she pulled open the desk drawers. "I'll consolidate my papers and belongings in two drawers so that you'll have room for yours. And, Almut, call me Jessie."

"Gesundheit," I said in perfect German and added, "I'll try, Jessie."

I returned to decorating the bulletin boards. In the front of the room I pinned up a colored map of Germany, issued by the *Deutsche Bundesbahn,* the German Federal Railroad. Bert had lettered *Guten Morgen* on one banner and *Guten Tag* on another, which I fastened across two corners of the map. On the bulletin board near the door, the sign read, "*Auf Wiedersehen!* over black, red, and golden-yellow construction paper, representing the colors of the German flag.

Jessie and I finished our chores at the same time. "Good luck, tomorrow," she said. "Remember: We are here to help you."

"Thank you. I admit, I am nervous about meeting my students. But now my family awaits my report. Our two older boys are anxious about their new teachers; especially Riko, who will enter first grade."

A S I P A R K E D T H E P A C K A R D in the driveway, our sons ran toward me. "How was it, Mutti? Do you like your school? Do you have a nice room? Did you eat a hot lunch?"

"Hi, boys. Yes, I like my school and the teachers. You can visit my room soon." I laughed, "I forgot to eat lunch, didn't even notice that until you mentioned it."

"Were you so overwhelmed by the new experience that you didn't listen to your stomach?" Honey asked.

"I suppose so, and worried I would not finish the necessary preparations."

"Your kids were good but restless. They, too, are trying to adjust."

"Can't wait to go to school with Veit," Riko said.

"You won't see much of me, other than on the bus where the big guys sit in the back."

"Oh." Riko was disappointed. He thought he was one of the big boys, now that kindergarten was behind him.

A F T E R D I N N E R , I showed my family the two texts from which I would teach. "Look at the print," I said. "The German II class is probably used to it. But for the three full German I sections

I'll need to show a lot of enthusiasm and encouragement to help the students over the initial hurdle."

"Are the dialogues appropriate for teenagers?" Bert asked. *"Eins und eins ist ..."*

"Zwei," Eitel called out jubilantly.

"I can do that," Riko added his voice.

"That's right, one and one is two." I caressed Eitel's cheek and patted Riko's arm.

"I am all for quick immersion into the language but not with childish examples. I'll adjust the exercises to the students' ages; do some arithmetic and introduce measurements," I said.

"Good idea," Bert agreed. "But now, let's catch a few balls before hitting the shower or bathtub. You want to shine tomorrow, don't you, guys?"

U N D E R   B L U E   S K I E S, with temperatures that promised a summer day, youngsters walked to school in first-day outfits; school buses with their noisy cargo rolled toward their destinations.

"Good morning, Mrs. Brown," I said as I deposited my briefcase in the small closet next to the door of Room 103.

"Good morning, Almut." She smiled. "You forgot! The next time you call me Mrs. Brown it will cost you a dime."

"I am sorry, Jessie. Bad timing to start the school year with a faulty memory, isn't it?"

"You'll be all right. Soon you'll establish a routine. Stick to it so your students know what you expect of them."

"Good advice. Thank you. I'll see you after homeroom."

M Y   C L A S S R O O M was near the student entrance. A steady stream of laughing, seemingly carefree sixteen-to-eighteen-year olds greeted each other on the way to their homerooms.

Printouts posted on the glass panels next to the doors listed student's names assigned to the respective rooms.

On the way to the office I was swept along the hallway. "Who is that?" I caught a question near me. "A new teacher?"

"Or an intern? Or a sub?"

"We'll find out soon enough."

The fragrances of freshly scrubbed bodies and lotions of personal grooming, together with those of new clothes, were never again as strong during the months of the school year. Usually, odors of anti-bacterial cleaning agents pervaded the building. *Not a bad sign, though.*

I picked up revised class lists from my mailbox and went on a get-acquainted stroll through the two-story building.

This walk allowed me to think about my planned strategies one more time. I decided to address my students in the so-called German polite form of dealing with second persons. From my school days in Germany I remembered the awkward but proud feeling of being treated as an adult. Often the same teachers who had addressed us with *du,* the familiar form, before the short Easter vacation switched to *Sie* at the sixth level of high school after Easter.

M Y N E R V E S D E M A N D E D a visit to the bathroom before the bell announced the end of the extended homeroom period.

When the students poured out of my classroom I stood aside.

"I can't believe I have the same math teacher again," one girl complained. "I'm going to Guidance and make a change."

"Good luck. They'll give you an appointment," a boy remarked.

"Okay, the room is yours," Jessie said to me. "I'll see you at lunch."

Here we go. I braced myself for the imminent evaluation by my charges. Moving to the inside of the door, I fielded first questions. "Is this the German classroom?"

"Yes. Come right in."

"Are you the teacher?"

"Yes," I said and nodded. "Find a seat you like."

"She doesn't assign seats," a boy of fullback stature said over his shoulder to a lanky classmate. They chortled. Of course, they chose adjoining seats in the last row. Now the word was out and the competition for preferred desks became lively.

Because of homogeneous grouping, this German I class consisted of about twenty-five gifted tenth-graders who settled down quickly after the bell rang.

"Mein Name ist Frau Metzroth," I said and pointed at the board where I had printed my name. *"Und Ihr Name ist?"* I addressed the girl in the third seat of the window row.

"Lizzy Munson," she answered.

"Guten Morgen, Lizzi." Looking at the class and making a sweeping motion with my arms to include all students before me, I repeated, *"Guten Morgen!"*

The response came slowly. After several repetitions I handed out the texts. "Please fill out the book receipts."

That task completed, the students passed the yellow slips to the front and perused their books. "I can't read this," one whispered. "Me neither," another responded.

"Before this shortened class period ends, open your books to page two where you see the German alphabet in Gothic print as well as in Roman letters, with which you are familiar. The third column shows how to pronounce the alphabet in German.

"Your assignment for tomorrow will be to acquaint yourself with that table. To get started, let's practice the pronunciation."

I was pleased with the students' cooperation.

"You are doing well. I have a suggestion: I'll teach you German and you can help me with my pronunciation of English. What do you think?"

"Well … okay," a timid voice relented.

"What's harder?" a wiseguy quipped.

Ah, the lanky boy. Is he the class clown?

"It's a deal," another young man said, getting bolder. "It's going to be a job."

"We'll see how well you do…in both jobs," I reacted.

THE GERMAN II STUDENTS entered my room second period. Talkative, they chose the seats they occupied the previous year, I gathered.

After taking attendance, I tried to involve my "advanced" students in a German conversation; greeting them with phrases used when meeting people; asking how they spent their summer vacation.

These juniors and seniors offered only embarrassed giggles and questioning looks at their neighbors. Suddenly a brave soul, Nancy, said, *"Wir verstehen nicht. Zu schnell."*

"You don't understand me because I speak too fast?" I asked.

Encouraged by my returning to English, several students spoke up and explained the situation. "We never practiced much oral work. Mr. Cox could not always meet with us when he was needed in the guidance department. So we had lots of written assignments–translations, you know?"

"But you can read the Gothic letters in the texts?"

"Yeah. We'll have to get back into it," Charlie suggested.

"Good. Take these books, then," I said.

They looked at the German II texts. "We can't do this work," John hesitated before adding, "We didn't get through half of *A First Course in German.*"

"Hmm," I pondered, "Let me find out how many of these books I need for German I. Perhaps we'll have enough for you to study the grammar lessons and enable you to use the texts meant for your level. Using last year's notes, please review the conjugations of *haben* and *sein,* to have and to be, as well as numerals from one to fifty for tomorrow."

"I don't think I kept any notes," Butch said with an air of nobody-told-me-to.

If he signed up for German II, how can he not save his notes?

"Come back after school. I'll prepare a ditto with the basics for you."

"I have football practice after school."

"The sheets will be ready. You can drop in and pick one up on your way to practice," I said.

"Jawohl, Herr General!"

"Dismissed," I said, surprising our football captain by echoing his military jargon. To my luck, the bell rang just in time.

P H E W ! L U N C H T I M E for the ground floor. *I can use a break.*

Cafeteria personnel set up hot meals buffet-style in the teachers' lounge. The aroma emanating from the food in the stainless steel containers filled the room. I carried my tray to a table for four and stopped at the available seat.

"May I join you?" I asked.

"Please," said the young, blonde woman. "I am Lynn and teach biology. I was new here last year. When I sat down to my first lunch, Mr. Cox asked me immediately, 'Do you prefer Bach or Beethoven?' I nearly choked on my first bite and thought, 'How about André Previn?' "

We laughed. "That describes Larry Cox," Eleanor Finnin said. "Do you like classical music, Almut?"

"I grew up listening to it. Because of the war, instruments were hard to find, I never had lessons. As soon as I heard American jazz I became a fan."

"This stew is tasty. The kitchen crew is starting the year right," the math teacher to my left said. "I hope they keep up the good work."

"Oops! Look at the time. I better leave to meet two more classes," I said.

T H E P E R I O D 3 A N D 4 G E R M A N 1 sections included students of all three high school classes. Juniors and seniors demonstrated their superiority by being loud. Sophomores were eager to have class started. To manage these groups with the older students' attempts at interrupting and diverting the subject at hand presented challenges.

"Settle down. To make this a successful year let's keep our aim in mind. By the end of this school year you are expected to express yourselves in elementary German. To that end, we report here to work, prepared. Together we can reach our goal," I stated.

When I stood at my door and said, *"Auf Wiedersehen!"* to the last group of the day, I felt bathed in sweat and hoped that it didn't show. *An entire year of this tension? Can I keep this up?*

*   *   *

OUR SONS EAGERLY AWAITED my return home that afternoon. Riko ran toward me, waving our afternoon newspaper above his head.

"See here, Mom! I'm in the paper." *Oh, it's Mom now instead of Mutti after one day in first grade and befitting an American boy.* "A man came to kindergarten last year and took my picture."

In the photograph, Riko sat on the floor among stacked-up textbooks he would be expected to study before graduating from high school.

I looked at the photo. "You appear pleased being surrounded by books. They don't scare you, do they? It's a good thing you like to read."

"Yeah, all of those in two years," Veit teased.

"Really, Mom?" Riko's face expressed concern.

"No," I said and nodded toward Veit to ease Riko's worry. "Ask your brother how many of the titles he recognizes because he studied the lessons of the books."

Riko turned toward Veit, "How many?"

"After this year, probably half. Right, Mom?" Veit said as he sought to impress our first grader.

"Perhaps." I handed Veit my briefcase and scooped up Eitel, who pulled on my skirt to gain attention. Honey Peterson was ready to leave.

"How did Greenfield's teenagers treat you?" she asked me.

"With circumspection," I said. "The feeling was mutual."

"What was most difficult?"

256

"Trying to take attendance and pronounce the students' names without causing uncontrollable laughter."

Honey looked puzzled. "What's so hard about that?"

"I didn't know whether the French and Polish surnames frequently found in Franklin County retained their native pronounciation or became Americanized. So I learned that Dupuis was read 'Dippy'; Dubois, 'Deboy'…until I met cousins of those students. Their pronunciation might vary again. And when I sounded the *ow* combination in Helstowski the European way, *Helstovski,* a boy objected, 'I'm not Russian. I am Polish!'"

"Do you speak Polish?" I asked.

"No, only my father does. My mother is Irish," he explained.

"Just call him Ski; we all do," his neighbor suggested.

"Yes, people have a lot of ethnic pride." Honey said. "Years ago, immigrants gave support to each other in their neighborhoods and founded social clubs. You find the Polish-American Club in Greenfield and the (German) Turnverein across the river in Turners Falls."

"I wonder whether any pupil or student learned as much on the first day of school as this teacher did," I said as I gave Honey the keys to the Packard.

"See you tomorrow." Honey waved goodbye to the boys and me.

*   *   *

JESSIE BROWN WAS RIGHT: An orderly routine moves work forward. Some of my students, notably the German II class, were not thrilled to be held accountable for their daily preparation. Only five young people in that group had clear, professional goals; the others took their time to convert from their previous habits of neglecting homework. To cover up their omissions they tried to distract teacher and classmates.

"What I was wondering," Bill drawled one day, hoping to waste time, "Do they have washing machines in Germany?"

257

"No, women beat their laundry against rocks in the river," I blurted out.

"Really?" was Bill's reaction. Others giggled, "Where have you been?"

Before losing control of the class, I apologized. "I did not mean to be facetious. Sixteen years after World War II, West Germany produces many machines and articles that are competitive in world trade.

"The next time we discuss social and economic issues again, we'll shine a light on the German *Wirtschaftswunder,* the economic miracle. Let's plan that for next Tuesday. Your assignment for that day—write it down—is to research the term; take notes. Also, check advertisements for German products, such as washers, cars, and more. Clip the ads if possible. We'll create a bulletin board display.

"All right. Back to our conversation in German about the calendar, the seasons, and the weather. Don't forget: quiz tomorrow."

B Y   T H E   T I M E the German I class reported after lunch, the *Frau's* momentary loss of patience was well known among the high school population. What would be the consequences?

I worried needlessly. Students, faculty, and administrators probably forgave me my first breach of good manners at GHS. *What a lesson! I won't allow that to happen again.*

*   *   *

"W H E R E   I S   G E R M A N Y ?" A German I student called out loud after I mentioned other countries and areas where people spoke German.

"Are you serious? You don't know that?" a boy sitting beside the questioner asked.

"Don't be judgmental. I'm sure Joe is not the only one who needs that question answered. I'll ask the Social Studies Department to lend us a wall map of Europe," I said.

Howard Boucher, the department head, did more than help us out with a map. "Your department must have money left in this year's budget. Perhaps you can order instructional items you need," he suggested.

"But we don't have anyone in charge. Who can make those decisions?"

"Here are some catalogs. When you find in them material that will enrich your students' learning, ask the principal for the money available to your department and for permission to order items."

Following Howard's advice, I took the necessary steps to obtain two up-to-date wall maps of the divided Germany and her adjoining countries, one map showing the geophysical features and the other indicating political boundaries, both with German titles.

When my fellow foreign language teachers saw my acquisitions, they immediately voiced needs. "Because we don't have a chairperson, the administration ordered our texts. Having taught here for decades we have relied on our stock of teaching aids. But we'd like some slides of modern street scenes of our target countries," the French teacher said.

"The office has foreign language catalogs," I informed my colleagues.

"Yes, we know. But you have just been through the ordering process. Would you mind filling out the forms for us?"

I stared, probably open-mouthed, at my esteemed fellow trilinguists. Should I, the novice in the U.S. school system, feel trusted, honored and accepted, or used?

"All r-right," I stammered. "Mark in the catalogs the titles and indicate quantities before you hand me your requests, please."

And all this developed from Joe's inquiring about Germany's place on our planet.

*   *   *

THE METZROTH FAMILY adjusted well to the extra tasks we had to perform. When we located a babysitter who would eat

259

the evening meal with us, Bert needed to provide transportation for Mrs. Snyder before work and after dinner.

The petite, elderly woman played the role of grandmother for our children. They adored her and she loved them. Keenly aware of the boys' talents and skills, she presented Eitel with animal figures, Riko with coloring books and crayons, and Veit with a chemistry set for their respective birthdays. Naturally, we restricted Veit to carrying out experiments on weekends only. In school, Veit, Riko, and I made good progress.

My students learned that I checked their assignments daily and recorded them in the back of my plan book. If I collected their work, I returned it the next day. The same was true for quizzes and, depending on their lengths, for tests. I could not afford to fall behind.

The gifted German I section surprised me in a positive way. More than half of the students' grades for written work were of A quality; seldom did any of them receive a C. At the time teachers had to determine first-quarter grades, I showed Ross Burns my marking sheet: eighteen A's, the rest B's.

"I can't grade this class on the bell curve," I said.

He looked at the names, then showed me his grades for this group. "The same A students. This class of '64 is remarkable."

"It's enjoyable to teach them. I don't have to repeat myself in that class."

THE OTHER THREE SECTIONS, however, presented challenges every day. With them I kept my resolve: don't smile much for the first six weeks. In German II, I created two groups and placed the five responsible students in the southeast corner of the room. They were destined for German III the following year. During half of the period I drilled on oral work with one group and assigned written exercises or homework to the other. Bill still made questionable observations, "Past participles? We don't have those in English, do we?"

"Yes, Bill, we do. But in English class, you students hear and forget grammatical terms because you think, 'I know how to speak English.' In a foreign language you pay attention to new patterns and sometimes," I smiled at him, "to grammar."

"Is that how you learned English?" Bill asked.

I know where this is going: Let's get the Frau off the subject, have her tell about her background.

"Yes," I said. "But before I share some of my school experiences with you, I'll write today's assignment on the board.

"Choose five of the irregular German verbs we studied today. Then use them in sentences, applying the imperfect and perfect tenses. And," I added, "be sure to hand in neat papers, written in pen rather than pencil. At your age you must rise above smudgy papers that only you can read. Moreover, neatness assures clarity. The reader will not have to guess at o, a, i, or e."

"Is that what you had to do in German schools?" Laura asked.

"Yes, again. But I don't want to convert the American school system. Instead, I suggest easier communication between you and me. It will save time and arguments."

"What about learning English?" Bill persisted.

I explained the difference between an American high school and a Lyzeum for girls and Gymnasium for boys.

"In my first year, at age ten, I began my English lessons as prescribed by the school's curriculum. Obviously, the teaching approach for that age group is different from one for teenagers."

"Why should it be?" Butch wanted to know.

"Because ten-year olds have yet to learn the details of grammar that you have mastered by now," I said, bestowing good will on my German II class.

"Hear, hear!" John, the future physicist, contributed from the corner of the brainy group, as their classmates called them.

"So, what was the approach?" Nancy asked.

"Memorization of sentences; putting together conversations. We liked acting them out."

"I hate memorization," Laura said. "What if I won't ever use those sentences?"

"Based on them, you learn patterns. Soon you'll have learned vocabulary that you plug into the patterns to express your thoughts."

"Can you show us?" Nancy asked.

I used the chalkboard to demonstrate examples.

"That looks like fun," the class decided. "Can we try that?"

"Sure. Do a good job with your homework. After checking your sentences tomorrow, we'll use them for pattern practice."

Phew! I hooked them: Learning looks like fun? Can't give them slack now; have to reel them in while I have their attention.

All of us were astonished when the bell rang. "Do we have short periods today?" Fred asked.

"No. It's lunchtime. You did well today. Quiz tomorrow," I said before my charges left.

The following day, my German II students individually wrote one example on the board and took suggestions for pattern changes from the class.

JUST WHEN I THOUGHT life in school and at home was harmonious; it challenged me in two events. First, the mother of my star pupil requested to meet with me after school. She made an unforgettable entrance to my room, pulling the door forcefully shut behind her.

"Mrs. Metzroth," she assailed me with words, "what have you done to my daughter?"

Rendered speechless, I looked at the well-groomed woman with ash-blonde hair. Her blue eyes seemed on fire as they penetrated mine.

"Hello, Mrs. Munson, please sit down." I pulled a chair next to my desk. "I don't understand your question."

"You gave Lizzi a B on her test. She has never had a B."

"Did you see the test?"

"Yes. She came home so upset but, initially, did not want to tell us why. Upon our insistence she revealed her poor grade and showed us her paper."

Poor grade? Poor girl! I could only imagine the pressure Lizzi's parents exerted on her.

"It took us years to bring our daughter out of her shell. Now she's being scared back into it."

"Mrs. Munson, if you had brought Lizzi's test with you, I could have explained my corrections of your daughter's mistakes to you. My comments include 'w.o. (word order)', 'sp(elling)', 'tense', and others with which the class is familiar." I waited for a reaction. When Mrs. Munson did not speak, I continued, "Lizzi is involved in several extra-curricular activities. Could it be that for once she could not find time to study for the German test?"

"I don't know. I'll ask her." She paused and then continued, "You know how competitive her class is. We always try to support Lizzy so she'll be accepted by the college of her choice."

"She'll make it," I assured this anxious mother. "She is only in tenth grade. Receiving a deserved lower grade once in a while will reinforce her desire to stay ahead of her gifted classmates."

Mrs. Munson rose to leave. She extended her hand to me. "Thank you for seeing me. I return home with a better knowledge of your good efforts. Should you have any concern about Lizzi's work, please call me." She smiled.

"I will," I said, taking her hand and holding the door open for Mrs. Munson's exit.

My first parent-teacher conference left me drained. I gathered my paperwork and headed home, where my happy bunch welcomed me.

T H E S E C O N D U N N E R V I N G I N C I D E N T during my early teaching days also took place after the end of a school day. Again I sat behind my desk correcting students' papers. Open windows and door allowed the air of a warm autumn day to waft through Room 103. Deeply involved in my task, I became startled by the door's closing. Before me stood a boy whom I saw once a week in the study period assigned to me in my room. Twisting a smile, he held a German officer's saber in his hands, palms up. With outstretched arms he moved toward my side of the desk as I rose to hasten away from him.

Images of Soviet soldiers manipulating looted sabers raced before my eyes.

"You are the German teacher. I wanted to show you what my father brought home from the war," he said, an eerie grin spreading over his face.

"Why don't you sit here?" I pointed at the student desk facing mine. "Then you can tell me about it."

The visitor followed my suggestion. I looked at the door and the glass panel to the right of it. *Why can't there be any traffic in the hall when I need help?* On the left side of the door was the telephone atop a filing cabinet.

Before I summoned courage to call the office, the boy unsheathed the saber and swung it through the air.

"See this?" he asked.

How can I not? "Yes. Does your father know you borrowed his souvenir?" I asked.

"He's dead."

"Then you should take care of it in his memory and keep it safely at home. Why don't you place it back into its scabbard now?"

"I will. But first I want to tell you…."

The tenth grader rambled on about wars and politics while I busied myself behind my desk. Occasionally, I looked at him and issued faint "Ohs" or "Ahas."

Finally I said, "I have to go to the office now and check for mail," hoping that he would not want any contact with authority.

"Yeah, I have to go, too," the intruder decided. "Bye." He left as abruptly as he had entered. Perhaps I met his need for conversation; perhaps he felt bringing a German object to a German teacher was an appropriate opener for a discussion. Whatever his reasons, I was scared enough to feel that iron ring around my neck again.

*   *   *

A S   M Y   F I R S T   Y E A R   of teaching at GHS progressed, I became more sure of my role and thus less tense in my personal life. I was amazed to realize how much I enjoyed teaching at this American school. As a student in Germany, I had observed my teachers' unquestioned methods and attitudes. Only in classes of mathematics and science did I feel as a participant in the classroom. Because of those early experiences, I had clear ideas about conducting my classes.

Of course, I slipped every so often in my good intentions— *remember washing the laundry in the river?*—but was never afraid to admit that I could not answer some of my students' questions. "Let's look it up together," I suggested when we had the resources at hand; otherwise I promised to research the problem before we met again in class.

"I never learned as much as when I taught," has been my refrain, from the time I dropped the eraser in front of the chalkboard to the day I received incorrect paychecks consecutively. Expecting helpful students to rush forward to pick up the fallen pad, I stepped aside quickly until I realized, *those days are over. Pick it up yourself.*

Aware that I was on the bottom rung of the teachers' pay scale and receiving the same amount as janitors in 1961, I believed my first two checks reflected miscalculations. When I asked the superintendent's secretary for clarification, she said in all seriousness, "I don't make mistakes." With great patience I led the woman through my earnings and deductions to let her see the errors. "I don't understand how this happened. I have never made mistakes," she mumbled, shook her head and made the adjustments.

Dealing with people in itself presents a learning experience.

*   *   *

IN THE SPRING OF 1962, Larry Cox notified Greenfield's Superintendent of Schools that the U.S. State Department wanted to retain him in Tokyo for another year.

"You have been successful with your students, Mrs. Metzroth. The anticipated enrollment for next year indicates three German I sections, two German II classes, and a level III group. Would you be willing to stay another year?" Dr. Downie asked.

"I have enjoyed my contact with the students. For such a weighty decision I'll have to consult our family council, though," I said, pleased with the offer. "May I give you our answer tomorrow?"

"That'll be fine."

MY FAMILY VOTED IN THE AFFIRMATIVE. "Eitel will be three years old next fall. He can enter The Roberts School on the Mohawk Trail." Bert turned to Eitel, "Would you like to go to school, too?"

"With Veit?"

"No, to a day school with boys and girls who are three and four years old. You can also learn to ski there. They have rope tows on the mountain behind their school," I explained.

"With Veit and Riko?"

"We can all go to Hogback on weekends," Veit said, referring to the Hogback Mountain ski area in Vermont less than an hour from Greenfield by car.

"Okay," Eitel said, returning to his wooden train set that snaked around the legs of the dining room table and a chair. He blew his metal whistle and called out, "All aboard!" copying Captain Kangaroo, whom he watched most mornings on television.

FOR THE SECOND YEAR, our superintendent obtained a state waiver for teaching requirements for me. This time it carried a condition. "The commissioner told me, 'Have her show an interest in education,' " Mr. Wright, our new superintendent said when he reported the outcome of his endeavor to me.

"What does that mean?" I asked.

266

"You are supposed to take the educational block, which means six courses, or eighteen credits, at the college level."

"How do I go about gaining admission?"

"I'll talk to Robert Vail, your new principal. Can you bring your German diplomas to my office? A federal agency will evaluate them."

"Certainly. I'll drop them off tomorrow."

"Good." We shook hands as Mr. Wright turned to leave. "And don't worry about your qualifications. You have demonstrated them. We'll put in a good word for you."

Within a week, Mr. Vail drove me to the University of Massachusetts in Amherst to meet the dean of admissions.

Mother Nature gave a party on that early summer day. She had willed the rain away and invited her helpers to toil the fertile land under the protective covers of the tobacco plants, to gather fruit from the endless rows of strawberry fields, or to water the decorative flowers near their dwellings.

"The Connecticut River valley reminds me of the countryside of my birth. I am glad we are living in New England," I said as we neared Amherst.

"Do you like the winters here, too?" Mr. Vail asked.

"Yes, better than the periods of high humidity."

Pleasant sights and light conversation barely masked my jittery nerves. I clutched my briefcase to steady them on the walk to the administration building.

The dean greeted us in his office. Less than six feet tall, he wore the professional garb of Chino slacks, a crisp white shirt topped with a bow tie. His tweed jacket with leather patches at the elbows hung over the back of a chair on this warm day. In an accommodating manner, the dean exchanged comments with us about the pressures at the end of the academic year.

"But you come here to explore solutions for the future." He steered the discussion toward my conditional waiver. "I read your superiors' recommendations. According to them, you must like teaching. I understand that Greenfield has planned a full schedule for you next year, which rules out full-time studies.

"Most definitely." I gasped at the thought.

"We could offer you a Special Student status," the dean indicated. "You would have the same obligations and privileges as our degree candidates but can take the education courses first, as the State demands. Should you decide to obtain an undergraduate degree, you would register for class status when you'll have the fulfillment of your requirements in sight. Does that sound manageable?"

Both the dean and Mr. Vail awaited my answer.

"I believe so but can only be sure when I learn to juggle and satisfy all my responsibilities." *The only thing you can give up is sleep,* my inner voice opined.

"That's right," the dean responded to my willingness to take advantage of the university's offer. "Here are forms for your application, in your case a mere formality, which will make you a member of our student body. Also, take this course schedule for the two summer semesters to get you started. Any questions?" he asked Mr. Vail and me.

"Not at this time," my principal said. "When any come up, we'll know where to look for answers."

Rising from my chair, I thanked the two men for their faith in me. "It will be a hill to climb. I have a cheering section at home, though, that has promised to help me reach the lookout."

With a golden setting sun at our back, Mr. Vail's nervous personality softened during our return trip to Greenfield. *Had he worried about the university rejecting his request?*

"Now we can plan for next year's German program with certainty," he said. "I have looked at your orders and support materials. Would you be so kind as to help your foreign language colleagues with choosing new releases of teaching aids?" he asked.

"I don't think I'd be comfortable doing that as the newest and least-educated member of the department," I said with conviction.

"Neither I nor your colleagues doubt your apprehension but would appreciate your assistance. Let me check my calendar. I'll set a date and time to meet with your department in my office and introduce the idea to your colleagues," our principal decided.

And so I came to be acting department head.

Before GHS's year ended, the first summer session at UMass began. I wrote, administered, and corrected final exams for my students during the initial two weeks of my university studies. Multi-tasking became my way of life years before the concept turned into an expression.

Our first car, 1949 Nash. Bert and Veit.

Vati and his three grandsons

CHAPTER 16

Being a Student Again

G R E E N F I E L D T E A C H E R S had a contractual obligation to earn four college credits in the span of three years. With UMass less than thirty miles away, many members of the faculty had driven on River Road or Route 5 and 10, and later on I-91 to Amherst to study for professional improvement; some called the university their alma mater. They shared rides most of the time.

Those of us who had enrolled in eight or nine o'clock classes came back to GHS to proctor the second exam of our students.

Every morning, Howard Boucher gathered his fares along the way. I learned much already from the discussions in the car, which dealt mostly with topics of our courses. Arguments became heated only when they dealt with Boston Red Sox actions at the previous game.

The School of Education sat at the north edge of the university grounds. I entered the school, a modern brick building, with trepidation. *It's been fifteen years since I left the Elisabeth-Charlotte Oberlyzeum in Bad Kreuznach. And the language of instruction was German.*

Howard noticed my hesitation as I opened the door to Dr. Anthony's room. "You can do it," he said.

270

"Welcome to History of Education," the professor greeted us. A young woman following me uttered, "Oops! Wrong class," and turned back into the hallway.

"I see we have undergrads and grads here, and one Special Student." Dr. Anthony looked at the class list. "When I call your name give me a short background sketch of your studies."

Our lanky, fortyish professor adjusted his dark-rimmed glasses and took attendance. After hearing the purpose of my presence at his lecture, he nodded and said, "Well, we can pursue a bit of comparative history. Much of our educational philosophy was based on European thought. In the twentieth century, however, American educators developed theories and plans suitable for our society."

I took copious notes in and for that class. Instead of a textbook, we had a long list of required reading. The subject for our first paper, due in three weeks, demanded of each student a desirable overhaul of our respective departments.

I had made adjustments and additions to the educational materials for my classes but never thought to revamp the German program at GHS. I considered the notion presumptuous for an interim teacher.

Accustomed to thorough research for an assignment and mindful of the title of Dr. Anthony's course I delivered my best effort to him. Anxious days followed until I held my graded paper in shaking hands. "B+" it said on the front page. "Exhaustive research but don't you have any ideas of your own?" read the comment.

That question set me free. By making improvements at my place of work I contributed to a change in the history of education. Dr. Anthony's comment could not have come at a more appropriate time: the beginning of my studies. Inhibiting caution had guided me. *Americans didn't wait for you to come over here and change their ways,* I had thought until now.

"Hello everyone!" I announced my return to our family that day. "Look what I have." Taking my brain child out of the briefcase I held it up proudly, front page facing Bert and the children.

"Weren't there any A's?" Veit asked. His face expressed doubt and disappointment. The boy who rarely received B's during his years at elementary school could not believe that his mother would do less well at her school.

"Yeah, Mom, you always tell us to do our best," Riko echoed.

Bert tried to explain to our sons the circumstances under which I performed my diverse tasks. "Mom will get A's," he assured them.

"Did you make any typos, Dad?" Veit alluded to my inability to type and Bert's second job: typing all my papers, eventually in three languages.

"Mom and I tried to correct those during repeated readings," Bert said.

Eitel took my hand and pulled me toward the living room. "I built a windmill." He pointed at the Tinker Toy tower. "I did my best," he said.

All of us laughed at his words. "Wait 'til you go to school," his big brother warned him.

"And I'll have to work for marks," I said in an aside to Bert, "Something I never believed in. Instead of Big Brother, young brothers are watching me."

"What is your eight-o'clock course like?" Bert asked.

"Like exercises in physics for which I lack the vocabulary in English. That class will require a lot of time and study. It's interesting, however, and will give me current knowledge in technology. Don't expect any A's in there for me."

Every morning, I reported to my audio-visual aids course with notebook, pencil, eraser, ruler, dividers, and protractor. True to my German schooling, I used my tools and feverishly copied Professor Wyman's diagrams from the chalkboard.

"Well, let's see what we have learned so far," Dr. Wyman said on the third day as he handed out a quiz.

A quiz at the university level? I panicked. I had counted on the German system that left processing their acquired knowledge to the students, expecting them to come prepared to their final exams. Until the end of the academic year at GHS I had no time for studying but on weekends.

I flunked the quiz, partly because I wasted precious minutes by using my tools. On the ride home my fellow summer students tried to cheer me up. "Chalk it up to another learning experience," Howard said.

Jim added, "Now you know what not to do. It was only a quiz. You'll pull up your grade."

More pressure.

AT THE END OF THE SUMMER of '62 I had accumulated twelve credits of the educational block, leaving a psychology class and student teaching for me to schedule. The first-semester psych course sections at UMass met during daytime only, so I enrolled in one in the evening at Westfield State College, about thirty miles south of Greenfield. "I'm going to make it," I said out loud as I drove home at ten o'clock once a week.

For the student teaching requirement, Dr. Thelen of UMass came to observe my teaching three times. "You obviously know what you are doing. I'll hand in your grade," he said.

Having satisfied the state's requirements, I wondered if GHS still needed me the following year.

Mr. Vail removed that doubt the day he swirled into my room in his customary hurrying way. "You're still here," he said. "It's four thirty."

"Yes, I want to correct yesterday's homework assignment before going home."

"I'm glad I caught you. Larry Cox answered our query concerning his plans. He is returning as a full-time guidance counselor. Our student enrollment has increased considerably. Are you willing to stay on as our German teacher?"

"I'd be happy to. Bert and I discussed this eventuality. We feel that our family has adjusted to my working outside the home."

"It's agreed, then. I'm going to Boston tomorrow to obtain certification for you.

"Don't stay too long and let the janitor sweep you out the room," Mr. Vail joked and hied out the door.

As I followed him with my eyes, I noticed a new sketch on the bulletin board near the door. *Another work of art by gifted John?* I rose to look at it and laughed out loud.

A popular song in the sixties was "The Sinking of the *Bismarck*," alluding to the German battleship, which planes from the British aircraft carrier *Ark Royal* and British battleships damaged in the North Atlantic. On May 26, 1941, the inoperable *Bismarck* sank.

My student John became inspired by people's comments and actions, class discussions, world events, or, in particular, by music to draw cartoons. In class he never lost track of ongoing activities and participated while doodling, as his friends called it. After class, on his way out, he would remove one of the tacks from the board to affix his latest drawing. I had missed his contribution that day.

His sketch depicted two anglers standing upright in a dinghy named *Bismarck*. Extending their fishing poles over the water, the men were singing and oblivious to the breaking up and sinking of their boat.

Teachers and students admired John for his friendly disposition, positive attitude and talents. According to his schoolmates, he played a mean sax.

"In what will you choose to major?" I asked him once.

"Probably in music and minor in art. I would like to have a syndicated cartoon strip some day," he mused, turning to look at the windows … and into the future?

JOHN WAS ONE OF THE STUDENTS who made me want to come to school every day. The bright lights among them unknowingly set examples for their peers and assured GHS of its good reputation. I hoped to be a part of the community for years to come.

The day after our principal's trip to Boston, he called me on the phone in Room 103. "Are you available to come to my office? I want to discuss the state waiver with you."

"I can meet you after lunch."

"Fine. Until then."

That sounds ominous. Two more classes before I'll find out.

When I entered Mr. Vail's sun-lit office after what had seemed too many hours, he pulled a chair up for me and sat beside me. "The criterion for teaching in Massachusetts has changed. No longer can you teach with only the educational block in your résumé. You need a bachelor's degree," he said without pausing.

"That will take years with a full teaching load," I whispered.

"Yes. It's up to you whether you want to pursue a degree. GHS would benefit from your staying with us. Moreover, you are already a student at UMass. You remember the offer the dean made last year."

"I do. I just don't know…Will Bert and our sons be ready for that long haul?" I wondered. *Time for another powwow.*

*   *   *

WITH MY FAMILY'S COOPERATION we embarked on the eight-year journey to our destination: Mom's BA in German.

Unlike the majority of college students, who begin their studies at age eighteen and think of them as four more years of school, I had one life behind me. In the early 1960s, few undergraduates were over thirty… that age being a stigma for the baby boomers. My fellow students had no problems accepting older classmates; some professors, though, acted toward older students in a disparate manner. *Do they think we should know more? Do they feel threatened?*

The enrollment process at the beginning of every semester was my biggest headache on campus. I had to select my courses according to the time they were scheduled because of my obligations to family and GHS.

"You should see the lines for signing up in the required courses," I said to Bert after returning from one registration. "There are advantages and disadvantages to being a Special Student: I don't have to take the necessary freshmen and sophomore courses in a specific order; and I can schedule German graduate classes at my convenience."

"Were you able to enroll in the European history course?"

"No. Special Students will be admitted only after registration day to be sure that history majors will have a seat. The sections may be closed tomorrow."

Over the years, nothing frustrated me more at UMass than closed sections because of my status—not that I passed all my courses without difficulty. For some of them I lacked the appropriate jargon, such as the social sciences.

"Why don't scholars of government and social scientists use the same expressions in their studies concerning the welfare of the population?" I asked Howard and Jim.

They laughed. "It takes a newcomer to our shores to point out the problem of communication our Federal agencies have," Jim said.

As in the audio-visual course, I had to learn new vocabulary for my math studies. When I heard the professor give an example containing the phrase "to the fifth power," I was confused. Power translated into German as *Kraft, Energie, Macht*, or strength, energy, might. *I better watch what he writes on the board when he uses that expression.*

At home I shared my new knowledge with our family.

"To the fifth power means *fünf hoch fünf*," I said.

"You didn't know that?" our junior high student, Veit, asked.

"What's five high five?" Riko wanted to know. To him, we had to explain the expression in reverse. "Oh," he said, turning back to his soldiers and the fort, which Opa had built for the boys on his recent visit from Germany.

BERT PUT THE FINISHING TOUCHES on a boat he built from a kit in the backyard. We could not wait for him to complete his project. I wanted more help and the boys were eager to launch our "*BRAVE.*" Veit thought up this acronym using our family members' first names.

"Will she float?" Bert asked as she separated from the submerged trailer at a nearby lake.

"Hurrah!" We shouted, laughed, and clapped applause.

"Can we board her?" Riko asked.

"Yes. Put your life vests on while I park the car and trailer," Bert said. "We'll take her for a ride along the edge of the lake."

Our *Brave* lived up to her name. She gave us years of pleasure on the Connecticut River, where Veit enjoyed water-skiing.

We spent many weekends on a sandy beach there and on French King Island, having picnics, diving off the boat and swimming in the clear, refreshing water.

Across a small channel from the island, the steep river bank invited teens to swing on ropes from mighty trees.

They wound the rope once around their body and grabbed it high above their heads. After running and pushing themselves off the ground, they clung to the rope with their feet, swinging toward the channel. When the youths cleared the edge of the bank, they freed their feet, let the rope unwind and let it go. With a cry of "Geronimo!" they dropped into the water.

All was well until one summer when Veit broke out in a rash clearly delineating the pattern of the rope all over his body from his hands to his feet: poison ivy!

Our boy was in agony. The summer heat allowed him to lie uncovered on the bottom sheet of his bed.

"Don't let the rash enter any orifice," Merle warned. "Wash his body down with water and apply calamine lotion. Give him frequent baths with Epsom salts."

Between the baths, we treated Veit as prescribed, turning him every thirty minutes, stopping only when he was able to sleep. Not to scratch took all his concentration. Teeth clenched, he crumpled the sheet in his hands.

"Why did this happen now?" he asked. We could not answer his question. Did the poison ivy invade the area only that year?

Helping Veit to overcome his suffering required twenty-four-hour care, which Bert and I shared.

I studied logic and a survey course of English literature that summer. "How am I going to pass these courses?" I asked Bert, "I can't even keep my eyes open, let alone read books, write papers, and memorize theorems."

"You have to make a decision," he answered. "What do you want to let go?"

"It's too late to drop a course. I'll attend both classes but focus on English lit. I like logic better but can't keep up with the daily assignments. I'm learning from every lecture, though."

When the grades came home, I stared at my first and only F.

"It's all right. Veit has recovered and we can go on vacation. I'll always remember the benefits of logical thinking: Know what you say; say what you mean; and mean what you say," I said to Bert.

"LANGUAGES REFLECT GEOGRAPHY, climate, history, and culture of every linguistic group," I began instructions to my eight o'clock class on a gloomy, overcast December day. "Can you name words we use in English that tell us their place of origin?"

"Bikini," Robert shouted. His face turned crimson when his classmates broke out in laughter and made pointed remarks.

"You should know," and, "Remember the Covered Bridge?" as they referred to summer fun and beach wear at one of the swimming holes at the Green River.

Infected by the joyful mood of my students, I said, "Your experience was memorable enough to state a perfect example for the lesson at hand. What other expressions come to mind?"

"Parka," Fred contributed.

"Correct. In America, people call their down-filled jackets by the name the Eskimos of the Aleutians gave their heavy jackets. As I grew up in Germany, I wore my anorak. This term stemmed from the early inhabitants of the European north."

"We baked napoleons in home ec," Betty said.

"Yummy. I love puffed pastry," came a comment from the back of the room.

"I'm glad you brought up food, which has been an important part of culture since the hunters and gatherers carried out their daily search," I said. "As we are preparing for Christmas I want to introduce you to holiday traditions of the German-speaking populations. Our Jewish students have agreed to share with us the history and customs of Hanukkah."

"Who brings the children their presents—Santa Claus?" Ed wanted to know.

"The answer to that question illustrates my initial statement about the origin of words. In southern regions, the *Christkind,* or Christchild shares gifts with children. In other areas, der *Weihnachtsmann,* literally translated as Christmas man, travels in a horse-drawn sleigh to deliver presents. His appearance differs from your Santa Claus in his stature: He is not as rotund as Jolly Old Nick; his beard is not always white as snow but has some gray hairs in. And I don't remember him smiling as jovially as Santa."

"Wouldn't he frighten children with a stern look?" Karen asked.

"In my youth, we didn't meet him at every store but saw his image in books. The mythical figure we had qualms about was *der Nikolaus.* He supposedly listened to our parents' reports about our being good or naughty."

"What was his role?" Butch asked.

"Yeah. You should worry," his buddy advised him.

"Der Nikolaus is an old, bearded, gaunt man, clothed in a dark, gray coat that touches his boots. He is the helper of the Weihnachtsmann; pictures show him walking next to his horse and holding the reins. To prepare for his visit during the night of December 5, children shined their shoes. They lined one of them with wrapping paper and inserted their *Wunschzettel,* or wish list. Before going to sleep, children placed one shoe outside their bedroom door. Nikolaus took the *Wunschzettel* to give it to the Weihnachtsmann. If the children had been good, Nikolaus filled the individual shoe with an apple, nuts, wrapped sweets and a small toy. If they needed a warning, they'd find *eine Rute,* a switch, across their shoe the next morning."

"What kind of switch?" Christine asked.

"Parents gathered thin branches autumn storms had blown off trees. They bundled them much like people had done for ages to fashion brooms," I said and turned to walk by my desk to the chalkboard.

"Starting with Jamie in the last seat at the window side and moving through the rows, every one of you name an item you want to write on your *Wunschzettel.* I'll write the German expressions on the board. Together we'll compose a list for tomorrow's quiz."

"I knew the fun couldn't last," Butch said.

"But think of the fun we'll have at our party where you can show off your German." I dangled the proverbial carrot before my class.

"A party? Does the office know about that?" my doubting charges wondered.

"Yes. I have cleared all the hurdles," *I hope all of them,* "with Mr. Vail and invited him to witness your accomplishments."

"I suppose you had to do that, huh?" Robert mused.

"Yes, again. And I expect you to make our effort a success so that we set a precedent."

"You mean for next year?"

"And the one after?"

The questions filled the room with excitement.

"What will we do?" "What about food?" "Will we have presents?"

During the following days, the students brought German family recipes to class. Also, I had them choose meals and desserts from my colorful cookbooks.

We drew names out of a bowl to find out for whom we would create a handmade present.

"I can't sew," one boy protested. "What are the guys supposed to do?"

"You remember the crafts you learned in earlier years, or in junior high shop classes, don't you? They'll be appropriate," I suggested.

Enthusiasm ran high. "Forget past participles. I never thought I'd learn useful vocabulary in German, like saw, drill, glue, and cinnamon and cookies," Bill said.

Our party filled Jessie Brown's spacious home ec kitchen with holiday spirit. The hand-crafted presents were worthy of an exhibit. Traditional holiday delicacies looked and tasted authentic; they included Rachel and Richard's contributions of strudel and blintzes.

The mandatory recitals of seasonal poems affected great glee, most notably when we listened to blond, fair-complexioned, blushing Fred, a tackle on the football team, address the imaginary Santa Claus, *"Lieber guter Weihnachtsmann ..."*

After doing the dishes, we sat around the tables and learned from Rachel to spin the dreidel in the customary game played at Hanukkah. Richard, who intended to make classical music his career, entertained us with his lute.

"So, when is the next party, Frau Metzroth?"

"That depends on your performance at the semester exams in January. As long as every one of you lives up to our posted motto, we can think of a costume party at *Karneval,* or Mardi gras."

At a student fundraiser I had bought a plastic-laminated picture that portrayed a busy squirrel gathering its winter provisions. The imprinted words "Move over for Excellence" could be read clearly from every desk, because I fastened the picture under the clock in front of the room. Students could not help but notice the poster whenever they checked the time.

*　　*　　*

M Y   O W N   S T U D I E S   P R O G R E S S E D according to plan. Although I did not have to take basic courses in German, I had to fulfill undergraduate requirements as a German major.

Like logic, the study of linguistics enriched my thinking process and stimulated my thirst for more knowledge. I found an added pleasure in that course when I discovered a familiar classmate: Susan, who was previously my student. Teachers experience great joy in their careers when they observe their former charges succeed in life; to realize some chose their mentor's field of study is humbling.

I   P E R C E I V E D   M Y   S P E C I A L   S T A T U S as a student to be more than the unlimited time I had to obtain an undergraduate degree. Life experience, maturity, and gratitude funneled my efforts toward my goal in *Sturm und Drang*-fashion.

Like the eighteenth-century German movement, I broke away from established ideas and practices. American educators gave me that freedom.

In courses of the UMass Department of German, I encountered among native German instructors attitudes I had rejected in my youth. I loathed teachers' unwillingness to admit errors and to say, "I don't know." So I sat in those courses vowing: *Don't you do that at GHS.*

The prime example for this genre of instructors was a man diminutive in stature, personality, and knowledge. As a graduate student, he had followed his *Doktorvater,* or advisor, for years to teaching appointments at different universities. In his late thirties, he became instructor of a German literature survey course. That summer, only four students enrolled: one graduate student, Beth;

282

Anita, majoring in Italian; a young man, Curly, who had just returned from a year's study in Germany; and I.

The variety of the students made this course as memorable as the instructor's antic performance.

"I'll tell you what's wrong with the world," he opened his tirades. Or, "People are unreliable. That includes my wife. I rely only on my car. But it's getting old...."

That course became a do-it-yourself project. We studied our text and readings on the reference list.

On the first day of the second summer session, three of us met to check our grades of the survey course.

"What?" I exclaimed. "He gave me a C?"

"*Ja.* Check this: the guy handed out an A for me," Beth read off the printout, "Anita got a B, and Curly, who attended classes less than fifty percent, passed with a D."

"We have to let the office know about this absurd grading," Anita said.

The department chair did not seem surprised. Beth said, "Almut taught us more over coffee in the Student Union than our instructor ever did. Even the *Sütterlin-Schrift.*"

"*Ja,* the German handwriting," Anita emphasized, "So we could read parts of early manuscripts."

"I'll look into this. Thank you for your report."

A week later my corrected grade arrived in the mail. I never ran into the instructor again as a student or a teacher.

A visiting professor from Germany also saw a problem in my attending required undergraduate courses. "I feel you have an advantage over the other students," he opined.

"Please consider that I study for thirty credits in my mother tongue and for ninety in a foreign language. This semester, for example, I take Astronomy 201. For that course I have to look up a lot of vocabulary before I can understand the subject matter," I said.

"*Alle Achtung!* Congratulations. You are right. You deserve your good grades."

My personal advisor, Bert, suggested I choose astronomy for my physical science, "...so the stars can help us with night cruising."

I enjoyed those two astronomy courses. During the first one, we students sat in the auditorium of Hasbrouck Hall, watching on television Apollo 11's approach and landing on the moon on July 20, 1964. Our young professor of renown elucidated the running commentary by NASA's mission control. The following evening we observed Neil Armstrong's memorable steps onto the lunar surface.

Having learned the needed scientific expressions, I comprehended the lectures and text better during the second course—and received an A.

"Today I'll introduce you to recent developments in radio astronomy. In the last ten years, scientists have identified stars whose emissions had earlier been too weak to detect," the lecturer said. "With improved instruments your instructor of the previous course, Dr. Dent, discovered that quasars, like pulsars, are pulsating."

"Wow. We can touch history," my lab partner, a nineteen-year-old senior, marveled. "I'm glad, I picked the right place," he added.

I N 1969, as I reached senior standing at UMass, I applied for a sabbatical leave, which the Greenfield School Committee granted. My capable intern graduated that spring from our alma mater and agreed to take over my classes at GHS so I could finish my studies.

Veit started college in Williamstown, Massachusetts, 43 miles over the Mohawk Trail, west of Greenfield. His freshman year at Williams coincided with my last semesters. Riko entered eighth grade and Eitel fourth.

*   *   *

J U B I L A T I O N over the victorious ending of WWII and the return to peaceful pursuit were interrupted by the Korean War in the early 1950s. The opposing forces signed an armistice in Pammunjon in 1953. To prevent another outbreak of hostilities, the U.S. and South Korea signed a mutual defense treaty, which requires American forces to protect the delicate truce in Korea. After a respite from turmoil in the international arena, the United States posted military advisors in South Vietnam.

The Vietnam War influenced the fabric of the American society in the 1960s. By 1964, skirmishes between North and South Vietnamese troops, and the South's U.S. supporters, escalated into full warfare. Thousands of American families had sent their men to the tropical battlefields in Indochina. American losses in troop strength through combat deaths and wounded soldiers sparked demonstrations in cities and on college campuses. The annual draft lottery caused anxiety and had the opposite of the designed effect on the population: Instead of lending support for the government policies, people shouted them down in public protests.

Greenfield High School mirrored the national unrest. Boys faced possible deployment overseas; girls shared the angst and reacted with defiance against authority. Attending school seemed a waste to teenagers.

For the first time, I mentioned to students my odysseys through high schools during wartime.

"You can't just give up and think, I'll never use any of this. Though we mourn losses, many people survive wars. You may encounter hardships not known before, like those experienced after natural disasters."

"What good would math do me?" Mary asked.

"I can see value in math and science," Tony said, "But foreign languages?"

"U.S. troops are stationed in Germany; you may be sent there. A few years ago one of my students said she wanted to learn French so she could understand French expressions on menus. Her classmates laughed at her. Today, she is married to an American officer, has lived in Germany and spent time in France. She writes cookbooks in English, having tried out and translated foreign recipes."

"What about history?" Ted queried. "Teachers always tell us we can learn from the study of the past. But do we?"

"Yeah. Look at the mess we are in," a disgruntled senior called out.

"Perhaps you'll run for office some day. Then you can make enlightened decisions based on your careful studies and your honest intentions to improve your constituents' lives," I ventured an opinion. "Now, let's continue to prepare you for future challenges. Please open your books to page 322."

"Karl der Grosse?" Tony read. "This must be about Charlemagne."

"Oh, boy. History in German yet," Nick groaned.

"Aren't you amazed at how much you can discuss without using English?" I asked.

"From now on we'll conduct all our social debates in German."

"That may be wishful thinking," Nick commented.

He was right.

S T U D E N T S   A T UMass, too, expressed their opposition to the Vietnam War, at first in isolated protests. By the spring of 1970 the majority joined the general student strike. To espouse their view, they wore white T-shirts with orange fists stenciled on them.

Shouting anti-war slogans that repeated the messages on their placards, the demonstrators caused professors to close windows during their lectures. Yet, the noise outside made it difficult to take notes in the stuffy classrooms.

During those unsettling months, the university introduced pass/fail options in its grading, which emboldened students to participate in political activities and still pass their courses.

As a senior, I felt secure enough with my grade point average to apply the new option to a course I feared taking, the Bible as literature. Due to the political climate in Germany during my youth, I had neither owned a Bible nor received religious instruction. As a language major now, I knew that profound literary works reflected in parts the writing of the Bible. I wanted that knowledge.

A young Amherst College professor had designed the course and each year attracted more students than the assigned oversize classroom could seat. But he accepted them all; and they used every inch on the sturdy window sills.

I was overwhelmed by the reading and my need to comprehend it all. My informed Jewish classmates participated in deep discourse about the Old Testament with our professor. I sat there in disbelief. *How can I absorb all of the information in one semester?*

To pass the course, students had to research a topic of their choice and base a project on the literature under study. *I can do that.* I immersed myself in books and articles, satisfying the specific desire that urged me to take the Bible course.

"That was the last hurdle," I told my family when I received my grades report.

"I'm glad. What's next?" Bert asked.

"The first course about the environment the university offers. It is open to selected seniors. A biology professor teaches it. You should see Morrill Hall inside. Green stickers greet you from the walls: Have you thanked a green plant today?"

"Mr. Card has one of those in his biology classroom," Riko said.

"Why should I thank a green plant?" Eitel wondered.

"Well, not literally." Riko laughed. In astonishingly simple terms he explained photosynthesis and the plant's interaction with the air we breathe to his younger brother.

"Foreshadowing the science major?" I whispered to Bert.

AMID AMERICANS' UNREST in 1970 over the war in Vietnam and their slow awakening to environmental concerns, I finished my undergraduate studies.

"Wouldn't you like to study for advanced degrees?" the department chair of Germanic Languages and Literature asked me when I returned reference books. "We need a person to specialize in Middle High German."

Middle High German was spoken from the eleventh to the fourteenth century. The language experienced significant enrichment during the Teutonic Order's expansion into Slavic territories in the thirteenth century, I recalled.

"This is an unexpected offer. Thank you for your confidence. Let me think it over, please."

I drove home dumfounded but elated.

In the back of my mind, I had occasionally contemplated a university career because of the schedule that would place me less in front of classes than at the high school level and allow me time to think. I liked research. The emphasis on publishing did not threaten me. *Yes, Dr. Anthony, I have many ideas of my own.*

Bert and our sons considered the news from their individual points of view. "Are you sure you can continue to carry the workload of the last several years?" Bert asked.

"Veit had you in high school. I thought you'd be there for us," Riko said, including Eitel in his concern. "You wouldn't be our German teacher. And you wouldn't see us at sports, would you?"

I looked at Riko in amazement. "I always thought my being your teacher may make you uncomfortable."

"Did Veit give you that impression?" Riko asked.

"No. As a matter of fact, he was never embarrassed when a rare 'But Mom' slipped out in discussions. In class his fellow students considered him to be one of them rather than the teacher's son."

"So, you'll stay and be our teacher, too?"

"If I go the university route, I would still be teaching at GHS until I had a master's degree. That would take two to three years. We would have no immediate changes at home. We could go on another tack when necessary."

"I guess it's up to you," Bert said, summing up the deliberations.

T H E R E L A X E D A T M O S P H E R E in German graduate courses belied the intense study and analysis of the target subjects by doctoral candidates. I delighted in the challenges and never tired of the assignments.

In the middle of October, my body signaled for attention. I had the flu. "This is not the flu season," I feebly uttered to Bert. "None of the students at GHS are absent with those symptoms."

"I called Dr. Haggett. He will meet us at the emergency room," Bert said.

While sitting in the waiting area of the ER, Dr. MacLean walked by, "Almut, is that you? You look stoned."

"Is that what it feels like?" I mumbled.

Dr. Haggett, Merle's successor, checked my vitals and sent me home with medication. "You need a rest," he advised in parting.

Helping me back into bed, Bert said with emphasis, "Something's got to give."

I could drop only one activity without interrupting our family life. Saddened, I became a grad school drop-out.

Sing-along at GHS German party in '66.
Mrs. M, Susan Borer, Roger Turton.

CHAPTER 17

Our Student Tours to Europe

MY COLLEAGUE AND FRIEND Marianne Keating had taken students from her Spanish classes to Spain in recent years. A French teacher offered visits to France. Small wonder, some of my students asked me, "Can't you show us Germany?"

When U.S. and Soviet rockets shot satellites into orbits, foreign language programs also received a big boost. The Cold War competition mobilized studies of science as well as languages.

Yet, at budget hearings we teachers of the arts and foreign tongues faced the strongest scrutiny about our financial requests.

"When I attended GHS we didn't have a language lab," a school committee member and father of three argued. "Only college-bound kids took two years of Latin or French. Now you offer five years of French, German, Spanish and two years of Latin. Can Greenfield afford that?"

As Greenfield's foreign language coordinator, I carefully suggested, "Consider how the world has changed since you went to school. America is more involved in international affairs than before. To say let others speak English is not to our advantage."

"I must admit, your programs interest a great number of students, many of whom stay for more years than colleges require," the chairman said.

"Colleges appreciate our sequential courses. GHS school seniors can now apply for acceptance as foreign language majors.

291

Earlier, only private school students had this opportunity," I pressed my point in defense of my budget requests.

"Yes, with the increased offerings in our academic areas, we don't lose many students to Deerfield Academy, Northfield-Mount Hermon and other private schools in our area," Mr. Jones, GHS principal, concurred.

"I hear you plan a student trip to Germany next April?" another committee member asked.

"You have good sources," I laughed. "When I have the itinerary worked out, I'll present it to you and request your approval."

"Why do you see a need for such travel?" the superintendent asked in an attempt to support my plan.

"When our charges study English, history, math and science, they can practice in daily life what they have learned. But who will speak German, French, or Spanish with them at this time in Greenfield? Also, despite the fact that they learn about the metric system in math, science and our programs, students have no experience in using it outside of school."

"You are right. In a global community we have to meet and understand our partners on common grounds," the chairman said. "We'll look forward to your presentation."

*   *   *

"D O Y O U R E A L I Z E you are trading the doctoral studies for a student trip to Germany?" Bert asked. "Think of all the necessary preparation."

"Hmm. I never looked at my present plans from that perspective," I reflected. "With this project, I don't feel the pressure of weekly deadlines in addition to my daily duties. On the contrary, the bubbly excitement of our prospective participants affects their classmates and me."

"Is your students' enthusiasm, and yours, backed by parents?"

"I believe so; otherwise their children would not be so excited. We'll find out the parents' sentiments in the first of monthly evening meetings I will schedule."

"Good luck. You know you have my support." Bert closed our exchange with a kiss. Leaving our den, he said, "Back to work. Finish your corrections. I'll check on the boys."

F R O M 1972 T O 1988, I designed seven biennial tours for GHS students of German as well as one student exchange with a German high school group. I based my itineraries on classroom lessons.

Over the years, the venerable foreign language teachers had retired. Young teachers who studied or traveled abroad chose books and supplementary materials of relevance to teenagers.

German I and II students "inhaled" the *Guten Tag* series, including films for every chapter. The dialogues presented every-day situations, which I had my students memorize. At a time when rote learning was not to be thought of, our beginners spouted their phrases in the halls, the cafeteria, or at other activities, *"Zu spät, zu spät!"* Too late.

"Was ist los?" What's the matter?

"Verzeihung, wo sind die Toiletten?" Excuse me. Where are the toilets?

With practical phrases imprinted on their minds, our travelers were able to ask for directions, places, and food. They could go shopping as well as express minor pains in German.

In German III, we concentrated on cultural topics, learning about the geography and history of German-speaking countries in addition to researching the influence of their famous citizens.

German IV and V students wrote personal journals, which I collected once a week to guide their self-expressions in German. We also studied the lives of writers, philosophers, and inventors with the help of level-graded booklets.

The acquired knowledge allowed my students to appreciate the sights and sounds of the countries we visited.

The following account is a composite of the student tours I led. It describes the activity leading to our travel to German-speaking countries, and to France on one occasion. Dramatized narration depicts also the impressions the countries, history, landscape, economy, and artifacts made on the participants. Cooperation developed into congeniality and affected personal growth.

Students and accompanying adults on these tours are too numerous to name. Their fictitious identities represent all who partook in our travels.

"S O, W H E R E A R E W E G O I N G , Mrs. M?" the daily questions began.

"I want to go to Munich," Alan requested. *Ins Deutsche Museum.*"

"You mean München," a friend corrected him. "Of course, you're interested in technology. Can we go to the Pinakothek, too? I like art."

More suggestions followed, "How about Switzerland? Walk in Wilhelm Tell's mountains."

"And Berlin? See the Wall?"

"Hold it!" I said to settle my students down. "Let's find out whether your parents want you to try your wings away from their nest. We'll have to explore the many issues involved in overseas travel with them. If they'll give their consent, we can finalize a plan."

A F T E R I H A D P R E S E N T E D a tentative itinerary, one father, Mr. O'Hara, rose from his chair and beamed with keen interest, "Where do I sign up?"

"Yes, I'd like to go, too," Mrs. Newley said.

"If you go, I'll stay at home," her son Kyle blurted out.

"You won't even know I'm around. All I want from you is one time to go with me and buy presents for our family," Kyle's mother pleaded.

"Okay," the son relented.

"I'm pleased with your reception of my plans," I said. "You are welcome to join our student group as fellow travelers. The only chaperones will be my husband and I. We cannot consider requests, such as, 'This town is so beautiful. Can't we stay here another day?' Our contracted schedule doesn't allow for changes of venues or set times."

"No problem," jovial Mr. O'Hara agreed. "Right, Mrs. Newley?"

"Right," she answered.

Marianne Keating had advised me to make clear from the outset that the term chaperone may wrongly suggest participation in decision making; it did not apply to the adults accompanying the GHS German Club.

I CHOSE A GERMAN TRAVEL AGENCY with offices in New York City to arrange transportation and hotel accommodations in Europe. Icelandic Airlines offered the lowest fare I could find for our price-conscious group, one hundred eighty dollars round trip per person. Another advantage was Icelandic's landing in Luxembourg, a small airport without the bustle of larger ones.

THE EAGER FUTURE TRAVELERS among my students established the GHS German Club, electing Riko as their president. Having spent a summer with an Outward Bound group in Germany at the Baltic Sea coast, Riko was fluent in German. The German Red Cross had sponsored the camp, where seven American teenagers joined more then ninety apprentices of Siemens, an international leader in technology. Riko's GHS peers believed he would be an effective troubleshooter if they needed one in Germany.

Club officers called for evening meetings because most of the members participated in clubs, sports, or band practice after school.

"Let's stick to the agenda," Riko reminded his flock. "We still have to do homework after this. How are our fundraisers coming?"

Treasurer Jill O'Hara reported that the car wash netted seventy dollars, which she deposited with the faculty treasurer who managed all student funds.

"How much did you credit me on my account?" Luke wanted to know.

"Well, you didn't put much time in and took off before cleanup. So, dividing seventy dollars by workers' hours resulted in two dollars for you," Jill said.

"And me?" Ryan asked.

"Seven dollars," Jill read from her entry for Ryan.

"Yeah, that's why your history paper was late," Luke revealed.

I broke into the discussion, "Remember our agreement: Your grades may not slide because of our club activities, which we call extracurricular. Your first responsibility is to your studies."

After a moment of reflection, Julie Schneider pointed at the boxes on the window sill. "Have the Advent calendars come in?"

"Yes, we'll hand them out after the Old Business," Vice President Molly Skrypek said, returning to the agenda. "If there are no questions, we can move on to New Business."

"What ideas do you have for other money-making projects?" Riko asked.

The students' suggestions included signing up for the refreshment stand at the football field, sharing it with the French and Spanish clubs; serving baked goods in the lobby during home basketball games; and in the spring, a public softball hitting contest.

I ruled against one popular fundraiser where people were invited to bang on wrecked cars with baseball bats. The liability was too great.

Although these activities consumed an enormous amount of time—I acted as faculty advisor, facilitator, mother, baker, as well as chauffeur to the students without drivers' licenses—I had two reasons for lending the GHS German Club my full support.

I believed the members' efforts in raising money as a contribution to their parents' expenses toward the trip made the students appreciate their opportunity more. Also, by working together, sophomores, juniors, and seniors became better acquainted with one another. This bond served them abroad when they needed to draw on a friend's more advanced vocabulary.

WITH ONE EXCEPTION, 1981, our excursions to Germany took place over spring break, which included April 19, Patriots' Day in Massachusetts. I applied to the school committee for permission to leave before the first weekend and to return on the second Sunday or Monday of that period.

"Why can't you restrict your travel to one week?" one committee member asked me.

"This trip may be the only chance most students will have to try out their German language skills with native speakers. Confidence to speak German builds up until they apply their knowledge on the third day. After all their hard work in preparation for this learning experience, we don't want to limit them to four days of practice."

"How many people are going?" the chairman inquired.

"Twenty-two students and seven adults."

"You'll not have a vacation," he smiled.

"But a validation of our program."

"Who will teach your classes in your absence?"

"Elizabeth Lachmann, my UMass intern, who has been with us since January."

"Well, I see you are prepared. Our best wishes go with you and your group."

AT THE LAST GERMAN CLUB MEETING with parents before our sanctioned tour, I handed out the itinerary, complete with hotel addresses and telephone numbers.   Club

297

officers collected forms containing emergency contacts and health information about all participants.

When the final question-and-answer period satisfied parents' concerns, I reiterated my expectations of the students.

"We prepared for this trip for nearly two years. We studied the language and the culture of the countries we will visit. We agreed to blend with that culture. We promised to be good ambassadors for America."

Making eye contact with everyone in the room, I continued, "As I pointed out before, wine and beer will be available to anyone over sixteen and will cost no more than a soda. I can't control what your children do on their free time. I have to rely on directions you gave them.

"Any behavior unbecoming a GHS student excludes that person from further travel with our group. If breaking our rules should occur, I would call to let you know at which airport your child will expect your arrangement for his or her return home at your expense."

In silence, all present kept their eyes on me.

Mr. Freeman rose and surveyed the gathering. "I assume I can speak for the parents and children here when I say that we are grateful for the opportunity you provide. Your students will not ruin what may be the trip of a lifetime for some of them."

None ever did.

An hour before our departure, the GHS chapter of the National Honor Society held its annual induction of new members, Riko among them. After the ceremony, the student travelers grabbed a quick hot lunch before lining up with their baggage on the sidewalk in front of the school.

"Where's Riko?" I asked everyone within earshot, including Bert and Eitel. We had included Eitel in our group so he could see his grandmother and family.

"He took our car home, followed by Kyle. They'll be right back," Bert said. "I wonder what's taken them so long," he added, scanning the parking lot.

Neither one of us expressed our latent fears. *Please, no accident.*

"All right. I'll sign us out. You may board the bus." I counted our participants. "Twenty-seven, plus Riko and me."

As I left the front office, Riko met me in the lobby. He handed me a long-stemmed rose.

"If you hadn't pushed me, I wouldn't have made the honor society," he said.

"Danke, mein Bub," thanks, son. I patted his arm, suppressing tears of joy and avoiding a hug that would have embarrassed him. "Now let's get the leader and the president on the bus, and my precious rose."

"Hey, Riko, congratulations," his friends greeted us. "If it weren't for our mothers, we'd all be digging ditches, huh?"

*   *   *

W H I L E   E N R O U T E   T O   New York's JFK airport, I overheard a voice saying, "Look at that blue-domed building with a statue of a horse on top."

"That's a colt, the trademark of Colt revolvers, which are manufactured here in Hartford," Mr. O'Hara explained.

Nancy, a shy but always alert junior, noticed the huge billboard announcing the home of Bic pens in Milford. "So this is where they come from," she said.

I realized then that several of my charges had never crossed the Massachusetts borders. Now they headed for Europe.

A T   T H E   A I R P O R T, people swarmed about as excited as bees circling a new hive.

"Remain together. Always follow me. Let's line up in three adjacent lines at the check-in counter. Don't lose your passports," I reminded my troop.

"I'll be relieved when our group is seated in the plane," Bert said to me.

"Me, too. We've had a long day. It's almost midnight. I'm tired but can't relax yet. Everything's gone according to plan, though. Perhaps our young people can take a nap before landing in Iceland for a stopover."

"The adults are cooperating models for your students and a calming influence," Bert observed.

O U R   Y O U T H S   W E R E   B U S Y eating dinner and perusing Icelandic's on-board magazine and Ice Mart catalog. They postponed their naps until the second leg of the flight.

"Save your shopping for the return trip," I advised my group. "You don't want to pack and repack your souvenirs for the next ten days, do you? But our stop at Keflavik will allow you to look over the Ice Mart's merchandise."

In 1970, Iceland's international airport consisted of one-story buildings of the World War II era. Gale-force winds shook our plane on its landing approach. Passengers' faces showed apprehension over the turbulence—mine, too, I am sure; but the native pilots guided their bird expertly onto the tarmac.

As we walked from the plane to the reception station, we had to lean into the wind at a forty-five degree angle. With great effort, I took a picture of our girls' waist-long hair trailing behind them in horizontal lines.

"Wow!" Mrs. Newley said in the tax-free store, admiring the displays of knitware, blankets, jewelry, and items crafted from lava. "All these things are handmade. Look at the variety of designs in the wool and in the glazed lava. Amazing."

"I guess a lot of winter wear will go to Masssachusetts in twelve days," Mr. O'Hara mused and smiled.

"Making plans, are you?" Ms. Oskiwicz, a GHS teacher, asked.

Soon an announcement over the intercom told us to reboard the plane. Crossing the tarmac was treacherous this time because the wind now caught us in the back, nearly pushing the feet from under us on the rain-slicked ground. Our girls had wisely tucked their hair inside their coats.

"I wouldn't want to live here," Kyle said, catching his breath on entering the plane.

A stewardess overheard his comment and assured Kyle that Iceland's weather had seasons, too. "It's not that blustery every day. In the summer we like camping on the northern shore," she said. "Check out the article in our magazine."

"*Ja,* Mrs. M," Jill agreed, "judging by the Ice Mart and the magazine, Iceland must be a cool place. Oops, that's a pun, isn't it? I meant to suggest that you stay over for twenty-four hours with your next group." Jill sounded like a public relations representative for Iceland. "Did you read, 'Twenty-four hours for twenty-four dollars?' You can stay in the new hotel where Bobby Fisher won his famous chess match."

"You may have a good idea. Bring it up when we report back home," I concurred. "I, too, would like to see Reykjavik and the system of hot water pipes through which water from the geysers flows to heat homes and businesses."

As our plane climbed through the fierce wind, we watched the geysers again, spewing their valuable resource into the air, creating steam.

"Not much longer before we step on German soil again," I said to Bert. "I remember when crossing the Atlantic in 1954 we counted days instead of hours. The wind in lower altitudes stirs the ocean as fiercely now as on many days during our voyage."

"*Ja,* the disturbances we encounter today are overcome in minutes. I trust the skills of the Icelandic pilots who live with the stormy weather patterns prevalent in this region."

One by one, our fellow travelers dozed despite the lively conversations by the Icelanders who had come aboard for a visit to Europe. The islanders wandered up and down the aisles, greeting friends and laughing heartily.

"How can people be so cheerful at this hour?" Luke asked Bert, who sat to his right.

"It's now eight o'clock, Icelandic time; four in Greenfield," Bert said. "The Icelanders got up to make this flight. You have not slept for about twenty-two hours. During that time you attended school from eight to twelve, sat on the bus, hung around JFK, and dropped in on a foreign country. You ought to be tired."

"*Ja,* and it's only the beginning. I better catch some winks before the fun begins."

"Maybe I can take forty of those," I said to Bert. "Could you keep your eyes open a little longer and respond to our group in case of need?"

"Sure. I'll wake you before I become too drowsy." He patted my hand reassuringly. I thanked him with a smile.

"In a few hours you'll see Mutter and Ina," I said.

He knows I'm grateful he took time off from work to help me; to check the boys' attendance before lights out.

S H O R T L Y B E F O R E N O O N, our plane landed in Luxembourg.

"See the people waving wildly on the visitors' gallery on top of the building?" Riko asked. "Aren't they Oma, Reiner and Inge?"

"And Ina and Walter?" Eitel added.

"Really! They couldn't wait until we came to Koblenz." Joy spread across our family's faces.

C L A I M I N G L U G G A G E and checking through customs took little time at this small terminal. We avoided the confusion and the delay associated with large airports and their traffic.

As soon as we exited the restricted area, Bert's relatives greeted us with open arms. They shook hands with everyone in our group and greeted them with, "Welcome to Europe!"

"*Guten Tag,*" they answered shyly.

"Let's get our gang on the bus," Bert said after a while.

"*Ja,* go ahead. We'll visit you after dinner at your hotel," Reiner promised.

D E S P I T E T H E E X T E N S I V E construction outside the provisional building, we easily spotted our bus. *Greenfield High*

School German Club read the banners attached to the sides of our light-green transportation for the coming twelve days.

Klaus, the driver, smiled a friendly Hello. About six feet tall, the muscular man in his late thirties looked trim in his sporty clothes. Klaus's engaging demeanor radiated confidence and service. Dark-blond wavy hair fell partly over his blue eyes and clean-shaven face as he bent over to stow the luggage in the designated compartment. Our young gentlemen assisted him.

"Klasse," Klaus said in an approving tone, acknowledg-ing their help.

"Why did he address us as class?" one of the students asked quietly as they passed by me to enter the bus.

"I wondered about that, too," I pondered. "Judging by his voice, smile and nod, I have the feeling *Klasse* may mean cool or neat in the sense of first rate."

"Replacing *prima?"* Justin asked.

"Probably not replacing it but expressing approval as we do with great."

"Well, it goes to show, German is a living language," our class clown John declared as he imitated me, "just like English. Right, Mrs. M?"

"Right." I joined the laughter that spread through the group as everyone became aware of our discussion.

During the trip Klaus used *Klasse* often and we adopted it eagerly; students and teacher learning together.

F R O M   T H E   A I R P O R T, our bus rolled through the rural landscape to the border. At the side, guards approached the driver's window and asked Klaus about his passengers. *"Eine amerikanische Schulgruppe,"* he said. At that point twenty-nine arms stretched upwards with blue passports in their hands, a droll sight.

"Okay," the guards said and waved us on.

The German officials, after observing their counterparts' action, let us pass.

"I didn't expect to just sail across the borders. I thought we'd all have to get off the bus, be searched, or something like that," Mrs. McDonald remarked.

"That happens when you cross the Iron Curtain," I explained. Western Europeans and North Americans are rarely checked as they change countries on their travels in the west."

"I see a city in the distance," Mrs. Newley said.

"That's Trier," her son Kyle volunteered," the oldest city in Germany. We'll visit it on our way back."

"You did your homework, huh?" John teased him.

After we skirted the city, Klaus drove us on the Autobahn through the Eifel mountain range to Koblenz. Our travelers fell silent; they had left their beds about twenty-six hours before.

WHEN THE BUS ENTERED KOBLENZ, the smooth rhythm of its tires along the highway turned into a stop-and-go pattern of urban traffic. Car horns pierced the dreams of our fellow tourists who rubbed their eyes and sat up straight. Trying to see everything beyond the windows at once, heads swiveled from side to side.

"There is one of those famous *Konditoreien,*" sweet-tooth Luke discovered, pointing at a well-lit pastry shop.

"Man, don't people drive anything but German cars here?" Justin asked.

Our group broke out in laughter. "Wake up! You are in Germany, m a n," Kyle reminded him.

"Look at the fashions," Mrs. McDonald observed. "We *are* coming from the hinterland, aren't we?"

"Look at the girls wearing them," John rhapsodized.

"They aren't exactly waiting for you. Besides you are on a study tour, dear boy," Molly broke John's spell.

I rose from my front seat and faced the passengers. With microphone in hand, I said, *"Bitte herhören!"* Please listen. "In a few minutes we'll reach today's destination, *Zur Weinlaube.* At the hotel desk I'll obtain our room assignments while you gather in the parking lot to pick up your luggage. Then come to the lobby, where you'll pick up your room keys. Take a good look at your rooms so you'll know how to leave them at our departure. Let us practice this routine as a model for the duration of our tour.

"Dinner will be served in thirty minutes. Follow the signs to the dining area."

"Isn't this place charming?' Ms. Oskiewicz eyed the building on our approach.

The small hotel had the perfect name: vine bower. Bright green window frames, shutters and doors complimented the white stucco exterior. Grape vines hugged the façade.

AFTER WASHING UP in our room, I cleaned the sink, filled it with water, and submerged the stem and leaves of my trimmed red rose. It had nearly drained its vial through the hole in the rubber lid.

In the dining room, tired but freshly scrubbed faces bent over their plates to appreciate the aroma and arrangement of pork roast, fresh vegetables and mashed potatoes.

The adults in our group tried local Rhein or Mosel wines: They relied on Bert's, the native *Rheinländer's* recommenda-tions. Most students stuck with soda that night; some ordered milk. Chris seemed to gag; others quietly made uneasy faces.

"What's wrong?" I asked, alarmed.

Chris hesitated with his answer, "I don't know about this milk."

"It's warm and so thick," Eitel filled us in. "Could we have some ice?"

Friendly waitresses in black dresses with white collars and half-aprons seemed astonished at this request but obliged.

"Americans put ice in their milk?" they asked.

"No," I explained politely, "but they are used to drinking it refrigerated, rather than at room temperature."

To our group I said, "As planned, I'll review our itinerary for the next day before we leave the nightly dinner table. Tomorrow, after breakfast, Klaus will drive us to the *Rheinanlagen*, a park along the Rhine River, or Rhein from now on, where we can walk to the *Deutsches Eck*, translated as German Corner. At its point, the Mosel, or Moselle River empties into the Rhein. Because of this confluence, Romans in AD 14 named their local fort *Confluentes*, which over the centuries became the city of Koblenz.

"From there, we'll join a guided walking tour and visit historic sites. You are going to see buildings, cobblestones, and art treasures, some of which are nearly two thousand years old. Frequent wars destroyed much of this city and others we have on our itinerary. For twenty-seven years after World War II, however, West Germans rebuilt and modernized the Federal Republic of Germany, supported by the Marshall Plan."

"Any questions so far?"

"Yeah, when do we eat?" Luke asked.

"The walking tour ends in the center of the city. You'll be on your own for two hours to try your German in restaurants or stores. Take care of each other; stay in groups of three or more."

"Where will you be?" Mr. O'Hara wanted to know.

"At the nearest bookstore," Molly answered for me.

"You are probably right." I chuckled. "I'll point out the spot where you can reach me during your free time."

B E R T' S F A M I L Y had waited in the Common Room until we joined them after dinner. They wanted to hear about Veit, and we asked about their life and concerns.

Our group sat at tables to write their first postcards home, play cards, or visit with one another. Soon the two parties mixed. Reiner, now an architect for the city of Koblenz, entertained us with jokes and anecdotes. He also warned us about the legal red-light district, where registered ladies of the night ply their trade without pimps. The government issues them work permits. Prostitutes are required to record their income and pay taxes. Health authorities schedule mandatory physicals.

"When you notice smaller and less attractive stores on the streets leading away from the shopping center, turn around before

306

you are accosted." He advised boundaries that everyone wrote down.

Catching the furtive smiles on the boy's faces, I added to Reiner's remarks, "Just don't cross the boundaries."

Before long, yawning became a competitive activity. Bert's family left. We travelers retired to our rooms to snuggle under the heavenly down comforters.

*   *   *

THE FOLLOWING DAY, the sun shone brightly on spring flowers and blossoming trees.

"How advanced the season is here, compared to Greenfield," Mrs. Newley said. "Our snowdrops and crocuses are just breaking through the soil; the buds on trees have not yet opened."

"Practically every house has flower boxes here," Mrs. McDonald added.

In the park, we noticed busy city employees remove dead flowers and leaves from the colorful groupings of perennials, and rake the walkways.

"You almost don't want to step on their patterns," Nancy said.

"Our cameras are getting a workout," Julie commented.

"Try to place people in your pictures as you create memories of sites," Bert suggested. "Later, you'll remember both."

"Yeah, come and stand in front of this fountain, guys," John called out.

We stood around the *Schängelbrunnen,* the Schängel Fountain. Nancy read from the brochure, "...a monument to the city's eternal 'naughty boy' and his joie de vivre."

As we moved along, three girls seemed to lag behind.

"Any blisters yet?" I asked my happy gang.

"*Ja*, I could use a band-aid," Nancy admitted.

"Here you are," Ms. Oskiwicz said, holding up a medium-size strip. "Let me help you."

CONCLUDING OUR GUIDED TOUR, we broke for lunch. The students as well as the accompanying adults chatted nervously.

"We're saved! There's a McDonald's," Luke said. "Let's go."

"Wait 'til they realize that the menu is in German," I said to Eitel.

"*Ja,* and the hamburgers and rolls taste different in Germany."

IN THE AFTERNOON, Klaus picked us up in back of the Löhr-Center, a mall. I counted twenty-eight people.

"Where is Don?" I asked.

"He was with Luke and me in a shoe store. We looked at Pumas and Adidases," Kyle said. "All of a sudden, he was gone."

Don was a loner. I felt his parents wanted to give him the opportunity to share new experiences with his age group. Was he uncomfortable being scheduled night and day with other people, some of them strangers?

"We'll wait a while," I said to Klaus.

Bert and Riko left to search for Don in the area. "You don't think he ended up in the district Reiner warned us about, do you?" Riko worried.

"I hope not. Let's go back to the bus. Maybe he's found his way."

As they returned on one street, Don ran toward us from another. Out of breath, he uttered, "I'm sorry. I lost my way for a bit."

"You had all of us worried," I reproved Don. "We'll talk about this later. Now let's join our group on the bus."

TO REACH OUR AFTERNOON DESTINATION, Klaus drove us via the *Rheinbrücke* to the right bank of the mighty river. Here, the *Festung Ehrenbreitstein,* a fortress, had its beginning as a castle around AD 1000. Between six and eight hundred years later, the defenders added living quarters and defense buildings.

Situated on a mountain top, this fortification overlooked the area in all directions, an advantage for its defense. As a consequence, enemy forces never conquered the *Ehrenbreitstein*. In 1801, however, Napoleon had the French army blow up the installation. Prussians rebuilt the fortress in neo-Classical style to look more defiant than before.

"I'm impressed," Mr. O'Hara said. "The buildings are in excellent repair."

"The reason is that they are in constant use as museums or for exhibits," Bert said.

"What a spectacular view," Ms. Oskiwicz marveled.

"Look at those guys over there kicking soccer balls around," Riko observed. "They are good."

"German boys are as fanatic about soccer as you are about baseball," Bert explained. "That group is probably staying at the youth hostel up here."

"Can we go into those buildings?" Molly asked.

"That's one purpose for our coming here," I said. "In the Regional Museum, you'll find, among other displays, an ornate cannon from 1524. Check out the Rheinmuseum, too. Its treasures will indicate the rich cultural and economic history of the Rheinland."

As our group dispersed toward the different buildings, I motioned to Don to meet me at a bench in front of the outdoor café.

"Why did you leave Luke and Kyle?"

"I was bored looking at sneakers with those jocks."

"Where did you go?"

"Just through the streets, taking in Koblenz."

"Did you feel lost?"

"Not really. I actually enjoyed ordering lunch at a stand-up seafood place and paying with German money. That probably took too much time, considering how far I had to run to our meeting place."

"You disregarded our rule never to explore local attractions by yourself. Luke and Kyle felt responsible."

"I'm sorry. I will tell them, too. It won't happen again."

"I know it won't. So let's catch up with our friends," I said to the remorseful sinner.

The weight of that incident had caused the ring of fear around my neck to tighten. *Relax. Don's infraction was a warning to the entire group. Coming at the beginning of our tour may prevent other transgressions.*

At dinner, I reminded my captive audience of our plans for the next day.

"As you know, we'll travel to Köln, or Cologne, by train to add a new experience for you. The *Deutsche Bundesbahn,* is known for its punctuality. Keep that in mind for the return trip. Stick together. If you miss a partner, report that to me as soon as possible; don't wait until departure time."

*   *   *

BERT, RIKO AND EITEL spent the third day in Koblenz with relatives. "We'll take care of Mrs. M," my students assured Bert.

"Thank you. And don't forget: You only have to count to twenty-six today," Bert said in parting.

The excursion on the train captivated our group with the Inter-City's speed, comfort and cleanliness. Frequent service by employees rolling pushcarts along the aisles, offering snacks and beverages drew oohs and look-at-thats from my troop.

"This scenery is fabulous," Mrs. Legrand said, looking out the windows. "We are lucky to have such beautiful spring weather that highlights the fresh colors of nature and the houses tucked in the valley as well as amid trees on mountain sides."

"Indeed. Most buildings look new," Margaret observed.

"Most buildings *are* new. Toward the end of World War II, many battles destroyed homes and industries. After more than twenty-five years of recovery, West Germany has a new look," I explained, remembering the war-torn area when Vati and I relocated to the Rheinland in 1946.

"What is that?" Debbie asked in disbelief, pointing at the vision she thought she had beyond the window.

"Oh, wow! Is that Cologne Cathedral?" Mr. O'Hara wondered.

Now all of us strained to gain window space and view the mighty edifice silhouetted against the horizon, miles before we reached Köln.

"How big is that cathedral? Will we get lost in it?" Kyle mused.

"We'll certainly feel small." I opened my notebook and continued, "The total length of its exterior is one hundred and forty-four meters, or more than four hundred seventy feet; the exterior height is forty-three and a half meters, one hundred forty-three feet. The ridge turret spikes upward to one hundred and nine meters, three hundred fifty-eight feet."

"Will this be in a quiz?" Luke joked, evoking laughter.

"I hadn't thought of that," I answered in mock seriousness.

"Well, don't consider it," Molly pleaded.

STANDING IN FRONT OF THE GOTHIC *Kölner Dom* quieted my group.

"Truly awesome," Mr. O'Hara said.

"Take as much time as you want to explore this architectural marvel. Its chancel dates back to 1248.

"At the entrance you can obtain a printed guide that details historical information. Notice also the blackened stones inside and outside, the result of centuries of smog and soot, especially from coal-fired locomotives passing beyond the plaza."

"When and where do you want to meet?" Mrs. Newley asked.

"At two o'clock, right here. Look about you: You have a choice of restaurants for lunch and a variety of stores to look into."

"Over there is a bookstore for Mrs. M," Nancy said. "Will you be there?"

"You guessed it," I admitted. "After two o'clock we'll take a short guided tour through a central district of the city. There, too, you'll be amazed at the new buildings because ninety percent of the inner city was laid in ruin during the war."

Saturated with knowledge, we returned to *Zur Weinlaube* for dinner and our last night in Koblenz.

*　　*　　*

T H E　F O U R T H　D A Y of our journey kept us on the bus for several hours. If we wanted to walk in Wilhelm Tell's mountains as German V students had requested after reading Schiller's drama, we had to bridge the distance between Koblenz and Switzerland with celerity.

Klaus whisked us on the Autobahn, which by-passed most communities, to Freiburg im Breisgau, in the Breis district.

"In the morning we left the beautiful Rhein valley. I can't believe we are now in just as scenic an area," Mrs. Legrand said.

"This is the *Schwarzwald,* or Black Forest ," Joan told her mom. "Famous for cuckoo clocks."

"Among diverse products, such as other time pieces and medical instruments." John referred to his travel brochure.

"And what towers over this city but another cathedral," Kyle remarked.

"Yes, the Freiburger *Münster,"* I said. "We'll check in at the hotel and freshen up. After lunch, we'll give our tourist legs a further workout and go sightseeing. Agreed?"

"Sounds good. I'm ready to eat," Riko confessed.

W E　M E A N T　T O　H A V E　L U N C H　T O G E T H E R so we could set out on our discovery tour as a group. On that first Sunday after Easter, however, our hotel and other big restaurants had reservations for First Holy Communion celebrations.

"Did you see the festive decorations in the dining room?" Mrs. Newley asked.

"Ja, all in white and green," Eitel said.

312

"Restaurants probably have some tables for two or four available. So, try your luck in small teams. We'll meet in two hours on the north side of the *Münster*," I decided.

Mrs. Newley, Kyle, Mrs. Legrand and Joan joined our family for the main meal of the day in the German tradition.

"Can that be true?" Riko asked and pointed at a plaque near the entrance of the restaurant. "Operated by eleven successive generations of one family? That goes back to the middle of the seventeenth century."

"I suppose city records can verify that," Bert said. "Perhaps this place will have room for us."

"See one of the parties coming toward us?" Mrs. Legrand asked. "The little girl looks adorable in her white dress, leggings and patent leather shoes as she walks ahead of her family and guests. How proudly she carries her tall candle in front of her."

"Look at her sweet, serious face and those long curls. Would you ask if I may take her picture?" Mrs. Newley requested of me.

"Consent granted," I informed her after my inquiry.

"A typical American tourist," Kyle said to and of his mother, shaking his head.

"That's all right." I patted his shoulder. "Tourists capture memories for themselves and to share with others."

When the eight of us succeeded in our search for an eatery with non-reserved seating, Bert and I had to translate the holiday menu.

"Well, what are you having?" the women wanted to know.

"*Leberknödel,* with sauerkraut and potatoes," we both answered.

"Liver dumplings?" our youngsters exclaimed.

"Yes, have you ever had any?" I asked.

"No, do I ever want any?" Kyle countered, grimacing.

"These dumplings are usually big. I'll have enough with one. The other, I'll divide into small portions and offer them to the adventurous. Then you can make up your mind. Meanwhile, choose your selections for today."

313

All of our small teams hurried to the meeting site near the *Münster* after lunch. They needed some time to chat about the meals they ordered and about the family gatherings they observed, which "were as big as some weddings."

"Mrs. M gave us samples of liver dumplings," Joan revealed.

"You ate those?" Luke expressed incredulity.

"Yes. At first I worried about their texture on my tongue, visualizing raw liver, you know? But they tasted pretty good thanks to the herbs in the mix; they felt like soft meatballs. I'll order some when I find them on a menu."

"Really? Will you let me try a morsel?"

"Sure."

"Me, too?" skeptic voices asked. "Any other regional specialty we should try?"

"I think you'll like *Spätzle,* home-made pasta in strips about five millimeters wide and one centimeter long. They go well with *Sauerbraten*," I suggested.

THE GUIDED TOUR of the *Münster* and the surrounding area began with a short history of the city.

"Founded in 1120 by Duke Konrad von Zähringen, this settlement became a trading center on the routes from neighboring *Schwaben,* or Suabia, in the east, across the *Schwarzwald* to the *Elsass,* or Alsace, and Burgundy to the west. In some of our streets you can still find remnants of the thirteenth-century sewage system, where waste water flowed down the street," a city employee recited.

We learned that the population suffered greatly during the Thirty-Years War when Austrian, Spanish, Swedish, and French armies took turns in conquering and ruling the city. Since 1806 Freiburg belongs to the *Land,* or state of, Baden.

"An intensive rebuilding program has replaced the ruins of World War II," the guide continued. "Now we turn our attention to the *Münster*."

314

She pointed out that building the cathedral took several centuries during which time architectural styles changed. As a consequence, the viewer notices Romanesque and Gothic influences along with some Rococo.

"The dimensions of the *Münster* are remarkable," our guide said. "The height of the tower is nearly equal to the length of the cathedral. Completed in 1513, this edifice underwent little change since then."

Pointing up to the tower, the woman directed our attention to the red- and blue-faced clock, divided into the signs of the Zodiac.

"In a moment, the bells will peal the full hour in their rich sound," she alerted us.

We did not enter the cathedral because of the services conducted at that hour but continued the tour through the city. From several hundred feet away, we heard the bells' rhythmic ringing resonate thanksgiving on this day.

Houses with bright colored stucco façades, some in medieval styles, others built after World War II, lined the streets. On the walkways, we saw elaborate pebble mosaics amid cobblestones.

"I'm beginning to understand why people call America the New World," John said at the conclusion of the city tour. "Here some scenes remind me of Disney World."

"Well, where do you think good old Walt got his ideas?" Kyle asked.

"Yes, to offer the people of the New World attractions they would visit, he started with Old World charm, fairy tales, and Robinson Crusoe to name a few, until his heirs added space age experiences," Mr. O'Hara said.

"Anybody hungry?" I asked.

"Yeah." The answer came in chorus strength.

"Time to take my shoes off and soak my feet," Mrs. McDonald sighed.

*   *   *

IT HAD TO RAIN SOME TIME. Perhaps the weather will improve while we're in transit to Schaffhausen.

Before our bus reached the highest elevation through which the secondary road led, we viewed pastoral scenes in the Black Forest that would move poets to write. Embraced by tall pines, old churches with traditional onion-shape spires stood alone or rose amid quaint villages.

"Hey, our heads are in the clouds, just like over Iceland," Justin said.

"That's a good sign. Deforestation after the war, due to imposed reparations, had such an impact on this area that the climate changed for years," I explained, "because clouds, unrestrained by trees, moved past the *Schwarzwald.* With time, planted seedlings grew tall and restored local weather patterns."

"We read about reparation costs in European history," Nancy said, "but I never thought about the effect they had on people or their land."

"As do wars," Ms. Oskiewicz contemplated.

K L A U S   S L O W E D   T H E   B U S as we approached the German-Swiss border. "I'll let you off at the parking lot," he announced through the microphone. "You can follow the signs and the stream of people to the viewing area of the *Rheinfall.*"

"*Rheinfall von Schaffhausen,*" Eitel read.

"So this is the European Niagara Falls?" Don asked. "It, too, sits on the border of two countries."

"But the *Rheinfall* isn't as high and its gorge isn't as wide," John said. He was the only student in our group who had visited the North American falls.

"Watch out!" Mr. O'Hara called out.

"Too late," I said, wet on my right side where a gust of wind blew spray toward me. "Brrr, that's cold."

We stood in the shade, the sun illuminating the falls and creating rainbow-colored drops across the gorge.

After a while of gazing and shivering—all of us having caught some moisture—we returned to Klaus and the bus.

"Onward to Konstanz," Kyle directed beside the open door." *Vierundzwanzig... sechsundzwanzig... neunundzwanzig.* All aboard." He grinned and entered last.

*　　*　　*

W E   A R R I V E D at our day's destination around noon.

When I had been in discussion about our arrangements with the travel agent, he mentioned the hotel in which he had made reservations for us.

"In Konstanz, you'll be staying at the Hotel Barbarossa."

"What?" I cried out in laughter.

Confused by my reaction, he wondered, "Do you know the place?"

"Yes," I said. "That's where my husband and I spent our honeymoon."

"Oh. So it'll be all right to book you there?"

"Yes, of course."

L O C A T E D   C E N T R A L L Y, the hotel provided opportunity for small team exploration without guidance.

After making my customary round of all the rooms occupied by our group, asking whether plumbing was in working order, and doors would lock, I returned to my room.

"Was that a knock at the door?" Bert asked a moment later.

"I'll get it," I said, leaving the sink with dripping hands.

Outside the door stood a tall young waiter dressed in a starched white shirt, black bow tie, black trousers and shoes; he held a bottle of champagne in a wine cooler. Next to him, a petite maid said, "Guten Tag!" She wore a black dress, accentuated by a white collar and cuffs. A white apron and headdress completed her outfit. She carried a tray with two glasses and a pink carnation in a vase.

"We didn't order room service," I explained. "You must have the wrong party."

"No," the waiter said. "This comes to you with the compliments of your travel agent and Hotel Barbarossa, in recognition of your first visit here." Both employees smiled knowingly.

"Our honeymoon—nearly twenty-three years ago... The agent must have informed the hotel of my comment."

"Please, come in and set your cooler and your tray down."

Bert thanked and tipped the messengers.

MY STUDENTS AND THE ADULTS in our group took advantage of the unscheduled time to go shopping. We had asked to have dinner late that day.

Before the meal, Debbie, Jill and Julie came to our room. "We wanted you to have a European rose when the American one dies," Debbie said with a broad smile.

"Thank you for your thoughtfulness and good timing. I think my red rose may not survive another night in the sink. But this yellow one will stand in a vase until we leave." I showed them the surprise delivery we had accepted earlier.

Dinner was served again in the table d'hôte style, one complete meal, including soup, salad, main course and dessert, as opposed to à la carte.

"I love German soups," Mr. O'Hara said.

"But their desserts are funny," Robert remarked, "always stewed fruit, never pies or ice cream."

"Germans eat their pastries or cake at their afternoon coffee break," I explained. "Ice cream becomes increasingly popular."

"And do they eat pork every day as we are getting?" Justin asked.

"No. I assume *that* meat is currently more economical to serve groups. Next year it may be chicken."

"Did you tell the gang about your present from the hotel?" Jill wondered.

"Not yet, but my husband and I would like to invite the adults to our room for a glass of champagne after dinner. The younger generation may stay at the table for ice cream, my treat. We'll see you before taps."

ON OUR GOOD-NIGHT ROUNDS, Bert and I noticed some rooms were overcrowded. Students sat on beds and the floor. Between showing each other the souvenirs they had bought, the young travelers found plenty to talk and chuckle about.

"We could've sold my sister," John said.

My heart raced. "What happened?"

"We were walking down a busy street," Riko explained, "when two Turks, attracted by Susan's long blonde hair, stopped us with their business proposition."

"Yeah, they pulled wads of money out of their pockets and asked in German how much we wanted for her." John recounted their adventure.

"What did you do?" I asked.

"We grabbed Susan's arms, yelled 'Nein, nein, nein,' and ran back to the hotel," Riko said.

Thank God this incident ended in our favor.

"Susan was in the right company," Robert said. "You two probably towered over the Turks."

"What other trouble did you get into?" Bert asked, adding, "Or get out of?"

"No trouble, but cultural enrichment," Kyle said with his head raised high, feigning intellectual superiority.

The group burst out in laughter. "You? What was the object of your curiosity?" They echoed Kyle's airs.

"Give me another cracker with Nutella and I'll tell you."

He continued, "Haven't you wondered why this hotel's name is Barbarossa? Why it advertises as *historisches Hotel?* Did you take the trouble of reading the plaques on the walls? That's where I gleaned much of my information. Let's review my findings and we can floor GHS's history teachers upon our return.

319

First, though, may I have a *Fanta,* please? Giving lectures makes me thirsty."

"Nutella will do that, too," Liz said as she handed Kyle the soft drink. "You can come down to earth now."

"Well," Kyle informed his listeners, "Friedrich I was born in 1122. He became known as Barbarossa, Italian for red beard. His reign began in 1152 as King of the Hohenstaufen. In 1167, he was crowned Emperor.

"Kaiser Rotbart, as we call him here," our lecturer went on, "fought and conquered many cities in Italy. In 1174, he bought Toscany, Sardinia, and Corsica. Difficulties arose in keeping his vast empire together. After the Lombards defeated the emperor, he signed a peace treaty with them in 1183 in the building, which is now the Hotel Barbarossa.

"He died in 1190 while on a crusade against the Saracens who had occupied Jerusalem. To be specific, Barbarossa drowned as he tried to cross a small river on horseback in Asia Minor."

Kyle bowed to loud applause and cheers, "Hear! Hear!"

I knew this young man for his politeness, attention in class and apt one-liners. With an interest in aviation, he was destined for a career in science.

"Good job, Kyle," I said. "Your history teachers will be proud of you."

"Yeah. Just don't tell them."

"All right, gang, get your rest. Tomorrow after lunch we leave for *die Schweiz.* "

* * *

UNDER AZURE SKIES, Klaus operated the bus skillfully toward the Glarner Alps. At times, only customary roadside barriers separated vehicles from a precipice that met a lake hundreds of feet below. Passengers with window seats leaned inward, as if shifting their weight could prevent crashing down the mountain. Later we laughed about their silent fear but at the time we heard little talk besides occasional nervous remarks.

"I suppose from a passenger car you can't even see the lake because of the barriers but from up here..." Mrs. McDonald said.

Our route led us in a southwesterly direction to Zurich. Passing the city, Klaus drove the bus south through Zug and Schwyz toward Altdorf, the capital of Uri Canton.

Having espied the Alps' silhouettes from afar, we soon became surrounded by them. Our group gazed in awe at the landscape. Villages filled the spaces below alpine pastures from which the cattle's lows and ringing cowbells reached our ears through the open bus windows. Deeper and deeper we penetrated the mountains; higher and higher the elevations reached toward the sky.

"Altdorf, over fifteen hundred feet above sea level, is home to eight thousand residents,"Alan quoted from the tourist brochure.

"They used their space well to accommodate all of them, didn't they?" Mrs. Legrand observed.

The town's main street seemed narrow as our touring bus rolled along toward that night's lodging.

The hotel sat like an outpost near the railroad station. When Klaus parked in the courtyard, people came to greet us, or so we guessed. After taking a look at the bus, they went back into the building.

"Why don't you remain seated," I advised our group. "I will register us at the desk and see what instructions I receive."

The owner and his wife avoided looking at me while processing our reception and handing me the keys.

Back at the bus I said, "They did expect us. The room assignments match our number and genders. Let's be at our best behavior."

Bert and I carried our luggage to the second floor. In our airy, clean room, beds with feather pillows promised a comfortable night.

"Are these all the towels for the two of us?" Bert asked.

"I don't see any drawers where more could be stored," I said. "And look how small and threadbare these towels are.

Perhaps the maid forgot to bring more. I'll look into it after I check all of our party's rooms."

Our fellow travelers were waiting for me, ready to voice similar complaints.

"The view from this room is spectacular. But what gives with these light-weight rags—I'm sorry, I mean towels?" Mr. O'Hara waved one to greet me.

"Everyone in our group is asking me that question. I'll see what I can do about it."

At the desk in the lobby, the owner listened to my inquiry but did not respond. Instead, he called his wife from the kitchen to help me. Without looking at me, she motioned me to follow her. Clutching her key, she opened a well-stocked linen closet and in a surly mood she counted out a stack of towels, heaping them onto my extended arms. When she realized that I would not be able to see where I was going, she brusquely took some and accompanied me to hand out the towels.

"Thank you," my contingent of Greenfielders said at every one of our stops.

"Ich höre, wir essen in einer halben Stunde im Tagesraum." I relayed the message the owner gave me.

"Dinner will be served in half an hour in the meeting room," the students informed our adult companions.

The meal did not vary much from those in Germany. The ample servings were delicious and colorfully arranged on each plate. The dinner conversation reflected the many new impressions our group tried to absorb. On that day, they continued to marvel at Mother Nature's grandiose display of her alps.

As our young people, with typical adolescent bottomless stomachs, cleared the last morsels from their plates, smiling waitresses brought bowls and platters heaped with additional meat, potatoes and vegetables to the table.

"Wow! Look at that!"

"More? For us?" My students could not believe their good fortune, especially after the frosty reception we received.

"Langt zu, wenn's schmeckt," the smiling chef in his white garb called from the door and winked at us. Help yourself if you like it.

Our teenagers needed no further encouragement. They finished off the unexpected offerings, too.

"Ice cream and fruit!" The group voiced their delight at the dessert as the owner approached our table.

"You have a well-behaved group," she said to me, nodding at several of us and including all with an outstretched motion of her arms. "If you'd like to, you can spend the evening in our restaurant. In one area, we have a piano your young people might want to play. And they could sing along."

"Thank you." *Why this change of attitude?*

Klaus told us later the owners and hotel employees had observed our polite and happy group at dinner.

"The people asked about my experience with your group. I assured them what they saw was real." Our chauffeur grinned.

"It's still a strange way to conduct business. Do all guests at this hotel have to prove themselves to the owners?" I asked.

Klaus shrugged. "Your people did. By the way, this place is a bit isolated from the town. The youngsters have been sitting most of the day. Would you mind if I took them downtown for a while?"

"That's kind of you. Let's find out how many want to go, and remind them of the buddy system."

As the mini-group of students left, accompanied by Bert and Ms. Oskiewicz, the woman owner joined me at the entrance where I waved a short goodbye to the departers.

"I must explain our hesitant reception at your arrival," she said. "When we accepted your reservations we noted only the designation German Club, rather than the Greenfield High School German Club. At your arrival we read the banner on your bus. 'Oh, no, teenagers' my husband said. 'How could we make that mistake?' "

"You were not going to accept students?" I asked.

"No more, we vowed after a private school group with international celebrities' teenagers cut holes in our blankets to

323

wear them as ponchos, used our towels to apply shoe polish, and stole the crucifix off the wall of many rooms."

"I hope we can restore your faith in young people."

"You already did. We replaced towels in all your rooms."

On my return to the restaurant, I noticed the owners' two children sitting with our students who drew pictures for them, or played *Schwarzer Peter*—in German.

GHS representatives practicing international relations, I thought, satisfied.

THE DAY OF OUR WILHELM TELL RESEARCH arrived. Before our trip I had distributed to all members of our group mimeographed details of the subject and relevant geographical sites.

In Altdorf, we first visited the *Historisches Museum von Uri* where we compared our notes and separated the historical background of Schiller's drama from the *"Märchen mit dem Hut und Apfel"*, the fairy tale of the hat and the apple, as the poet phrased it.

From the museum, Klaus drove us to the eastern part of town. Dominating the square at the foot of the forested mountains stood the *Telldenkmal*. This Tell monument shared its foundation with a tower, the lower half of which showed murals of local scenery and people during the time of the *Rütli* vow. The upper half featured two stories of boarded-up windows on the four sides under a church-type steeple.

With the *Rütli* vow, the men of three cantons, Schwyz, Uri, and Unterwalden, founded a confederation, determined to achieve freedom from the yoke of the Austrian empire. Into this history Schiller wove the efforts of Swiss freedom fighters in the Middle Ages.

At the *Schillerdenkmal* we split into small groups and continued our walking tour independently until after lunch.

Back on the bus, excited voices exchanged new impressions.

"Did you see the inlaid patterns on the tile roofs?"

"*Ja,* and the modern cars in front of historic buildings."

"We walked by an inn called Goethe-Haus. Is that one of those claiming that Goethe slept there?" Mrs. McDonald asked.

"Probably," I said. "Goethe, a friend of Schiller's, was as impressed with the natural beauty of this area and the *Vierwaldstättersee* as we are. He planned to write an epic poem about it but, at the time was too occupied with other works he had begun. He offered Schiller to use the material in his stead."

"Unbelievable....Did that really happen?" Liz asked.

"That's what I've been taught," I said. "But for now admire the majesty of the mountains and the deep blue water of the *Urnersee* as Klaus takes us to the *Tellkapelle,* a small chapel by the road."

"I'm glad I brought my camera," Mrs. Legrand said. "I'll never forget these alps. But how do you describe them to people who've never seen them?"

ON OUR FINAL EVENING at the hotel in Altdorf the owners treated us like family. Their children ate with us and after dinner would not leave the sides of my students. Later, townspeople filled the restaurant. Some wanted to talk to our group. My students, however, could not understand the Swiss intonation. Bert and I translated all evening. In the end, a Swiss-American songfest broke out, one side encouraging the other, ending with American and Swiss lullabies.

*   *   *

THE NEXT DESTINATION on our itinerary was well west of Altdorf. To reach Biel/Bienne we had to leave the Glarner Alpen, thread our way by the Vierwaldstättersee and Luzerne in a northeasterly direction, then turn southwest in Langenthal toward Bern. Shortly before Bern, we took a route to Biel on Lake Biel, or *Bienne au Lac de Bienne,* for those of us who spoke French.

The Bieler tourist brochure stated that of the town's population about two-thirds spoke German, one third French.

325

Officially bilingual, Biel/Bienne was the largest bilingual town in Switzerland, an economic advantage.

We made Biel our intermediate stop before leaving *die Schweiz*. The group explored the town before and after dinner unescorted.

"Keep your eyes open and share your discoveries when we get together again; try your French as well and watch over your buddies," I said before my giggling charges fluttered out of the hotel.

"Compared to Altdorf, Biel has a city flavor, don't you think so?" Ms. Oskiewicz asked as she met Bert and me in the business district. Liz, Debbie and Margaret accompanied her. With big eyes, which reflected the lights of the store windows and the sparkle of the displayed gems and watches, the girls tried to absorb yet more impressions of Europe.

"Yes, like the difference between Greenfield and Northampton," I mused. "Biel draws its vitality from commerce, however, and Northampton from the many colleges in its area."

"Okay, see you later." The three *Graces* and their teacher waved as they left.

Bert and I checked out the historical sites listed in the brochure, the Gothic church built in 1451 and the town hall in 1534.

"Biel looks so peaceful and prosperous," I said to Bert.

"*Ja,* but the Swiss had their struggles, too, as we learned in school in our youth," he refreshed my memory about Germany's shared history with her neighbors.

"You're right, Schiller reminded us of that."

O V E R   D I N N E R, our companions' mouths were as busy relating the high points of the afternoon as they were chewing.

"How many Swiss army knives will travel to Greenfield?" Mr. O'Hara asked.

Seven arms went up.

"How many cowbells?" We counted twenty-three.

How many watches did the adults buy for their families?

"Let it not be said that we were interested only in material things," Chris declared.

"Of course not," Kyle concurred. "We made sure to advance our knowledge of foreign tongues: *Schokolade oder chocolat* tastes good in either."

Big guy Chris blushed. *"Ja, sie schmeckt gut,"* it tastes good. "But I was talking about the history lessons along the way. Celts, Romans, Scandinavians, Napoleon... all of them stopped here. Their wanderlust was greater than our group's."

"Ja, I think I'll call my first son Belenus," Ryan chuckled.

"Belenus?" More than one asked. "Why?"

"In memory of Biel, which was settled by Celts and named after a deity, Belenus."

"We'll remind you of that," John promised.

"I know what I'll remember: the vibrating beds in this hotel. Have you tried them yet?" Molly asked. "They substitute nicely for lullabies."

"Please do not ruin the mechanisms. We want to keep our good reputation," I cautioned my enthusiastic youths.

When I returned to our room for the night, I found a white rose and a note in front of the door. "Here is your Swiss rose. Thanks for a great time. The Gang."

*   *   *

"B I D   F A R E W E L L   T O   T H E   A L P S," I said to my group from the front of the rolling bus. "We are crossing the northern mountains of the Jura on a curvy route to Basel."

"...in another one of three-country triangles you find on this continent," Chris said.

"Oh, is that where we enter France?" Joan asked.

"Oui," Kyle said, exhausting his knowledge of French, or what he remembered from the seventh-grade experiment.

"Look at us," John observed, "none of us boys here chose French or Spanish for five years. But some of these girls did and have studied three years of German, too."

"Well, that's why they'll make fine guides for us in *Strassburg,* as we 'Germans' say," Kyle simpered.

"But you remember, 'when in Rome…' don't you know?" Nancy countered Kyle. "So in *Strasbourg* you do as the French do."

Dollars for education well spent.

A T T H E B O R D E R C R O S S I N G, our travelers were again surprised that only Klaus had to show papers through the window of the driver's side. Guards of the receiving country always asked for proof of vehicle insurance.

"I guess we can tuck away our passports," Mr. O'Hara said.

"See the sign?" Eitel asked, "Mulhouse, 35 kilometres."

"Albert Schweitzer country," Nancy said.

"The landscape with its forested mountains, hills and grassy slopes is truly similar to the area of Great Barrington as you told us on our field trip to the Schweitzer House, Mrs. M," Alan said.

"*Ja,* that was a neat place; the park, too. It's a shame their funds ran out," his sister Trudy added.

"Now let's look at the sites we read about and saw in films back in Massachusettts," I encouraged the group.

"I appreciate the facts you mimeographed for us, detailing Schweitzer's life and work," Mrs. Newley said. "As a nurse, I heard of him as a doctor in Africa and an expert in tropical diseases but never of his accomplishments in music."

"Or in philosophy and theology," Liz, one of our French majors, remarked.

"*Ehrfurcht vor dem Leben,*" Riko quoted Schweitzer's maxim: reverence for life.

"Here is Mülhausen, where Schweitzer attended the Gymnasium," Justin remembered as he noticed the sign at Mulhouse's city limits.

Colmar was the next city we passed on our way to Strasbourg.

"I forgot," Jill said. "What happened here?"

"Only an event that changed Schweitzer's life," Joan, who intended to have a medical career, refreshed Jill's memory. "Here he decided to study medicine to help the natives of Africa as a missionary doctor."

"But what moved him in Colmar to change his direction from the study of music?" Mrs. Newley asked.

"Looking at a statue, Schweitzer contemplated the suffering expressed in the face of a native African," Joan said.

Pondering Schweitzer's momentous resolve, our fellow travelers fell silent while gazing at the scenery.

When I stood up to explain the timetable for our stay in Strasbourg, I noticed a passport lying in the isle.

We are fortunate the owner dropped it in the bus and not outside. Don't even imagine the worst possible predicament, I thought with consternation.

"Who lost his passport?" I asked. On purpose I did not go to pick it up and silently return it to its owner. Instead, I made it a preventive object lesson.

"Oh heavens! It's mine," Mrs. McDonald exclaimed. "I'm sorry. I'll be more careful."

IN STRASBOURG, we stepped off the bus near the imposing cathedral. The square before the front entrance teemed with representatives of various countries. In many cases, their clothes or gear disclosed their homeland. African women wore colorful dresses and turbans. Germans wore Birkenstocks. American and Japanese tourists pointed cameras at people and edifices. Numerous languages mixed with laughter and the shouts of aggressive street vendors.

"This is a busy place," I said. "Try to have lunch nearby in small groups. We'll meet here again in an hour."

Bert and I tried several restaurants before we found one that could accommodate us and our entourage.

"The European way of seating more than one party at a table does make sense at crunch times," Mrs. Legrand said.

"Otherwise, people might miss a meal and restaurants would lose business."

"*Ja,* but you don't have privacy," her daughter Joan added.

"So, discuss the weather," Eitel quipped, evoking laughter and approval.

"I smell sauerkraut," Molly said.

"Yes, it's a popular Alsatian side dish. They'll probably serve it with sausages," I concurred.

"Or liver dumplings?" Jill surveyed neighboring tables. "Do you see any?" she asked Molly.

"Girls, girls!" Mrs. Legrand spoke up. "Mind your manners."

"Sorry," Jill apologized. "I'm afraid I couldn't read the French menu. I would like to order those dumplings."

"They'll never believe you," Joan sang in a low voice, imitating a crooner.

"Well, I have lots of witnesses, don't I?"

The waiter served Jill a huge portion to satisfy her acquired taste. "Wow, this is enough for two. You guys have to help me," she pleaded.

To my surprise, Robert and Eitel obliged.

W H E N O U R G R E E N F I E L D G R O U P gathered at the appointed time for our tour of the *Strassburger Münster,* or the Cathedral of Strasbourg, we felt captivated by its architectural magnificence. Like its sisters of European medieval basilicas, this *Münster* examplified the great technical skills of the designers and craftsmen who for generations applied themselves in faithful adherence to their church and work. Supported by bishops and rulers, master masons erected a vaulted structure upon foundations laid in the early eleventh century, the Romanesque period.

Because the construction of an edifice of this magnitude takes place over centuries, later work reflected the Gothic style in the steep roofs and flying buttresses.

Everyone in our group walked silently through the nave, sometimes sitting down on a chair to gaze up to the ceiling or at the prominent rose window.

"The sculptures at the entrance and the Doomsday Pillar are indescribably beautiful," Mr. O'Hara whispered.

Mrs. Legrand marveled at the pulpit. "I could sit in front of it for hours and study the extraordinary artistry bestowed on the statues and ornaments."

"What a blessing that the ravages of war didn't destroy the monumental witnesses to human creativity and devotion," Mrs. Newley noted in awe, her eyes beholding the stained-glass windows.

Our youths congregated in front of the astronomical clock, which Swiss clockmakers assembled from 1571-1574. Its original mechanism stopped in the 1830s, and another clockmaker, Jean-Baptiste Schwilgué, placed a more complex mechanism into the 16th century casing and set it in motion in 1842.

"Look at the base. It says here in the brochure that every year on the 31st of December the left partition shows the dates of the new moon for the following year and thus determines Easter. Fascinating, isn't it?" Don said.

"And here you see the perpetual calendar, indicating actual time," Riko pointed at two hands in the middle partition, denoting sunrise and sunset.

"What does this do?" Don asked about the right partition.

"This mechanism regulates the travel of sun and moon, it seems," Riko said. "I'll buy a brochure of this mechanical wonder to figure it out."

As he turned to move along, Riko noticed the remnants of the first astronomical clock. "Incredible," he declared. "This one dates back to 1354."

S A T U R A T E D with new knowledge, we started to leave the cathedral.

"Wait. Don't forget to take a look at the organ, which Schweitzer played and whose sound he praised," I reminded my retinue.

"It looks imposing with its guilded framework. Too bad, we can't listen to it," Debbie remarked.

"Another place to revisit in my lifetime," Luke said. "Will it ever happen?"

"I see our bus; time to move on. We want to be in Saarbrücken for dinner," I guided my group to our conveyance. Inside, I found a pink rose on my seat. "Your French rose, Mrs. M," Mary called from the back of the bus.

"Thank you," I acknowledged my joy over their regards.

*　　　*　　　*

O U R   I T I N E R A R Y called for a return to Germany and an overnight stay in Saarbrücken. "From there, we'll be in Trier in two hours," Klaus announced.

After a pork dinner, to which we had become accustomed, we stayed at the long, cleared table.

"Who would like to prepare us for tomorrow's visit to our last stop on GHS Club's first study tour of Germany?" I asked.

"I can do that," Alan volunteered, blushing.

Great! What change this trip brought about in reserved Alan, I thought, surprised and pleased.

"Trier's history goes back more than two thousand years. Old chronicles report that Trebata founded this settlement thirteen hundred years before Rome. Modern studies date the first colonization in this area at 3000 BCE, when Celtic-Germanic tribes established a sanctuary here.

"Who wants to go on?" Alan said.

Chris continued, "According to research, Roman legions under Gajus Julius Caesar came next, Emperor Augustus called this colony *Augusta Treverorum.*

"Later, Trier, or Trèves, became a capital of the West Roman Empire. Under Constantine, many of the buildings and bridges were built; we'll see their ruins or remnants tomorrow. There are also thermal baths, an amphitheater, and palaces."

Applause rewarded our lecturers. Both blushed and bowed.

"No cathedral?" Jill asked.

"Yes, you'll notice the *Trierer Dom* is quite different from the cathedrals you saw in Köln, Freiburg and Strassburg," I said. "And wait till you stand in the Protestant *Basilika,* a restored palace hall of Roman Emperors of the fourth century.

"All right. Trier is a fascinating city, which we'll explore on a walking tour until mid-afternoon. You'll be free to shop for souvenirs until dinner. Now get a good rest."

ON THE LAST OF OUR DISCOVERY DAYS, we arrived at the Dorint Hotel in the morning—too early to occupy our rooms.

"You can leave your luggage on the bus," Klaus said. "We access the parking lot, which is behind the hotel, through a gate. Your belongings will be protected."

"That's a good solution." I agreed, "Our group will have a quicker start at the tour if we skip going to our rooms first."

"We can stop at the lavatories near the lobby, before taking off, can't we?" Mrs. Newley asked as some of our youths already headed that way.

"Of course. We'll leave from here when we count twenty-nine again," I said.

AFTER CROSSING THE BUSY NORDALLEE, or North Avenue, from the front of the hotel, our travelers faced the *Porta Nigra*, an awesome structure.

"You couldn't start your Trier experience from a more fitting entrance than the old north gate, built in the second century AD. Of the original four fortified gates allowing passage through the city wall, only this one still exists," Bert remarked.

"But why is it black?" Kyle asked.

"Listen!" Bert directed Kyle's attention to a tour guide nearby, speaking to a group of British tourists.

"Environmental impact over the centuries left its mark on this edifice. Since the Middle Ages, residents of Trier have called it the Black Gate."

I motioned our German Club treasurer Jill aside. "We still have sufficient funds to afford a city guide, don't we?"

"Yes." After a moment, she added, "I see an information sign beyond the gate. I'll check the prices."

"I'll go with you. Let's find out whether we can 'buy' us a guide. With her knowledge, she would also save us time and the effort of combing through our notes and brochures."

Jill and I returned to our fellow travelers accompanied by Frau Schulz, a blonde, heavy-set guide in her mid-sixties. Her British pronunciation challenged our participants' comprehension at first and demanded their close attention. Occasionally, the woman saw the spelling of a word more than she remembered its sound—a pitfall for many of us who speak a foreign language.

In her description of the early fortifications of the Porta Nigra, our guide explained that the hinges of the gates were pushed into hollowed rock cavities, filled with molten lead, to which she referred as 'leed'.

Showing us a former room for sentries, Frau Schulz smiled and pointed at weathered scratches in a wall. "We don't always bring these ancient graffiti to people's notice. Since you are language students, I thought you may appreciate the message Roman legionnaires left behind. This inscription is the ancient equivalent of 'Kilroy was here.' "

Next to the Porta Nigra, we stepped into the oldest monastery courtyard in Germany, which fronts the Simeonstift, built in 1037. Over the centuries it fell into disuse and eventual ruin.

"In the 1930s, sections were restored in the Roman style. As you can see, the Tourist Office and the City Museum are located within," our guide said. "Now let us proceed along the Simeonstrasse to the *Dreikönigenhaus.*"

Before reaching the House of the Three Magi, my charges and the adults noticed the many stores' modern window displays in this business district. "I know where we can go after our walking tour," Mr. O'Hara said.

Frau Schulz continued, "I suppose you did not expect a house decorated in Moorish patterns among Trier's historic sites. Research tells us that Frederick II, Holy Roman Emperor in the 1200s, had lived in Sicily; from there he brought the artistic style of the local Arab colony to Roman holdings. Built in 1230, this Gothic-style house is one of the oldest in Germany. Like so many in Trier, it was restored after World War II."

Turning to Mary, who had raised her hand, the guide asked, "Do you have a question?"

"Yes. Why is there a door on the second floor? Did it open to a balcony at one time?"

"No, but you are more observant than most of our visitors. For defensive purposes, the ground floor had no entrance from the front. People gained entry to the second story by a wooden staircase, which inhabitants removed when they installed a front door below in later years.

"We will now proceed to the *Haupmarkt,* the Main Market. On the way, I'll point out to you the *Judengasse,* the Medieval Jewish Quarter. Records show that a rabbi lived in Trier in 1066. In the thirteenth century, Jewish families occupied four houses beyond this arched passage. They shared an escape tunnel."

Miss Oskiewicz shook her head, "The Jewish people always had to provide for escape from persecution."

At the *Hauptmarkt* we learned about the *Marktkreuz,* a Celtic cross erected in 958, a monument and symbol of bishopric authority.

"A few feet ahead, you see St. Peter's Fountain," Frau Schulz said. "It, too, represents the wise government of our city in accordance with the virtues of Justitia, Fortitudo, Temperentia, and Prudentia. Each statue displays its symbols. Can you name them?"

"We know what the sword and scale stand for," several of my eager students commented.

"But I never saw Fortitudo with a broken column," John added, "Or Temperentia with urns of wine and water."

"I like Prudentia because of the snake and mirror," Jill said.

Mr. O'Hara remarked. "There is so much to learn all around the market square, especially the different styles of architecture, indicating the centuries during which they prevailed."

"Indeed," the guide nodded. "The students at Trier University have rich opportunities to back up their studies with ancient witnesses. One of the most dominant in terms of ground occupied is the *Trierer Dom,* which we approach through this side street."

"Wow, it's massive," Ryan said in amazement.

"The difference between this cathedral and those we've seen on our trip is that it is so closely surrounded by dwellings as well as another church," said John. "That makes it look more enormous than others."

Frau Schulz had overheard our young men's reaction and commented, "Well, because of its longer history, this *Dom* underwent more frequent destruction, rebuilding and expansion. The earlier construction on the origin of this edifice dates back to AD 325 under Constantine the Great."

Our guide described the growth and layout of the cathedral as they developed. When she mentioned the Salic imperial period, Susan said, "Never heard of it."

Bert assured her that the history of the Salians, a Germanic tribe, was too remote for a course in ancient history in American high schools. "Frau Schulz wants us to recognize the characteristics of the architectural styles represented by the *Trierer Dom.*"

"As long as we don't have a quiz on it," Susan said, looking at me.

"Of course not. Just share the awe we all feel, recognizing the skills of people in ancient times."

"And without the use of modern tools," Robert marveled.

The awesomeness of the cathedral's interior hushed our voices. Walking under the high arches of the vaults in the galleries or resting in the spacious nave made us aware of the magnificence builders and artisans created through their religious faith. "What little space we humans fill," I whispered to Eitel.

He nodded and asked, "Are we going to the burial place of Dad's cousin?"

"Yes, when Frau Schulz guides us through the arcades to the courtyard."

Heinrich Metzroth was a *Weihbischof* at the Diocese of Trier. He is buried in the arcade reserved for auxiliary bishops.

When our family wanted to leave for a short visit to the burial site, Frau Schulz asked, "Perhaps we may all go with you? I knew Bischof Heinrich."

"Certainly," Bert said.

Standing before the Bischof's grave, I thought, *Family history connected to the ages through these surroundings.*

A F T E R   L U N C H, we gathered in front of the Basilica. "True to the definition of its name, this vast rectangular brick building served as the throne room of the Roman emperor," our guide explained. Inside she continued, "Please notice that this undivided space of 65 by 28 meters with the height of 30 meters has no supports."

Double rows of gigantic arched windows admitted daylight into the *Aula Palatina.* The whitewashed walls emphasized the hall's stark simplicity. Visitors focused on the beauty of the colorful mosaic pattern of the pulpit, sparkling in the sun's rays.

"I didn't expect to see modern décor in this ancient building," John noted admiringly.

"Through the centuries, the Basilica has suffered damage from fires and warfare. City fathers have always restored the building, mindful of the original plans. Today you see again wooden ceiling squares that resemble Roman design. Since 1856 the Basilica has been a Protestant place of worship," Frau Schulz elucidated. "After the ruinations of WWII, the Church furnished the interior with benches of blond wood. Their modern simplicity, along with mosaic designs, blend well with that of the Roman building.

"Let us proceed to the *Kurfürstliches Palais,* or the Electoral Palace, adjacent to this building. You will probably be surprised again."

"Really," Mrs. Newley said. "After the awe-inspiring monuments to ancient history, this addition to the Basilica seems to have a happy face."

"Well, this building has always housed government offices and has gone through architectural changes. The rococo wing with its pink stucco façade and ornamentations over the formal pillared entrance is a fitting background for the elaborate landscaping of the Palace Gardens." Then our guide turned, and with a sweep of her right arm, introduced us to the park and the statues lining the paths.

"Here my tour ends," Frau Schulz announced. "Your group has been attentive and polite. You indicated you wanted to visit the Imperial Baths, which you can see from here, can't you? Cross these gardens and you will be at the entrance to the spas."

"Thank you for your informative guidance," I said. "You are right; our group will now go to explore the ruins and layout of the Roman public baths."

"Bye!" "Thanks." My students waived to Frau Schulz and moved unrestrained toward our next goal, the *Kaiserthermen.*

"Hey, who wants some marzipan?"

"You have some left, Julie?" Molly asked.

"*Ja,* but I finished my mints."

"I can't wait to get some *Sprudel.*" Justin was thirsty and wanted sparkling water.

"You'll have to wait. I don't see any stores around here," Don said.

From blue skies, the sun warmed the April day and persuaded blossoms in the park to share their fragrances.

At the *Kaiserthermen,* I thought of Ellen Pierce, GHS's former Latin teacher; how she threatened to send her Roman legions to my gate if I called Latin a dead language again. She would have enjoyed being with us on this trip.

We followed the signs indicating the *caldarium,* hot water bath, the *tepidarium,* warm air room, *sudaterium,* sweat room, and *frigidarium,* cold water bath.

"There are still ruins of all these installations," Mr. O'Hara marveled. "Some are sixteen hundred years old!" Amazed, he looked inside a tower with a spiral staircase.

"Look how thin the bricks are, about half the thickness of those today," Molly said.

"Yes. Don't break off any souvenirs, though," I warned my charges. "Imagine, if every person touching these walls during the last four hundred years had broken off a piece... How big would the ruins be today?"

"I saw a brick with an inscription," Riko said.

"A Roman brick maker stamped his name and place of production on the bricks, ensuring quality control," Bert enlightened us. "Today, archeologists and historians appreciate such information for their research."

"Where did the water for these baths come from?" Mary wanted to know.

"At first, large basins collected it from brooks and wells. Later, the Ruwer River supplied diverted water that flowed through improved conduits," I explained.

Everyone in our group admired the remains of the intricate water and heating systems.

"People advanced this technical knowledge of the Romans only in the early 1800s," Bert said. "Also, besides using their public baths for the care of their bodies, Romans enriched their minds at the social center of the spas."

"*Ja,* John, Riko and I walked one of the oval paths, pretending we were Roman scholars as they are pictured in history books," Kyle said.

"Like Plutarch felt on his visits to Rome," John added in a tutorial manner, "I had 'no leisure while there to study and exercise the Latin' — I mean the German — 'tongue...' "

Our group rewarded John with laughter and applause.

"Let it not be said," I echoed my student's oratory, "that we did not allow time for nourishment, rest and recreation."

"Good. *Wir haben Hunger, Hunger...*" Molly started the round I had taught some classes; more and more of us chimed in, catching the repetition.

"I am glad Klaus is waiting to drive us back to the Dorint," Mrs. Legrand said. "My feet hurt."

Mr. O'Hara wondered how luxurious our rooms would be. "For our last night in Europe, we stay at a classy hotel."

*   *   *

THE GHS GERMAN CLUB students and their accompanying adults delighted in the spacious, clean rooms. Excited, they checked out each other's *Zimmer*.

"Cool," Liz said to Jill. "Every room comes with a full bath. We haven't had this much comfort since the *Barbarossa* in Konstanz."

"You forgot the shaking beds in Biel already?" Julie asked.

"Oh yeah! Thanks for reminding me. Can't leave those out of the reports to our classmates. I was thinking of the bathrooms and tubs down the hall in some of our inns."

"Or the enclosed shower stalls in our rooms at others," Debbie added.

In the dining room, the hostess led us to tables for three to five guests, a change from the group seating we had grown used to.

"White linen tablecloths and napkins," Mrs. Newley said.

"*Ja.* Don, mind your manners," Kyle teased his friend. "One last time: fork in the left hand, knife in the right, without putting either down while you eat."

"Okay. I'll watch you," Don countered, pointing a finger at Kyle.

After our meal I went from table to table and repeated instructions for the following day.

"Wake-up call comes at six o'clock. The Dorint serves breakfast buffet style. Be sure to be at the bus ready to leave for

Luxembourg at half past seven. As you know from our itinerary, we will visit the American and German WWII military cemeteries outside of Luxembourg City; from there, Klaus will take us to the airport."

*   *   *

W E L E F T T R I E R, the modern vibrant city with ancient roots and numerous cultural witnesses to the ages and said goodbye to Germany.

Less than an hour later, we arrived at two memorial sites created to honor fallen soldiers during our shared recent U.S. and German history, the World War II era.

The American Battle Monument Commission established the American Cemetery on a site liberated by U.S. troops in 1944. The Grand Ducal government granted the use of fifty acres as a permanent burial ground free of charge.

Our group had been quiet on the bus. The early morning hours spent packing and rushing through breakfast to be on time for departure had an exhausting effect on all of us. Realizing that our trip was nearly over, participants took in last impressions of the rural landscape we passed on our way to the engrossing locale.

In this prevailing somber mood, we entered the American cemetery through a wrought iron gate. The path led us beyond the Visitors' Building where American employees keep records of U.S. military cemeteries abroad. As soon as we stepped on the stone terrace surrounding the memorial, our friends gasped at the white sea of more than four thousand, seven hundred marble crosses as headstones, over one hundred Stars of David and one hundred and one headstones marking the resting places of unidentified soldiers.

And countless loved ones still grieve these losses.

Like magnets the grave sites attracted my students who spread out to read the inscriptions on the markers.

"Heavens! This man was younger than I am now," one of the seniors said with reverence.

"Here lie the remains of a member of the Army Air Corps my father's age when he fought in the European theater," Kyle said. "My father was a pilot, too...but he came home."

The adults in our group visited the chapel first. Resembling a square column, it stretched fifty feet toward the sky.

The eight gold panels of the entrance door, which symbolize the virtues of a soldier, impressed me enough to write them down. I wanted to share them with my classes as desirable traits in human beings: Physical Fitness, Fidelity, Proficiency, Sacrifice, Valor, Family Ties, Fortitude, and Faith.

Upon entering the chapel we faced the altar, which was flanked by two American flags. The inscription on the altar read, "I shall give them eternal life and they shall never perish."

A stained-glass window above the altar depicted the insignia of the major U.S. units fighting in the region during WWII. The ceiling displayed a many-hued mosaic of the Holy Spirit as a dove, surrounded by four angels.

Later, walking toward the gravesites, we stopped at the two pylons to study the operations maps of the Battle of the Bulge and the final drive to end the war.

"I had read that General Patton was buried in Europe," Eitel said as we met him at the general's final resting place between the memorial terrace and the multitude of graves under a blanket of extraordinarily maintained lawns.

"Yes, he wanted to be with his troops, even in death," Mrs. Newley commented.

"At a few graves I saw fresh flowers. Who might have placed them there?" Mary asked me.

"Perhaps visitors from the States did; perhaps Americans stationed in Europe carried out requests by relatives back home, or European kin brought them."

"I never thought of relatives of earlier immigrants to our country fighting against our troops," Robert pondered.

Riko refreshed Robert's memory, "But you know about my father's service as a German paratrooper and his POW time in Florida and England."

"Yes," he contemplated. "I had never thought about it in that context…"

"We're gaining more insight on this trip than we anticipated," said Mr. O'Hara.

"That's why I told the school committee we'd go on a study tour. No one can gain knowledge and understanding from books alone."

"Why don't we see more visitors here?" Ryan wondered.

"Think about it," Ms. Oskiewicz reasoned. "It's early on a work day in April, which is not the height of traveling season."

"You're right," Bert said. "One year, our family was here in mid-summer. We had to search for a parking space."

When most of our group walked toward us, I sent them ahead to the bus. "I'll wait for the photographers among us. We should be with you in a few minutes."

Resting for a moment on one of the benches along the walkway between the separate large plots, the gardener in me appreciated the plantings. Activated sprinklers and the sun's caressing rays enticed the surrounding trees and hedges—some of the in bloom—to emit a promising spring scent. Rhododendrons and roses were pregnant with buds.

In this peaceful environment the fallen warriors found their final rest after brutal battles. The brutality of war has stayed with me. Why did I survive? Dr. Card's words came to mind as he had explained Nicord's condition, "We always think why me, never why not me?"

I gratefully accept the gift of life and will share its joy with my family and the people I meet.

THE RIDE FROM THE AMERICAN CEMETERY to the *Deutscher Soldatenfriedhof in Sandweiler,* the burial ground of nearly eleven thousand German soldiers, took only a few minutes.

We could have walked if we did not have a long travel day before us.

The similarity between the two graveyards lay in the quiescence of their location. In all other visual aspects they were dissimilar. At the American cemetery the bright colors of headstones, buildings, paved stone walks, and fountains created an aura of serenity. The German *Soldatenfriedhof* with its basalt building, headstones and mass grave evoked somber feelings. Each cemetery reflected its people's culture.

Most members of our group picked up brochures offered on tables in the arcade through which we reached the graveyard. Erect crosses as well as embedded headstones bore names, dates, and military units of the buried.

Slowly we walked on paths or through rows.

"Look," Joan said to me, "some of these names we read at the American cemetery, too. And some we find in Greenfield: Schneider, Beck, Becker, Müller, Schmidt, Metzger…"

"*Ja*. Although at times people had to adjust the spelling because of umlauts, as in Mueller, or for purposes of pronunciation."

"Like my middle name, Yens, Y instead of J," Eitel said before he left to catch up with his dad and Riko.

As on our previous family visits, Bert pointed out the ages of the fallen soldiers, the youngest from his birth year—1926—to WW I veterans. When several students joined him and our sons, he translated abbreviated ranks, and units with which the soldiers had served.

Several steps led up to the platform where the remains of four thousand, eight hundred and forty-nine bodies lie interred in a mass grave. Eight hundred and ten are of unknown soldiers.

Around the platform's perimeter, tablets showed engraved names. A large stone cross, the memorial, towered over us as we circled it, overlooking the site.

"The landscaping looks less regimented here than at the American cemetery," Mrs. Legrand said. "Trees amid the graves seem to stand guard, their rustling leaves whispering comfort."

"I see more visitors here, and flowers by more graves," Debbie observed. "Well, of course! Bereaved Germans live closer to these stark reminders of the devastating war than Americans."

"Why must we have wars?" one youthful voice asked. The question remained unanswered.

With reflections like these our group returned to the bus.

"One last drive with Klaus," Jill said, to which Alan added, "*Ja, und dann geht's zurück nach Island.*"

"What's that?" Mrs. McDonald asked.

Helping his mother out, Robert translated, "And then it's back to Iceland."

WHILE IN TRANSIT to the airport, our group's members talked about their recent solemn experience, easing the weight of its impact.

At our final destination in Europe, we said *Auf Wiedersehen* to Klaus and thanked him for his care beyond expected service.

"*Ihre Betreuung war Klasse,*" Riko told him as he shook hands with our driver.

"*Ja, Klasse!*" my students assured Klaus, "You did a great job."

"That's one of the German expressions I'll take home," Mrs. McDonald said, "and '*Wieviel kostet das?*'"

"But be sure to ask for a price in English the next time you go to Wilson's," Kyle reminded his mother, referring to Greenfield's department store.

"Let's check our baggage," I said as I led the way to the counters. "Then you'll have time for bathrooms, lunch and final purchases."

"Yeah, food!" my hungry teenagers responded in near unison.

"I haven't had time to eat the rolls I fixed for myself from the buffet table at the Dorint," Justin said.

"Weren't those offerings delectable?" Mrs. Legrand asked. "I'll miss German rolls."

"Me, too. But I'll tell my mom to hold off with pork delights for a while," Molly emphasized her remark with determined nods.

"Maybe we should open a *Konditorei,* when we grow up," Don suggested.

"A pastry shop? Naw, a home brewery," Chris threw in. "Both emit tempting smells, though."

"You are beginning your review of the trip early. That's good. Think about what else you want to share in class," Miss Oskiewicz said.

"And what not!" Kyle cautioned.

"All right. Listen to the loudspeakers. We'll gather at the boarding gate when called and only pass through it after I count to twenty-nine," I reminded our party.

Many of my students and I met at the newsstand to load up on German and French magazines. Some bought stickers: *Baby an Bord,* or *Iss dich fit.*

"I need that one: eat yourself fit," Molly said. "I'll put it on our fridge."

At the restaurant, people could pay with francs, marks, or dollars. As the bills stated the amounts owed in currency, our group was busy converting their remaining European bills and coins with arguments and laughter.

"Don't any of you tell Mr. J how rusty our math talents have become," John worried.

"Well, we have improved in many other areas." Thinking of her blistered feet, Susan continued, "Aside from the languages, we practiced phys. ed. on our walks, climbing stairs up towers, and carrying luggage. Right, Ms.Oskiewicz?"

"Yes. I must give up smoking." She caught Susan's message and raised her hands, palms up in an I-give-in motion.

"Hurrah, teacher!" The girls sitting at her table applauded her.

Before I left the restaurant, I left my French rose on the table, unable to take it into the United States.

WHEN TIME CAME TO BOARD THE PLANE, we crossed the tarmac, sending parting glances around us, deeply inhaling the fresh air.

"Goodbye! Farewell," Mrs. Newley said.

Mr. O'Hara looked at her, "I like the German and French farewell expressions better. They embrace expectation to see you again, to return."

The sky had become overcast. "Doesn't it look like rain?" Mrs. Legrand asked me.

"*Ja, wenn Engel reisen, weint der Himmel,* says a German proverb." Heaven cries when angels travel.

"We aren't angels, Mom," Eitel reminded me. "Isn't that why Heaven cries?"

"Good point. At any rate, let's hope we don't fly into a storm."

MINUTES AFTER TAKE-OFF, the pilot announced that weather conditions over Iceland made landing in Reykjavik impossible. Refueling would instead take place at the Shannon airport in Ireland.

"You said we should do our shopping at the Ice Mart on our return trip, Mrs. M. Now we won't be able to," the disappointed faction of our group reproved me.

The members of Irish descent were happy. "I have never set foot on Irish soil." Ryan's face mirrored his pleasure. "Think of the bonus to our trip: We add another country."

COMPARED TO THE ATTRACTIVE ICE MART, the duty-free store at Shannon resembled a warehouse. The merchandise, however, reflected Ireland's crafts and knitwear as much as Iceland did its lava items and Nordic clothing.

Elated Mr. O'Hara now selected white and green sweaters rather than the white and ice-blue ones he had planned on taking home to his family. The women in our group enthusiastically stocked up on Irish table linen.

ON THE FLIGHT TO JFK, our plane crossed the Atlantic on a route south of Iceland.

"Look at that black wall to the north," Riko said. "Doesn't it seem to touch the sea? With sights like these, no wonder Pythagoras and other Greeks after him had a hard time convincing people the earth was round."

"Really. That must be the weather front coming from Iceland." Eitel stared wide-eyed through the window. "I'm glad we didn't go there."

"Me, too," his neighbor, Nancy, said. "Remember how we blew across the tarmac the last time?"

"Uh-huh."

Most of my charges reclined in their seats to rest. I, too, closed my eyes. Although our trip was not yet complete, I felt I could relax, at least until we left the plane. In my mind, I reviewed our travels. Had I met my objectives? Were my students better informed about the people whose language and culture they studied? Their questions and comments proved to me that they had enriched their knowledge while they enjoyed getting away from classrooms and homework.

C L E A R I N G   C U S T O M S in New York went smoothly for our group. I called Mr. Jones, GHS principal, to advise him of the group's safe return to home soil. He, in turn, shared this information with the first parents on the list to be notified. From there, the chain of call went down the list.

Outside the terminal, a Greenfield bus waited at curbside. "Come on, guys, let's load our precious souvenirs into the luggage hold," Mr. O'Hara said. "Then you can sleep."

I counted twenty-nine heads for the final time. In our seats, none of us needed encouragement to follow Mr. O'Hara's suggestion.

We arrived at the GHS parking lot around midnight. Parents and relatives received our travelers with hugs and relief. Of course they had worried about their children's welfare abroad.

As Bert drove us home, I squeezed his arm in gratitude and said, "Thank Heaven, together we got them all home without greater injuries than blisters."

GHS GERMAN CLUB TRAVELERS contributed richly to my classes. Their shared observations of German customs, food, dwellings, and historic sites gave credence to my teaching. They had seen the results of a people's resolve to rebuild a war-torn country, its industry and its confidence.

"I won't forget the awe-inspiring nature of the Rhine Valley and the Alps, nor the splendor and craftsmanship of the ancient buildings and installations," Jill said. "But little, practical things like door handles instead of knobs impressed me. You can open every room's door with your elbow when you have to carry a load in your arms."

"...or the windows that open three ways," Justin added. "I had to figure out how to open them. Just like you told us about your initial problem with our windows, Mrs. M."

Susan promised herself that some day she'd have window boxes on her house, with multicolored petunias overflowing them.

"But then you can't air your featherbeds every morning," Robert teased her.

Because of remarks like these, students paid closer attention to the films accompanying our texts. They memorized the dialogues they heard, or variations, and mimicked the mannerisms of the German actors with pathos.

"Verzeihung! Sind Sie Herr Müller?" Excuse me, are you Mr. Müller?

"Nein, ich heisse Schneider." No, my name is Schneider.

Our travelers' enthusiasm stimulated an increase in enrollment in the foreign languages and in future travel.

Before long, many GHS students and their parents counted on teachers' willingness to conduct frequent tours. They showed their gratitude at welcome-home reunions where we recounted highlights and episodes of the trip, looked at each other's photographs and took orders for copies.

Amid the lightness of the parties, a club officer called for attention. "For your tireless care on our trip we'd like you to accept this token,—at times, a collector's piece from the local Lunt

349

Silversmiths— of our appreciation, Mrs. M. May you recuperate from the stress of the undertaking to give another GHS group the opportunity of a study tour abroad with you."

*   *   *

O V E R   T H E   Y E A R S, my seven itineraries reflected the material we had studied in the classroom and included students' suggestions such as an overnight stay in Keflavik.

The year we wanted to admire the German Alps near Garmisch, clouds hovered over roads and villages, enveloping higher regions. We never saw the mountains.

At our stay in Bonn, then the capital of the Federal Republic of Germany, we visited Beethoven's birthplace.

During one February vacation we used a Eurail-Pass from Frankfurt to München, instead of bus transportation. We stopped off at cities along the route. In München, the venues of the 1972 Olympic Games and the dramatic kidnapping of Israeli athletes grabbed our attention.

One year our itinerary included a tour of the U.S. Memorial site at Bastogne, Belgium. The huge star-shaped monument is dedicated to the GIs who had fought the fierce winter battles of 1944 and were killed in action on those grounds.

On another trip I had made reservations for a guided walking tour through the Mercedes-Benz plant near Stuttgart. There, even customers who came to pick up their new models watched assembly lines only from minibuses. My students, however, were able to interact with workers.

"Did you see Aki?" our teens asked each other with reference to the chapter in their textbook in which a Turkish apprentice learned German on his job.

I enjoyed the tours as much as my companions did, learning along with them. Through shared experiences individuals united. One mother summed up her sentiments about her partnership in one of our tours, "It was the best thing next to my wedding day."

CHAPTER 18

New Challenges

B Y T H E 1980s, steep price increases for airline tickets and hotel accommodations coincided with my desire to explore new fields.

Veit graduated Williams College and married in the early '70s. Riko received his Bachelor's from Skidmore College, and Eitel had served in the U.S. Marine Corps. They had gained independence.

"What would you say if I told you I wanted to study for my master's in education?" I surprised Bert one day.

"Are you sure you want more hurdles to jump?"

"I need new skills, and the foreign language department needs computers. The graduate courses I took would already count toward the degree. With a sabbatical I could finish my studies within one year."

"Let's do it, then."

My students were not happy with my decision, especially the seniors.

"I'll still write your recommendations for college," I assured them.

*   *   *

P R E P A R I N G T O C A R R Y O U T my decades-old pledge to write about the horrors of war and their impact on civilians, I had spent three weeks at the *Bundesarchiv,* the Federal Archives, in

351

Koblenz in the summer of 1976. Thirty years after WWII, formerly secret documents became available for research. The reams of information I had collected waited to be used.

Always keeping my goal in mind, I took courses at UMass in social and diplomatic history to gain insight and credibility.

A creative writing class helped facilitate my endeavor. After reading my purpose driven exercises for his course, Professor Charles Kay Smith commented, "It needs to be told." I committed his words to memory and chose them for the title of my master's thesis.

After transferring my graduate credits to Cambridge College in Northampton, I filled my schedule with computer and grant-writing courses.

When students had to declare their thesis topics, my advisor, Dr. Joseph DeFazio, asked, "And what is your proposal?"

"I suppose you expect me to write about computers in the foreign language classroom."

"I expect you to write a thesis. What subject do you want to treat?"

He had opened the flood gates! Words poured out of my mouth. Might the plan I had entertained and nourished for years materialize?

Dr. DeFazio smiled, "I can tell your topic has been on your mind. Go ahead. I approve."

As anticipated, I received my M.Ed. in administration in 1984. Moreover, after eight years I was finally able to send a copy of my thesis to the *Bundesarchiv* in understood compensation for the use of their documents free of charge.

*   *   *

FOR SEVERAL YEARS, Greenfield families hosted foreign students from Europe, the Middle East and South America who attended GHS for a year. But our teens, or their families, never took advantage of existing international programs to go abroad.

I felt strongly about the value of understanding other cultures.

"You could be ambassadors of our country at the same time that you learn about foreign ways of life," I tried to encourage my charges.

"Can't you come with us?" they asked.

That question and my desire to leave a vehicle in place to start GHS students on the road to an expanded weltanschauung before my retirement, led me to the German-American Partnership Program, GAPP.

The *Goethe-Institut* sponsored this program with support from the Department for Cultural Affairs of the *Bundesrepublik*. The U.S. government sanctioned the exchange. Based on these solid credentials, the Greenfield school administration and school board consented to our participation.

I chose the *Gymnasium auf der Karthause* in Koblenz as partner for GHS. At a three-day workshop at the Goethe House New York, I studied the intricacies of international exchanges.

Ten GHS students and their families agreed to open their homes to ten students from Koblenz for three weeks. Our students and I, their advisor and resource, traveled to Koblenz in the spring of 1988 to meet their host families. Bert's niece and her husband, Iris and Jochem Bröhl, had invited me. The Greenfield teens and their counterparts attended classes and all planned activities together. I taught English to several groups of Koblenzer students but also observed my students on occasion to monitor their level of understanding.

Whereas our teenagers communicated well with their host families, they, of course, experienced difficulties at cultural events. Who can say that we understand every word of an opera presented in our native language? My students, however, sat bravely through the première of the chamber opera *William Ratcliff* by Jens-Peter Ostendorf on a Koblenz stage, later humming strains of the music they had heard.

"Nein! Niemals!" No! Never! was the line they adopted from the opera and repeated whenever a simple no would have sufficed.

An hour-long ride by bus to a branch of the Max-Planck-Institut and the *Bonner Universität* landed us at the *Radiotelescop Effelsberg* in the Eifel Mountains. If films and slides had not supported the lectures given by physicists, Greenfield's bright lights would have gone out. Observing an international tracking station at work, however, made lasting impressions on teachers and students.

Another memorable field trip took us to Mainz, the *Johannes-Gutenberg-Stadt.* Proudly proclaiming that Gutenberg was the city's greatest son, the university and the World Museum of Printing also bear his name.

The museum traced the history of printing in Germany. Displays showed woodcuts, copperplate engraving, etching and lithography. A vault housed the Gutenberg Bible.

During WWII, three air raids devastated St. Stephen's. For the reconstructed church, Marc Chagall, the noted French artist, designed several stained-glass windows. Their blue hues not only dominate the depicted scenes of the Bible but also bathe the meditating congregation in its soothing light. Chagall donated some of his work in the spirit of French and German friendship.

At the *Sektkellerei Kupferberg,* our GAPP group appreciated the personal attention we received on our visit to the seven-storied underground cellars where cellar managers supervised the process of turning select grapes into world-class sparkling wines.

Our guide pointed out an interesting historical fact: During ferocious WWII air attacks on Mainz, the cellars served as air raid shelters and saved countless lives.

A reception in Mainz by the state government of Rheinland-Pfalz was a high point of our three-week stay. We sat in a front row when our presence was announced at a session of the *Landtag,* the diet. As in the opera, most of the proceedings went over the Greenfield students' heads. But the honor accorded them kept them attentive.

The city of Koblenz, too, recognized our efforts at promoting international friendships. At that reception the mayor presented us with an old framed lithograph of Confluentia to be hung at GHS. I received a blue silk scarf with the city's coat of arms.

Greenfield would reciprocate when the *Karthausers* came to see us in the fall.

Our present to the *Gymnasium* was a copy of *The Conservative Rebel, a Social History of Greenfield, Massachusetts,* by Paul Jenkins. Published in 1982, the book's author included recent history that let our German guests anticipate the small-town life they would encounter.

"H O W C A N W E C O M P E T E with the events the Koblenzers staged for us?" my students worried.

"We don't want to compete," I said. "Our town, school, and families will do their best to welcome our guests. In our midst they'll experience the New England way of life."

The German teens and their teacher tasted corn on the cob, maple products, American sandwiches, and lobster. Some picked McIntosh apples; some raked and photographed the colorful fall foliage. Because they were under age, they missed the beer accessible to them in Germany. I was also worried that they might try to coax their hosts into letting them drive cars.

"Being a good host doesn't mean you should disregard rules and safety," I said to my students. "Consider the responsibilities your parents accepted for your guests' well-being, and the efforts they make to entertain them. Your reputation is at stake here, now and after your friends' visit."

The three weeks of the Koblenzers' visit robbed me of more sleep than seven tours with GHS students; largely, because I had to also teach my classes and carry out departmental duties. The group's accompanying teacher, however, did not involve himself too closely with the program.

In school, the guest students had no problems following our teachers' instructions. After six to eight years of studying English, visiting England, and listening to British and American pop music, the *Karthauser* contingent participated in every class they attended at GHS. Their knowledge at every age level was superior to that of our students. They acted, however, like children. Our teens had more maturity, probably because they had held part-time jobs for months if not years. I credit also American team spirit as practiced in extra-curricular activities for their greater cooperation.

The Greenfield School Committee functioned as the town's welcoming body and heard first hand of the differences between American and German school systems.

On field trips to Old Deerfield, our guests learned about the tribulations the first settlers endured during wars with Indians. At Plimouth Plantation, our group observed the reenactments of daily chores in the life of the early British immigrants in the 1600s. When visiting Boston with our German friends, we walked the Freedom Trail, visited Faneuil Hall, its Marketplace, and the Museum of Fine Arts. On the way home, we stopped at Lexington and Concord, where the American Revolution broke out in 1775.

Host families treated their guests on weekend outings to tourist sites throughout New England and to Niagara Falls.

Courtesy of Hotel Barbarossa

Print shop at Gutenberg Museum, Mainz

At town square, Bastogne, Belgium

At the U.S. WW II Memorial near Bastogne, Belgium

*GHS student group at Gymnasium auf der
Karthause, Koblenz, Germany, 1988*

Presenting The Conservative Rebel *to DirectorSchneider
of Koblenz high school, 1988.*

THE *GYMNASIUM AUF DER KARTHAUSE*, Greenfield High School, the participating students and host families considered our mutual efforts to establish a continuing exchange program a success. Because of budget restraints, decreasing enrollment in challenging courses, and my retirement in 1989, Greenfield stopped offering German in its curriculum. The *Gymnasium auf der Karthause* needed to find a new partner.

*   *   *

BERT AND I had prepared ourselves for the next challenge. We sold Metzroth Graphics and our house. Then, after ten years of summer sailing in Maine waters on our *Brave II*, an Ericson 29 sloop, we traded her for a more manageable boat. With the double-ender *Stettin*, we moved to Stuart, Florida.

"Now we can put our training to work and cross the Gulf Stream on our boat," I said to Bert. "The Bahamas are waiting. Let's go sailing!"

Epilogue

I TOOK WEEKS in the summer of 1989 to separate myself from Greenfield High School. After absolving my administrative duties I checked the language laboratory for needed repairs and service, recalling who of my students had sat in which booth. Next, I shelved the textbooks and audio-visual materials. How much of my files would be helpful to the foreign language department? Who would find use for the German resources?

Change is a reality. I was always able to adapt to my life's stages, applying the lessons of the past to create a future. Retirement gave me the freedom to reach goals I had postponed, among them to record the events that ended my childhood. Over the years, our sons kept reminding me of my pledge; they wanted to share knowledge of their roots with their children.

People have wondered how I could remember the details of my experiences. I told them that it was others who made situations memorable. Their presence affected my decision-making. In discourse, we revealed our ideas; meaningful exchanges left imprints on my mind. Prevailing public sentiments, however, may color readers' understanding of my resolve to be truthful.

My personal life reflects the impact of political actions as they determine history. Stated historical data are documented. If I could not substantiate occurrences, I omitted them.

Family gave me shelter in my youth and later provided the anchor in home port. Jobs led Veit, Riko and their families to California. Eitel settled in Connecticut.

As our family grew—we have five spirited grandsons— death claimed its due. Bert's parents left us in the previous century; Omi and Opi died in 2002. Nephew Reiner who stole away at age nine rather than bidding us farewell in 1954 passed away too soon. My school friend Inge and the Friedebergers Burkhard and Gerhard also departed.

Death brings irreversible change. Scientific and social innovations necessitate reformed attitudes. With my children and students I stressed the need to consider the consequences of their actions and the value of all life. Students rewarded me with their parting words, "We may forget much of our German but will remember the discussions about attitude, or, as we say, weltanschauung."

B E S I D E S   M Y   N E E D to write this book, I harbored another unfulfilled desire: I wanted to see my hometown again.

In 1996 Bert and I crossed the German-Polish border by car at Pomellen.

The signpost read Szczecin 7 km, pointing in a northerly direction. Along the road, we observed fields sprouting tall weeds instead of planted grains, potatoes or crops I expected to see near Stettin. Fifty-one years after World War II the landscape and buildings still showed scars of that brutal conflict.

"Do you know where we are?" Bert asked after entering the city.

"No. Everything looks so different. And I can't read the street signs. Wait. There is a police car. Perhaps the officers can understand my memorized Polish phrases."

When I advanced toward them, they left.

"Let's follow the signs to the *Centrum,*" I encouraged Bert.

Suddenly I noticed a high stuccoed wall topped with rolled barbed wire. "That's the jail," I cried out. "Therefore my high school has to be across this broad avenue."

Instead of the four-storied brick building, one reduced to two stories fronted the street. Remembering our burned-out school and noticing a playground beyond the old iron fence, I said, "That looks like an elementary school now.

"All right. I know where we are and can guide you to the Radisson Hotel. There we'll find a taxi to take us to the places Felix marked on the city plan."

Family and friends in the Rheinland had assured us we would find a German-speaking driver. The first man Bert approached with his request in German shook his head and said, "I speak English, though." Our American clothing had given us away.

Jacek—he wanted to be called Jack—drove us all day to the sites I wanted to revisit. Great-grandmother Omchen's estate was now, thanks to its size, an orphanage. My grandparents' house showed an addition for a photolab.

Our second-floor apartment in the Pionierstrasse seemed restored. I walked through the heavy wooden entrance door of the building into the lobby where a half-eaten loaf of bread and other food stuff lay on the ground. The *Hinterhof* no longer had grass and flowers but asphalt in need of attention. The façades of the buildings were blackened, their interior probably hollow after the fires but later reconstructed. Curtains indicated tenants living in the apartments. I saw no one and was glad to leave.

Throughout the day I sensed a subdued atmosphere pervading the city. On the way to Neu-Podejuch, Jack, a former teacher, talked with chagrin about "our" opera house. Apparently, the *Stettiner Stadttheater* had survived the war, served as a cultural center, but later fell victim to a new priority: widened streets. We saw two cars as we passed the site on a normal weekday.

Crossing the Oder River we noticed just one freighter docked in front of the row of warehouses in one of the largest ports on the Baltic Sea.

Along the boulevard Stettiners called *die Lastadie,* I searched for Paul Schlegel's warehouse: nothing left but rubble.

Soon I pointed out the tall poplar trees that had surrounded the international airport. About half the trees still flanked the weed-covered area.

"Szczecin had an airport?" Jack asked.

I nodded and thought, *Stettin did.* "Don't you have one now?"

"No. The nearest Polish airport is in Warsaw. However, you can always catch a flight in Berlin."

WE COULD NOT ACCESS our family orchard despite Jack's inquiries at a restaurant down the hill from it. Mysteriously, people clammed up whenever Jack probed into the reason. Even eating lunch at our dead end did not change the innkeeper's mind.

Driving back into the city, our route took us again through Finkenwalde, a formerly affluent suburb. There, nothing reminded me of its earlier beauty. Inhabitable housing still showed the damage of war action and had not seen fresh paint.

We experienced a pleasant surprise at our visit to the rebuilt *Jakobi-Kirche,* or Jakobi Basilika. Its history goes back to 1187. In my memory, apartment blocks closely surrounded the mighty church so that one could never see the entire structure. After the removal of the ruined dwellings, the imposing brick cathedral dominates its surroundings.

Our next stop was at the Luisenstrasse. I was surprised to see the banks and government buildings here to appear untouched by the war. Their restoration was remarkable. After the air raid in April 1943, I had witnessed the wreckers bring down two structures among those buildings: No 10, the Preussenhof, Stettin's most formidable hotel, and its neighbor, Nr. 9, Paul Schlegel's business of glass and fine china. In place of these two enterprises several fifty-year-old trees shaded a courtyard and a snack bar—an odd interruption of the stately architecture on this street.

Joyful memories of visits to my uncles at my maternal family's business and the apartment above outweigh the sadness I felt on this side trip to the Luisenstrasse.

BERT AND I FINISHED OUR EXCURSION to Stettin on a happy note. At the Glambecksee I showed him a much-changed swimming pool where I had taken various long-distance and diving tests. We walked half-way around the lake and back at the edge of the forest, enjoying the solitude on the sunny autumn day.

"I'm glad you could see some of the places I told you about, though they differed from my descriptions. It's no longer my city as Jack mentioned unwittingly; it's his."

We left Stettin before sundown. I did not look back. The city and I had changed.

Bert and Almut, San Francisco, CA, 2002

Acknowledgments

I am grateful to:

Rick Metzroth, my editor, for his astute prodding;

Diane Desrochers, my reader, for her sensitivity to my repressed feelings;

The members of two Florida writers groups: Morningside in Port St. Lucie and Melody Lane in Fort Pierce. Their input converted occasional German or British phraseology into American English;

Bert, my husband, for your support and your typing skills;

Veit, Riko, and Eitel for believing I could deliver on your request: tracing your maternal roots.

Glossary

Aachen: Aix-la-Chapelle
Alle aussteigen: All get off
Abonnement: Season's ticket
Besser machen: Do better
CARE: Cooperative for American Relief; American
  organization sending relief throughout the world
Flucht: Flight; escape
Frau: Woman; Mrs.
Führer: Leader
Gehilfin: Journeywoman
Gehilfen: Journeymen and –women
Gemeinde: Precinct; community
Gepäckträger: carrier on bicycle
Guten Morgen: Good morning
Guten Tag: Good day, hello
Gymnasium: High school for boys
Hamstertouren: Hoarding trips
Handwagen: Handcart
Heimat: Home town; -state; -country
Hinterhaus: Apartment buildings not facing street
Hof: Courtyard
Kaiserin: Empress
Kaiserin-Auguste-Victoria (KAV): Name of *Oberschule*
Kinderlandverschickung (KLV): Evacuation of children
Kleiderkarte: Ration card for clothing
Kristallwaren: Items of crystal glass
Landwirt: Agriculturist
Lehrstelle: Place of apprenticeship
Lyzeum: High school for girls
Meister: Master (s)
Mitläufer: Nominal member
Mutti: Mom
Nationalsozialistische Deutsche Arbeiterpartei (NSDAP):
  National Socialist German Worker's Party; 1919-1945.
  Contraction: Nazi party
Nazi: Active member of Nazi party, fascist
Oberschule für Mädchen: High school for girls
Oma: Grandma

Glossary

Onkel: Uncle
Opa: Grandpa
Ostsee: Baltic Sea
Pilz: Mushroom
Polizeipräsident: Police commissioner
Porzellan: Porcelain
Rheinländer: Resident of the Rheinland
Saalschutz (SS): Originally organized to keep order at Nazi party meetings
Sie können gehen: You can go, leave
Strasse: Street
Sturmabteilung (SA): Storm Troopers, Brown Shirts
Tante: Aunt
U-Boot: Submarine
Vater Rhein: Father Rhine
Vati: Dad (dy)
Vorderhaus: Apartment building facing street
Zimmer: Room(s)

Bibliography

Amt für Volkswohlfahrt. *Pommern: Elternbrief der erweiterten Kinderlandverschickung. Gau Pommern.* Druck: F. Hessenland, Stettin, Juni 1943.

Blattner, Karl. *Englisch für Kaufleute: Handelskorrespondenz und Handelskunde.* Langenscheidts Handbücher der Handelskorrespondenz. Berlin-Schöneberg: Verlag der Langenscheidt-Sprachwerke. 1949.

Braudel, Fernand. *The Structures of Everyday Life.* Vol. 1. New York: Harper & Row. Publishers, 1979.

Bruhns, Wibke. *Meines Vaters Land: Geschichte einer deutschen Familie.* Berlin: Ullstein Buchverlage GmbH, 2005.

Bundesarchiv Koblenz. Federal Republic of Germany. *Ost-Documentation.* Ost-Dok. 1, 1944-1951; Ost-Dok. 2; 1949-1956; Ost-Dok. 8, 1952-1967.

Caldwell, Gail. *A Strong West Wind.* New York: Random House Trade Paperbacks, 2007.

Campbell, James. *The Bombing of Nuremberg: The Gripping Recreation of the Most Disastrous Allied Night Raid of World War II.* Garden City, New York: Doubleday & Co., Inc., 1974.

Clemens, Diane Shaver. *Yalta.* New York: Oxford University Press, 1970.

de Zayas, Alfred M. *Nemesis at Potsdam: The Anglo-Americans and the Expulsion of the Germans; Background, Execution,*

Bibliography

Consequences. London: Routledge and Kegan
Paul, 1977.

Dönhoff, Marion Gräfin. *Kindheit in Ostpreussen.*
Berlin: Wolf Jobst Siedler Verlag GmbH, März
1998.

Fest, Joachim. *Ich nicht: Erinnerungen an eine
Kindheit und Jugend.* Reinbek bei Hamburg:
Rowohlt Verlag GmbH. 2. Auflage. September
2006.

Frankl, Viktor E. *Man's Search for Meaning: An
Introduction to Logotherapy.* New York: A
touchstone Book: Published by Simon & Schuster,
1984.

Grass, Günter. *Beim Häuten der Zwiebel.* Göttingen:
Steidl Verlag. Zweite Auflage. September 2006.

Grube, Frank, and Richter, Gerhard. *Flucht und
Vertreibung: Deutschland zwischen 1944 und
1947.* Hamburg: Hoffmann und Campe, 1981.

Grun, Bernhard. *The Timetables of History:
A Historical Linkage of People and Events.*
New, Updated Edition. English Edition,
New York: Simon & Schuster, Inc., 1979.

Hegi, Ursula. *The Vision of Emma Blau.* New York:
Simon & Schuster, 2000.

Hoster, Joseph. *Guide to Cologne Cathedral.* Köln:
Greven Verlag.

Irving, David. *The Destruction of Dresden.* Morley,
Yorkshire: The Elmfield Press, 1974.

371

Bibliography

Jenkins, Paul. *The Conservative Rebel: A Social History of Greenfield, Massachusetts.* Published by the town of Greenfield, Massachusetts 1982.

Klein-Ehrminger, Madeleine. *The Cathedral of Strasbourg.* Lyon: Lescuyer.

Koblenz. Verlag und Druck. *Koblenzer Festungsjournal.* Mittelrhein Verlag GmbH. 7. Ausgabe Saison 2006.

Knopp, Guido. *Die grosse Flucht: Das Schicksal der Vertriebenen.* München: Egon Ullstein List Verlag GmbH & Co. KG, 2001.

Lord, M.G. *Astro Turf: The Private Life of Rocket Science.* New York: Walker Publishing Company, 2005.

MacLeod, Katrina. *Guten Tag, Koblenz.* In *Exponent.* Vol. LXXXIII No. 5. Greenfield Massachusetts: Greenfield High School, May 1981.

McCourt, Frank. *Teacher Man.* New York: Scribner, 2005.

Metzroth, Almut H. *It Needs To Be Told: The Plight of German Civilians in World War II.* Master's Thesis. Northampton Massachusetts: Cambridge College, June 1984.

Presseamt der Stadt Konstanz. *Konstanz im Blickpunkt,* Nr. 2. Radolfzell: Verlag Hans Lämmer, 15 April 1974.

Samuel, Wolfgang W.E. *German Boy: A Child in War.* Jackson, MS. The University Press of Misssissippi, 2000.

Schweizerische Verkehrszentrale (SVZ). *Schweiz.* Zürich, 1983.

Stadt Koblenz. Presse und Fremdenverkehrsamt. *Koblenz an Rhein und Mosel.* Koblenz: Görres-Druckerei GmbH.

Städtisches Verkehrsamt,. *Trier: A Guide to the Monuments.* Trier: Cusanus-Verlag GmbH. Volksfreund-Druckerei Nik. Koch.

Verkehrsverein Mainz e. V. *Mainz am Rhein.*

von Kardorff, Ursula. *Diary of a Nightmare: Berlin 1942-1945.* Translated by Ewan Butler. New York: The John Day Company, 1966.

Wald Leveton, Eva. *Eva's Berlin*: *Memories of a Wartime Childhood.* Fairfax, California: Thumbprint Press, 2000.

INDEX